Picture Chord Encyclopedia

INTRODUCTION

The Picture Chord Encyclopedia is designed to serve two purposes: first, it's a reference guide to chords; second, it's a collection of popular guitar sounds.

Use it when you're learning a new song and you come across a chord that's unfamiliar to you. Use it when you're composing your own music and looking for "just the right chord." Use it to explore the guitar fretboard, to improve your chord playing, to increase your understanding of chord theory, or just to discover new and unusual sounds. The applications are almost limitless.

The Picture Chord Encyclopedia is a comprehensive source for chords, for all playing styles and levels. One word of warning, though: it does not contain *every* guitar chord in existence; no book could. It does contain five easy-to-play voicings of 44 chord qualities for each of the twelve musical keys. All totaled, that's 2,640 chords at your fingertips! These chords and their fingerings have been chosen for their playability and their practicality, ensuring a wealth of usable fingerings for any musical situation. So, whether you're a beginner looking for your first C major chord, or a budding jazz guitarist searching for a new voicing for C7♭5(♯9), you'll find what you're looking for here.

Enjoy!

CONTENTS

How to Use This Book ii

Choosing the Best Voicing iii

Chord Construction iv
    What's a Chord? iv
    How Does a Chord Get Its Name? iv
    How Do I Build a Chord? v
    What About Other Keys? v
    Triads vii
    Sevenths vii
    Extended Chords vii
    Inversions & Voicings viii

The Chords
    C 1
    D♭ 23
    D 45
    E♭ 67
    E 89
    F 111
    F♯ 133
    G 155
    A♭ 177
    A 199
    B♭ 221
    B 243

ISBN 978-0-7935-8491-8

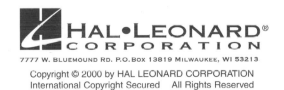

HAL•LEONARD®
CORPORATION

7777 W. BLUEMOUND RD. P.O. BOX 13819 MILWAUKEE, WI 53213

Visit Hal Leonard Online at
www.halleonard.com

HOW TO USE THIS BOOK

The Picture Chord Encyclopedia contains 2640 chord voicings and over 500 unique chord types. To help you find your way to the chord you need, all the chords are organized first by root (C, C#, D, E♭, E, etc.) and then by quality or type (major, minor, seventh, etc.)

Each chord is identified by its symbol: **Csus4**

By its full name: **C suspended fourth**

And by its spelling:

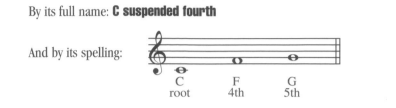

Then, you are given a choice of five voicings, which are presented in chord frames and photos. In a chord frame, the six vertical lines represent the six strings on the guitar, from low E to high E, moving left to right. The horizontal lines represent the frets:

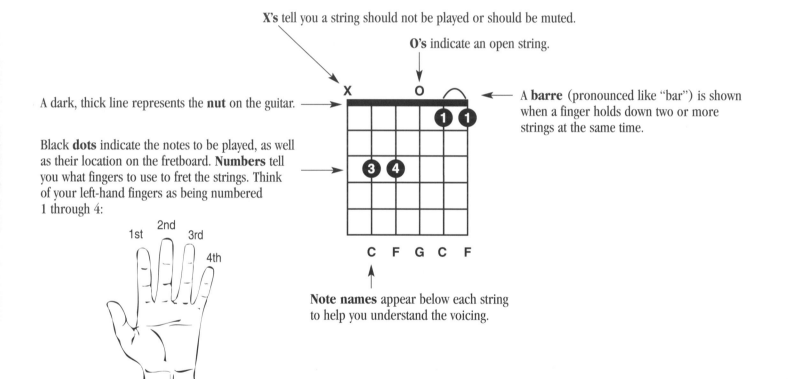

X's tell you a string should not be played or should be muted.

O's indicate an open string.

A dark, thick line represents the **nut** on the guitar.

A **barre** (pronounced like "bar") is shown when a finger holds down two or more strings at the same time.

Black **dots** indicate the notes to be played, as well as their location on the fretboard. **Numbers** tell you what fingers to use to fret the strings. Think of your left-hand fingers as being numbered 1 through 4:

Note names appear below each string to help you understand the voicing.

Chords above the fifth fret use a **fret number** (e.g., "5 fr") to the right of the chord frame. This tells you to move your hand up to that fret to position your fingers.

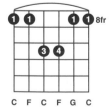

☛ One of the goals of this book is to provide "playable" chord fingerings. The fingerings in this book were chosen for their ease of play and transition between other chords in a progression. If you feel more comfortable with an alternate fingering, feel free to use it. Remember, these fingerings are only recommended. There is no single right way to play these chords.

CHOOSING THE BEST VOICING

Any chord can have a number of different voicings. A *voicing* refers to how the notes of the chord are arranged—which corresponds to where the chord is played on the guitar, and how it's fingered. Each chord quality in this book is presented with *five* different voicings. Typically, the first chord voicing presented is in the lowest position on the fretboard. The rest of the voicings gradually move up the neck. Within these sets of voicings, you will encounter open chords, barre chords, broken-set chords, and adjacent-set chords:

Open Chords

Open chords occur within the first five frets of the guitar and contain at least one open string. These chords are often the most appropriate choice for strumming purposes. They're also typically the easiest voicings to learn when you're a beginner.

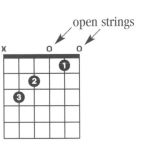

open strings

Barre Chords

Barre chords can occur anywhere on the neck and serve as a type of "all-purpose" chord voicing; that is, they can be strummed, plucked, or played fingerstyle, and can be used in almost any musical setting.

Barre chords require you to lay a finger flat across a fret and press down all the indicated strings simultaneously. This can be challenging for a beginning guitarist. If you find these chords to be especially difficult at first, don't give up. Just keep practicing, and be patient.

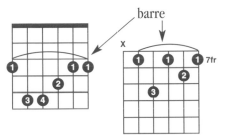

barre

Broken-Set Chords

Broken-set chords also provide good, multipurpose chord voicings. These chords contain a bass note on the fifth or sixth string and two or three notes on the higher strings, with at least one interior string muted, or not played. These often work best in a jazz or blues setting, especially when playing solo.

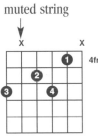

muted string

Adjacent-Set Chords

Adjacent-set chords contain notes on the middle or top four strings. These chords also work well within the jazz or blues idioms, especially for chord-melody techniques or when playing with another instrument that provides a bass line.

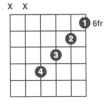

Ultimately, which chord voicing you choose will depend on either your playing level or the situation at hand. Musically speaking, if you're playing a chord sequence high on the neck, a chord voiced down low would probably sound out of place. Likewise, if you're playing a progression of open chords, jumping up high on the neck for a particular chord would likely sound and feel awkward.

That said, you should become familiar with as many voicings of a chord as you can. They do not all sound the same. Practice switching between different voicings of the same chord, and compare how they sound. If you like, go ahead and practice a progression where you jump from high to low on the neck—there really are no rules in music that can't be broken.

CHORD CONSTRUCTION

WHAT'S A CHORD?

In order to effectively choose and utilize the chords in this book, it is important to have a basic understanding of how chords are constructed. So, *what is a chord?* A chord is simply defined as *three or more notes* played at the same time. Typically, its function is to provide the harmony that supports the melody of a song.

HOW DOES A CHORD GET ITS NAME?

A chord gets its name from its root note. For example, the root of a G major chord is G. The remaining notes in the chord determine its *quality,* or *type.* This is indicated by the chord suffix. So, in a Bm7♭5 chord, B is the root, and m7♭5 is the suffix that indicates the quality of the chord.

root   quality or type

This book contains 44 chord types. Here is a summary table to help you keep track of the suffix for each chord type:

SUFFIX	CHORD TYPE	SUFFIX	CHORD TYPE
no suffix	major	m11	minor eleventh
5(no 3rd)	fifth (power chord)	m13	minor thirteenth
sus4	suspended fourth	7	dominant seventh
sus2	suspended second	7sus4	seventh, suspended fourth
add9	added ninth	7♭5	seventh, flat fifth
6	sixth	9	ninth
6/9	sixth, added ninth	9sus4	ninth, suspended fourth
maj7	major seventh	9♭5	ninth, flat fifth
maj9	major ninth	7♭9	seventh, flat ninth
maj7♯11	major seventh, sharp eleventh	7♯9	seventh, sharp ninth
maj13	major thirteenth	7♭5(♯9)	seventh, flat fifth, sharp ninth
m	minor	11	eleventh
m(add9)	minor, added ninth	7♯11	seventh, sharp eleventh
m6	minor sixth	13	thirteenth
m♭6	minor, flat sixth	13sus4	thirteenth, suspended fourth
m6/9	minor sixth, added ninth	+	augmented
m7	minor seventh	+7	seventh, sharp fifth
m7♭5	minor seventh, flat fifth	+9	ninth, sharp fifth
m(maj7)	minor, major seventh	+7♭9	seventh, sharp fifth, flat ninth
m9	minor ninth	+7♯9	seventh, sharp fifth, sharp ninth
m9♭5	minor ninth, flat fifth	°	diminished
m9(maj7)	minor ninth, major seventh	°7	diminished seventh

HOW DO I BUILD A CHORD?

All chords are constructed using intervals. An interval is the distance between any two notes. Though there are many types of intervals, there are only five categories: *major, minor, perfect, augmented,* and *diminished.* Interestingly, the major scale contains only major and perfect intervals:

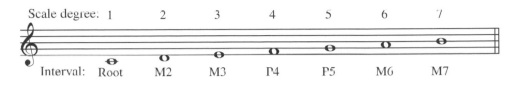

The major scale also happens to be a great starting point from which to construct chords. For example, if we start at the root (C) and add the interval of a major third (E) and a perfect fifth (G), we have constructed a C major chord.

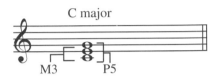

In order to construct a chord other than a major chord, at least one of the major or perfect intervals needs to be altered. For example, take the C major chord you just constructed, and lower the third degree (E) one half step. We now have a C minor chord: C-E♭-G. By lowering the major third by one half step, we create a new interval called a *minor* third.

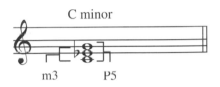

We can further alter the chord by flatting the perfect fifth (G). The chord is now a C°: C-E♭-G♭. The G♭ represents a *diminished* fifth interval.

This leads us to a basic rule of thumb to help remember interval alterations:

A major interval lowered one half step is a minor interval.

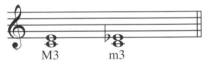

A perfect interval lowered one half step is a diminished interval.

A perfect interval raised one half step is an augmented interval.

☞ Half steps and whole steps are the building blocks of intervals; they determine an interval's quality—major, minor, etc. On the guitar, a *half step* is just the distance from one fret to the next. A *whole step* is equal to two half steps, or two frets.

WHAT ABOUT OTHER KEYS?

Notice that we assigned a numerical value to each note in the major scale, as well as labeling the intervals. These numerical values, termed *scale degrees,* allow us to "generically" construct chords, regardless of key. For example, a major chord consists of the root (1), major third (3), and perfect fifth (5). Substitute any major scale for the C major scale above, select scale degrees 1, 3, and 5, and you will have a major chord for the scale you selected.

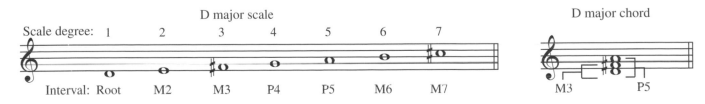

The chart below is a construction summary of the chord types in this book (based on the key of C only) using the scale degree method:

CHORD TYPE	FORMULA	NOTES	CHORD NAME
major	1-3-5	C-E-G	C
fifth (power chord)	1-5	C-G	C5
suspended fourth	1-4-5	C-F-G	Csus4
suspended second	1-2-5	C-D-G	Csus2
added ninth	1-3-5-9	C-E-G-D	Cadd9
sixth	1-3-5-6	C-E-G-A	C6
sixth, added ninth	1-3-5-6-9	C-E-G-A-D	C6/9
major seventh	1-3-5-7	C-E-G-B	Cmaj7
major ninth	1-3-5-7-9	C-E-G-B-D	Cmaj9
major seventh, sharp eleventh	1-3-5-7-♯11	C-E-G-B-F♯	Cmaj7♯11
major thirteenth	1-3-5-7-9-13	C-E-G-B-D-A	Cmaj13
minor	1-♭3-5	C-E♭-G	Cm
minor, added ninth	1-♭3-5-9	C-E♭-G-D	Cm(add9)
minor sixth	1-♭3-5-6	C-E♭-G-A	Cm6
minor, flat sixth	1-♭3-5-♭6	C-E♭-G-A♭	Cm♭6
minor sixth, added ninth	1-♭3-5-6-9	C-Eb-G-A-D	Cm6/9
minor seventh	1-♭3-5-♭7	C-E♭-G-B♭	Cm7
minor seventh, flat fifth	1-♭3-♭5-♭7	C-E♭-G♭-B♭	Cm7♭5
minor, major seventh	1-♭3-5-7	C-E♭-G-B	Cm(maj7)
minor ninth	1-♭3-5-♭7-9	C-E♭-G-B♭-D	Cm9
minor ninth, flat fifth	1-♭3-♭5-♭7-9	C-E♭-G♭-B♭-D	Cm9♭5
minor ninth, major seventh	1-♭3-5-7-9	C-E♭-G-B-D	Cm9(maj7)
minor eleventh	1-♭3-5-♭7-9-11	C-E♭-G-B♭-D-F	Cm11
minor thirteenth	1-♭3-5-♭7-9-11-13	C-E♭-G-B♭-D-F-A	Cm13
dominant seventh	1-3-5-♭7	C-E-G-B♭	C7
seventh, suspended fourth	1-4-5-♭7	C-F-G-B♭	C7sus4
seventh, flat fifth	1-3-♭5-♭7	C-E-G♭-B♭	C7♭5
ninth	1-3-5-♭7-9	C-E-G-B♭-D	C9
ninth, suspended fourth	1-4-5-♭7-9	C-F-G-B♭-D	C9sus4
ninth, flat fifth	1-3-♭5-♭7-9	C-E-G♭-B♭-D	C9♭5
seventh, flat ninth	1-3-5-♭7-♭9	C-E-G-B♭-D♭	C7♭9
seventh, sharp ninth	1-3-5-♭7-♯9	C-E-G-B♭-D♯	C7♯9
seventh, flat fifth, sharp ninth	1-3-♭5-♭7-♯9	C-E-G♭-B♭-D♯	C7♭5(♯9)
eleventh	1-5-♭7-9-11	C-G-B♭-D-F	C11
seventh, sharp eleventh	1-3-5-♭7-♯11	C-E-G-B♭-F♯	C7♯11
thirteenth	1-3-5-♭7-9-13	C-E-G-B♭-D-A	C13
thirteenth, suspended fourth	1-4-5-♭7-9-13	C-F-G-B♭-D-A	C13sus4
augmented	1-3-♯5	C-E-G♯	C+
seventh, sharp fifth	1-3-♯5-♭7	C-E-G♯-B♭	C+7
ninth, sharp fifth	1-3-♯5-♭7-9	C-E-G♯-B♭-D	C+9
seventh, sharp fifth, flat ninth	1-3-♯5-♭7-♭9	C-E-G♯-B♭-D♭	C+7♭9
seventh, sharp fifth, sharp ninth	1-3-♯5-♭7-♯9	C-E-G♯-B♭-D♯	C+7♯9
diminished	1-♭3-♭5	C-E♭-G♭	C°
diminished seventh	1-♭3-♭5-♭♭7	C-E♭-G♭-B♭♭	C°7

TRIADS

The most basic chords in this book are called triads. A *triad* is a chord that is made up of only three notes. For example, a simple G major chord is a triad consisting of the notes G, B, and D. There are several types of triads, including major, minor, diminished, augmented, and suspended. All of these chords are constructed by simply altering the relationships between the root note and the intervals.

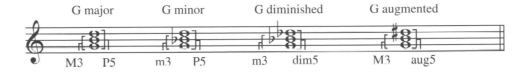

SEVENTHS

To create more interesting harmony, we can take the familiar triad and add another interval: the seventh. Seventh chords are comprised of four notes: the three notes of the triad plus a major or minor seventh interval. For example, if we use the G major triad (G-B-D) and add a major seventh interval (F♯), the Gmaj7 chord is formed. Likewise, if we substitute the minor seventh interval (F) for the F♯, we have a new seventh chord, the G7. This is also known as a dominant seventh chord, popularly used in blues and jazz music. As with the triads, seventh chords come in many types, including major, minor, diminished, augmented, suspended, and others.

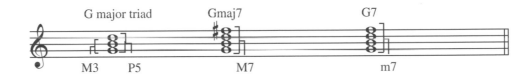

EXTENDED CHORDS

Extended chords are those that include notes beyond the seventh scale degree. These chords have a rich, complex harmony that is very common in jazz music. These include ninths, elevenths, and thirteenth chords. For example, if we take a Gmaj7 chord and add a major ninth interval (A), we get a Gmaj9 chord (G-B-D-F♯-A). We can then add an additional interval, a major thirteenth (E), to form a Gmaj13 chord (G-B-D-F♯-A-E). Note that the interval of a major eleventh is omitted. This is because the major eleventh sonically conflicts with the major third interval, creating a dissonance.

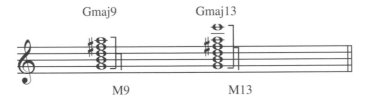

By the way, you may have noticed that these last two chords, Gmaj9 and Gmaj13, contain five and six notes, respectively; however, we only have four fingers in the left hand! Since the use of a barre chord or open-string chord is not always possible, we often need to choose the four notes of the chord that are most important to play. The harmonic theory that underlies these choices is beyond the scope of this book, but not to worry—it has already been done for you where necessary. Below are two examples to demonstrate these chord "trimmings."

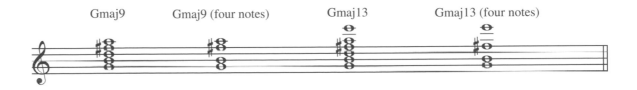

Generally speaking, the root, third, and seventh are the most crucial notes to include in an extended chord, along with the uppermost extension (ninth, thirteenth, etc.).

INVERSIONS & VOICINGS

This brings us to our last topic. Though a typical chord might consist of only three or four notes—a C triad, for example, consists of just a root, third, and fifth; a G7 chord consists of a root, third, fifth, and seventh—these notes do not necessarily have to appear in that same order, from bottom to top, in the actual chords you play. Inversions are produced when you rearrange the notes of a chord:

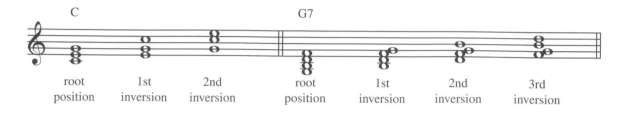

Practically speaking, on the guitar, notes of a chord are often inverted (rearranged), doubled (used more than once), and even omitted to create different voicings. Each voicing is unique and yet similar—kind of like different shades of the same color.

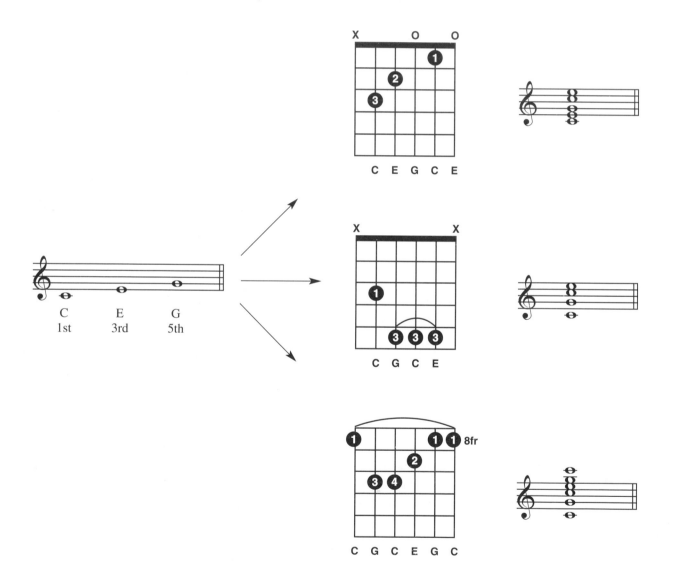

Once again, the possible voicings of a chord are many. The voicings in this book were chosen because they are some of the most popular, useful, and attractive chord voicings playable on the guitar.

C (Cmaj)
C major

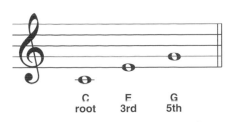

C root   F 3rd   G 5th

C5 (C no 3rd)
C fifth (power chord)

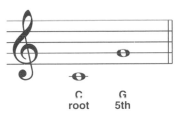

C root   G 5th

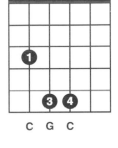

X O O
C E G C E

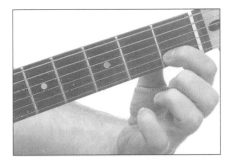
X X X O X
G C

X X
C G C E

X X X X
C G C

X 5fr
C E G C E

X X 5fr
G C G C

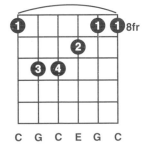
8fr
C G C E G C

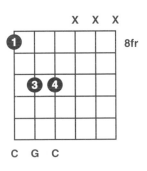
X X X 8fr
C G C

X X X 12fr
E G C

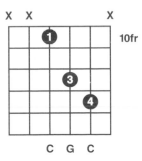
X X X 10fr
C G C

Csus4 (Csus)
C suspended fourth

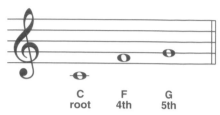

C root   F 4th   G 5th

X   O

C F G C F

3fr

G C G C F

X X   5fr

G C F C

8fr

C F C F G C

X X   10fr

C G C F

Csus2 (C5add2)
C suspended second

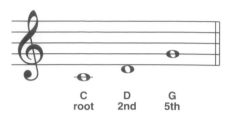

C root   D 2nd   G 5th

X O O

C D G C G

X   X X   3fr

C G D

X   5fr

D G C G C

X X   7fr

C D G D

X   10fr

D G D G C

Cadd9
C added ninth

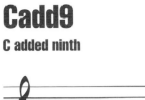

C	E	G	D
root	3rd	5th	9th

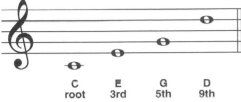

X   O

C E G D G

X

① ... ① 3fr

② ... ③

④

C G D E G

X   X

① ① ① ① 5fr

D G C E

X   X

① ... ② 7fr

③ ④

E   D G C

X   X

① ... ① 10fr

③

④

C G C D

C6
C sixth

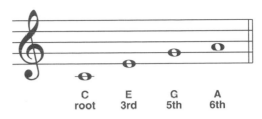

C	E	G	A
root	3rd	5th	6th

X   O

①
② ③

④

C E A C E

X

①

③ ③ ③ ③

C G C E A

X   X

① 7fr
② ... ③

④

C   A E G

X   X

① 8fr

②

③   ④

C E A C

X   X

① ... ②   ④ 12fr

③

A   G C E

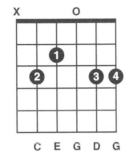
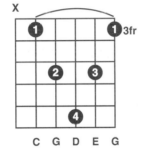
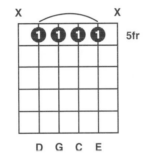
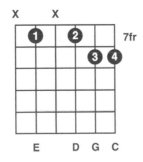
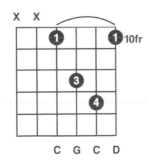
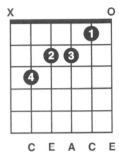
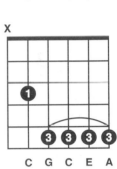
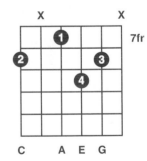
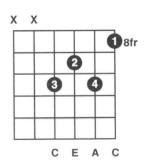
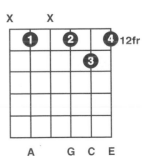

C6/9 (C6add9)
C sixth, added ninth

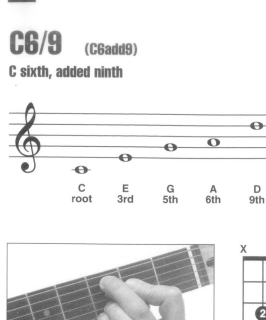

C	E	G	A	D
root	3rd	5th	6th	9th

X

C E A D G

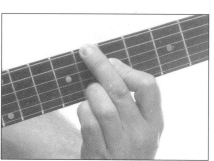

X

D G C E A

X X

7fr

C A D G

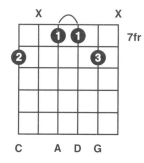

X X

9fr

C E A D

X

12fr

A D G C E

Cmaj7 (CM7)
C major seventh

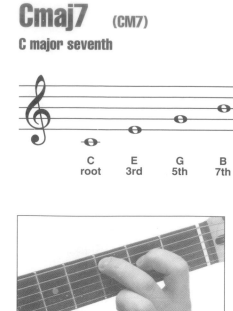

C	E	G	B
root	3rd	5th	7th

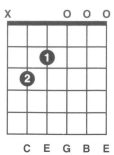

X O O O

C E G B E

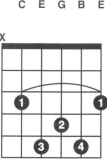

X

C G B E G

X X

5fr

G C E B

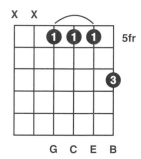

X X

8fr

C B E G

X X

10fr

C G B E

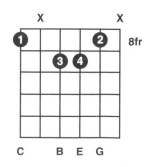

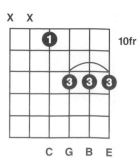

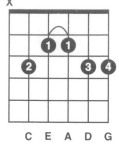

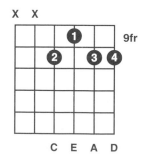

Cmaj9 (CM9)
C major ninth

C	E	G	B	D
root	3rd	5th	7th	9th

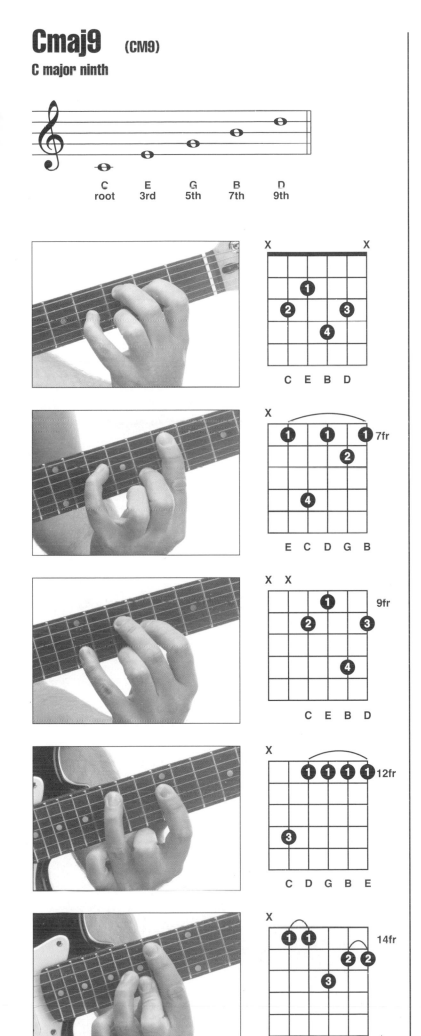

X ... X
C E B D

X
E C D G B — 7fr

X X
C E B D — 9fr

X
C D G B E — 12fr

X
B E B D G — 14fr

Cmaj7#11 (CM7#11)
C major seventh, sharp eleventh

C	E	G	B	F#
root	3rd	5th	7th	#11th

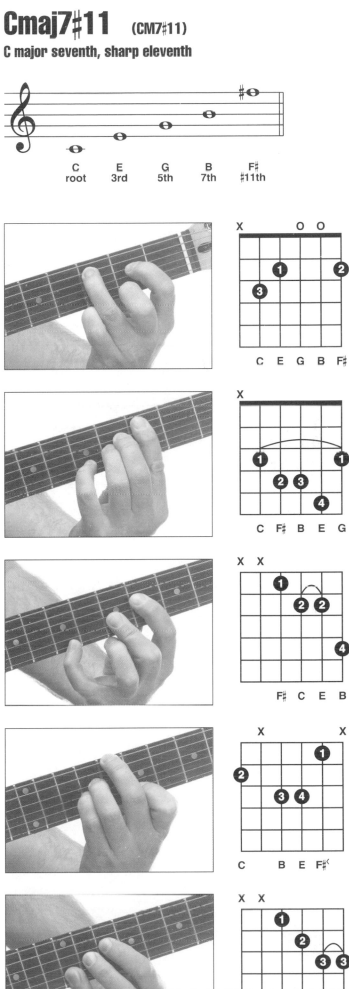

X O O
C E G B F#

X
C F# B E G

X X
F# C E B — 4fr

X X
C B E F#< — 7fr

X X
C F# B E — 10fr

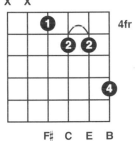
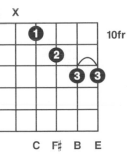

Cmaj13 (CM13)
C major thirteenth

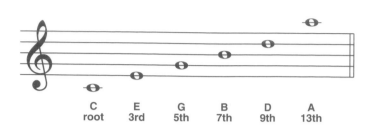

C	E	G	B	D	A
root	3rd	5th	7th	9th	13th

G C D A B E

C B E A

C E A D G B — 7fr

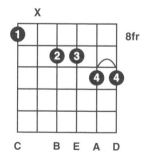
C B E A D — 8fr

A C G B E — 10fr

Cm (Cmin, C-)
C minor

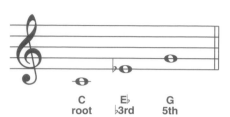

C	E♭	G
root	♭3rd	5th

C E♭ G C

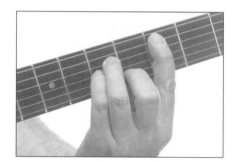
C G C E♭ G

C G C E♭ G C — 8fr

E♭ C G C — 10fr

E♭ G C E♭ — 11fr

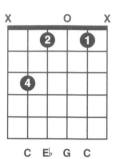
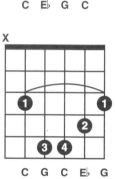
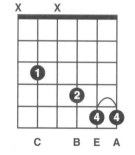
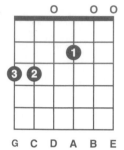

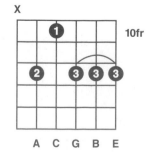
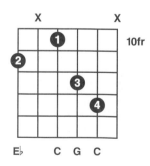
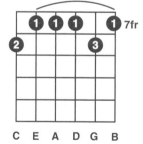
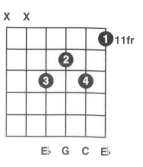

Cm(add9)
C minor, added ninth

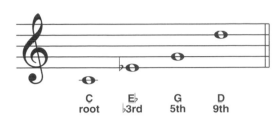

C	E♭	G	D
root	♭3rd	5th	9th

X   O

C E♭ G D G

X   X 3fr

E♭ G C D

X   X 6fr

E♭ D G C

X X 8fr

C E♭ G D

X X 11fr

D G C E♭

Cm6 (Cmin6, C-6)
C minor sixth

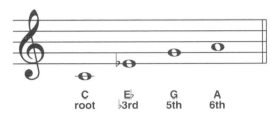

C	E♭	G	A
root	♭3rd	5th	6th

X

C E♭ A C G

X X 4fr

G C E♭ A

X   X 7fr

C A E♭ G

X   X 10fr

E♭ C G A

X X 13fr

E♭ A C G

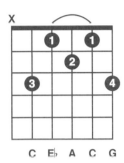
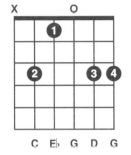
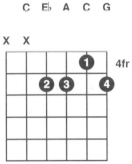
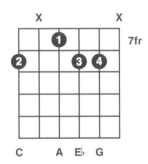
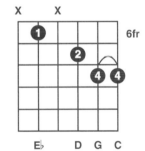
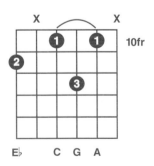
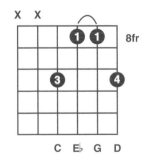
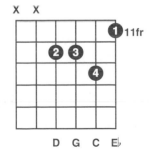
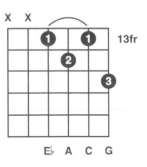

Cm♭6 <small>(C-(♭6), Cmin♭6)</small>
C minor, flat sixth

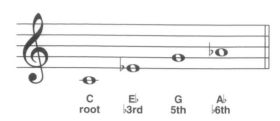

C	E♭	G	A♭
root	♭3rd	5th	♭6th

C E♭ A C G

4fr

A♭ G C E♭

6fr

C A♭ E♭ G

8fr

G C E♭ A♭

11fr

A♭ E♭ G C E♭

Cm6/9
C minor sixth, added ninth

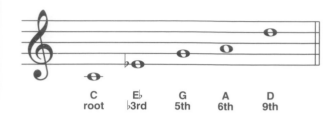

C	E♭	G	A	D
root	♭3rd	5th	6th	9th

E♭ A D G

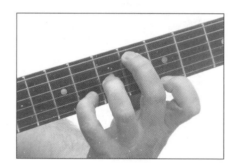

5fr

E♭ D G A

6fr

E♭ A D G C

7fr

A E♭ G D

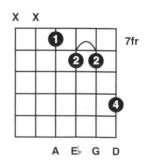

11fr

D A C E♭

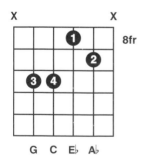
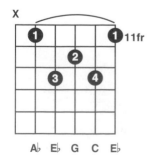
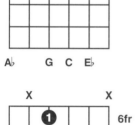
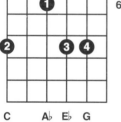
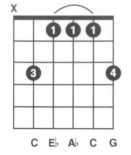
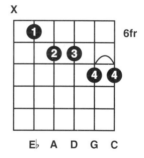
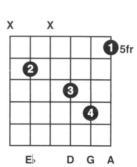
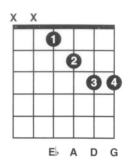

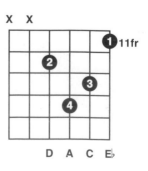

Cm7 (Cmin7, C-7)
C minor seventh

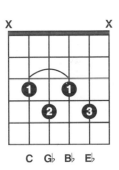

C root   E♭ ♭3rd   G 5th   B♭ ♭7th

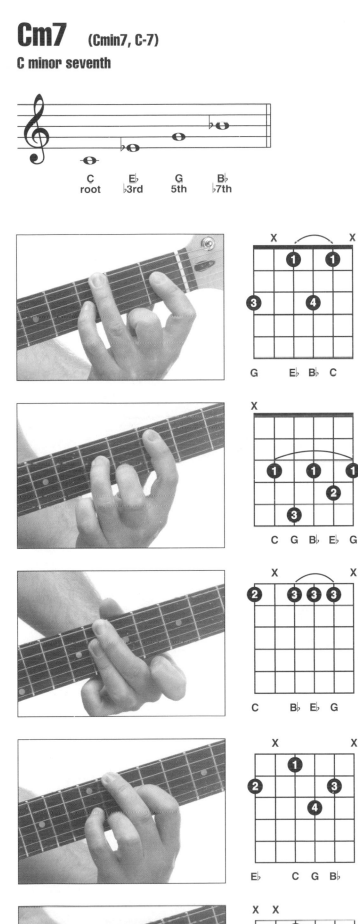

X   X

G   E♭   B♭   C

X

C G B♭ E♭ G

X   X   8fr

C   B♭ E♭ G

X   X   10fr

E♭   C G B♭

X   X   10fr

C G B♭ E♭

Cm7♭5 (C-7(♭5), Cmin7-5)
C minor seventh, flat fifth

C root   F♭ ♭3rd   G♭ ♭5th   B♭ ♭7th

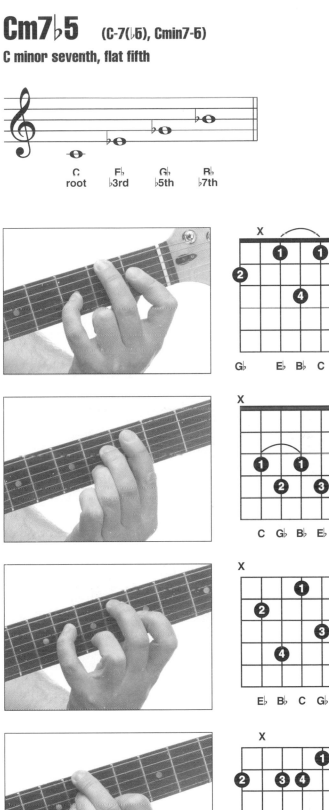

X   X

G♭   E♭   B♭   C

X   X

C G♭ B♭ E♭

X   X   5fr

E♭ B♭ C G♭

X   X   7fr

C   B♭ E♭ G♭

X   X   10fr

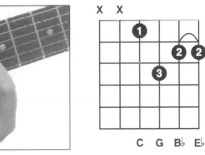

C G♭ B♭ E♭

Cm(maj7) (Cm(+7))
C minor, major seventh

C	E♭	G	B
root	♭3rd	5th	7th

Cm9 (Cmin9, C-9)
C minor ninth

C	E♭	G	B♭	D
root	♭3rd	5th	♭7th	9th

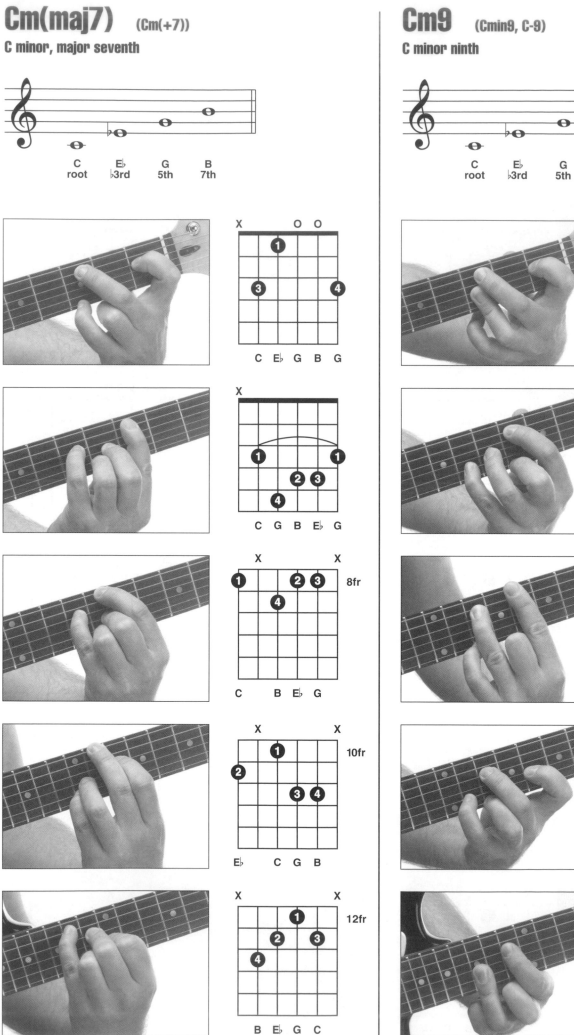

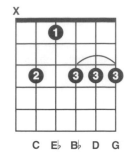

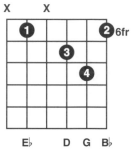

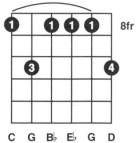

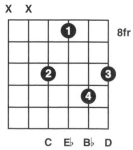

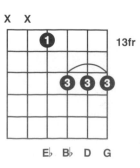

Cm9♭5 (Cm9-5, Cmin9♭5)
C minor ninth, flat fifth

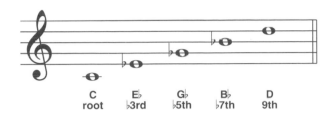

C	E♭	G♭	B♭	D
root	♭3rd	♭5th	♭7th	9th

Cm9(maj7) (Cm9+7, C-θ+7)
C minor ninth, major seventh

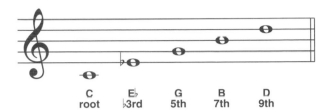

C	E♭	G	B	D
root	♭3rd	5th	7th	9th

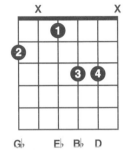

G♭   E♭ B♭ D

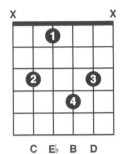

C E♭ B D

6fr

E♭   D G♭ B♭

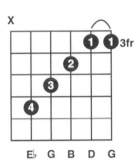

3fr

E♭ G B D G

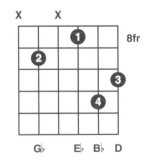

8fr

C G♭ B♭ E♭ B♭ D

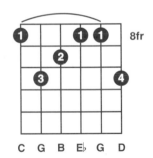

8fr

C G B E♭ G D

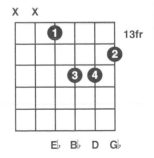

8fr

G♭   E♭ B♭ D

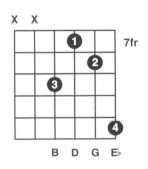

7fr

B D G E♭

13fr

E♭ B♭ D G♭

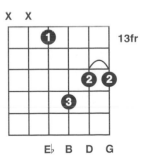

13fr

E♭ B D G

Cm11 (C-11, Cmin11)
C minor eleventh

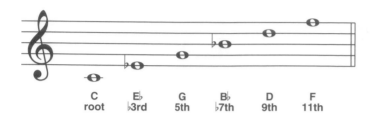

C	E♭	G	B♭	D	F
root	♭3rd	5th	♭7th	9th	11th

Cm13 (C-13, Cmin13)
C minor thirteenth

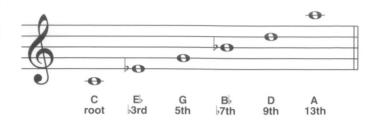

C	E♭	G	B♭	D	A
root	♭3rd	5th	♭7th	9th	13th

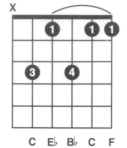
C E♭ B♭ C F

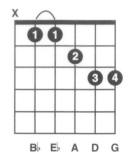
B♭ E♭ A D G

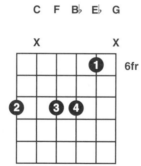
C F B♭ E♭ G

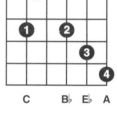
C B♭ E♭ A

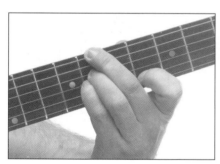
6fr
C B♭ E♭ F

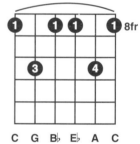
8fr
C G B♭ E♭ A C

10fr
C F B♭ E♭

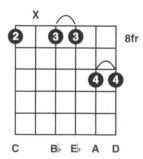
8fr
C B♭ E♭ A D

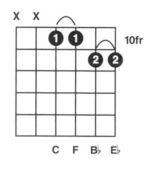
13fr
C B♭ E♭ F

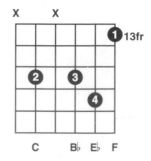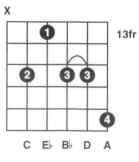
13fr
C E♭ B♭ D A

C7 (Cdom7)
C dominant seventh

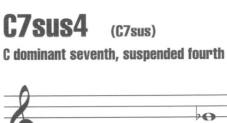

C E G B♭
root 3rd 5th ♭7th

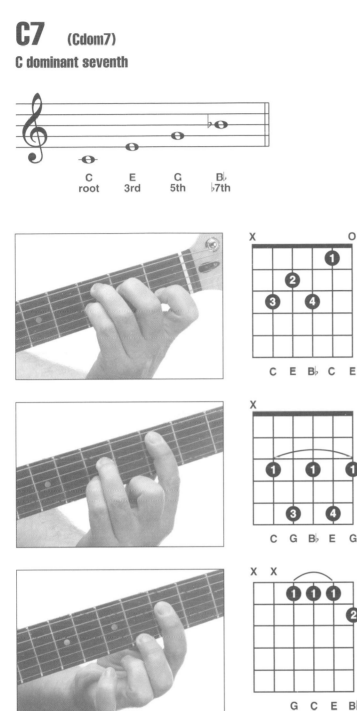

X   O

C E B♭ C E

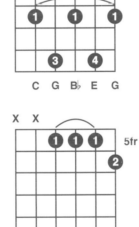

X

C G B♭ E G

X X

5fr

G C E B♭

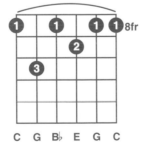

8fr

C G B♭ E G C

X X

10fr

C G B♭ E

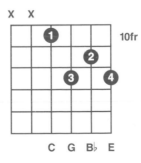

C7sus4 (C7sus)
C dominant seventh, suspended fourth

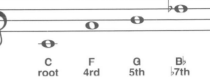

C F G B♭
root 4rd 5th ♭7th

X   X

C F B♭ C

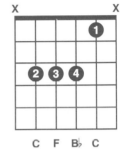

3fr

C G B♭ F G

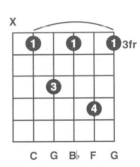

X X

5fr

G C F B♭

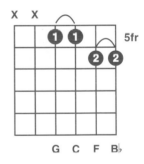

8fr

C G B♭ F G C

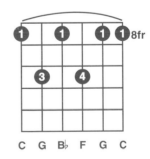

X X

10fr

C G B♭ F

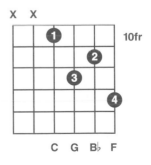

C7♭5 (C7-5, Cdom7♭5)
C dominant seventh, flat fifth

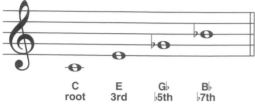

C	E	G♭	B♭
root	3rd	♭5th	♭7th

C9
C ninth

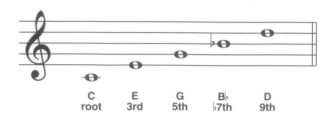

C	E	G	B♭	D
root	3rd	5th	♭7th	9th

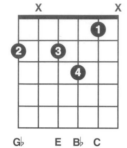
G♭ E B♭ C

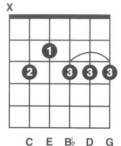
C E B♭ D G

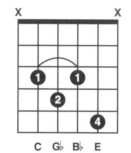
C G♭ B♭ E

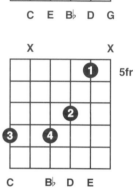
5fr
C B♭ D E

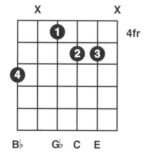
4fr
B♭ G♭ C E

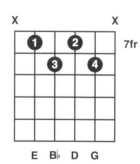
7fr
E B♭ D G

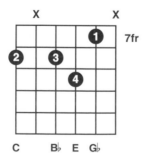
7fr
C B♭ E G♭

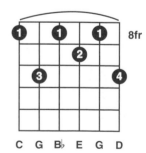
8fr
C G B♭ E G D

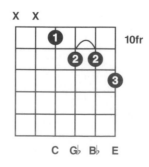
10fr
C G♭ B♭ E

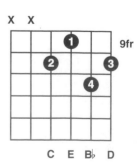
9fr
C E B♭ D

C

C9sus4 (C9sus)
C ninth, suspended fourth

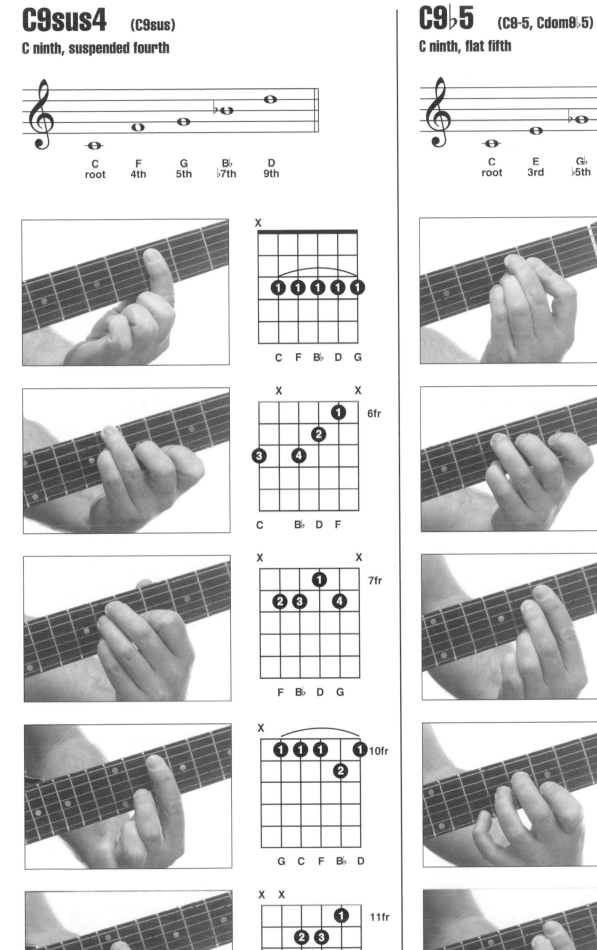

C F G B♭ D
root 4th 5th ♭7th 9th

C F B♭ D G

X

X   X
1   6fr
2
3   4

C   B♭ D F

X   X
1   7fr
2 3   4

F B♭ D G

X
1 1 1   1 10fr
2

G C F B♭ D

X X
1   11fr
2 3
4

D G B♭ F

C9♭5 (C⊖-5, Cdom9♭5)
C ninth, flat fifth

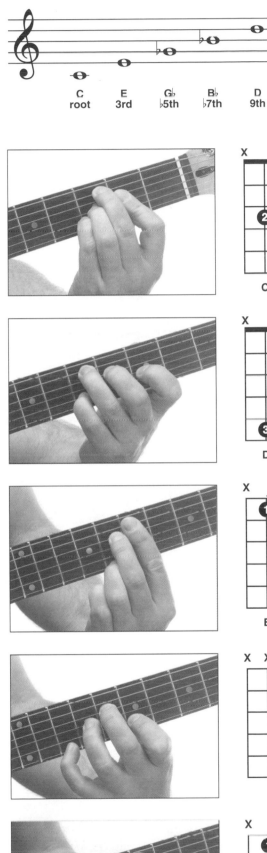
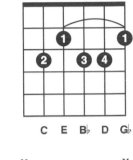
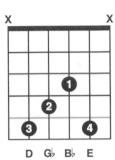
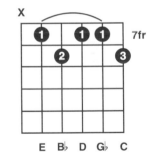
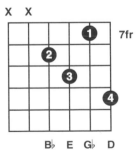
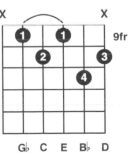

C E G♭ B♭ D
root 3rd ♭5th ♭7th 9th

X
1   1
2   3 4

C E B♭ D G♭

X   X
1
2
3   4

D G♭ B♭ E

X
1 1 1 7fr
2   3

E B♭ D G♭ C

X X
1 7fr
2
3
4

B♭ E G♭ D

X   X
1 1   9fr
2   3
4

G♭ C E B♭ D

C7♭9 (C7-9, Cdom7♭9)
C dominant seventh, flat ninth

C   E   G   B♭   D♭
root 3rd   5th   ♭7th ♭9th

C7♯9 (C7+9, Cdom7♯9)
C dominant seventh, sharp ninth

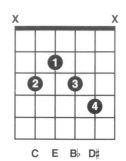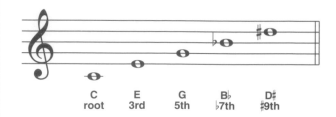

C   E   G   B♭   D♯
root 3rd   5th   ♭7th ♯9th

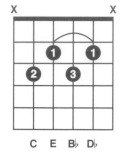

X   X

① ①
② ③

C E B♭ D♭

X   X

①
②
③ ④

C E B♭ D♯

X   X

①
②
③ ④

D♭ G B♭ E

①
③ ③ ③ ③ 7fr

E B♭ D♯ G C

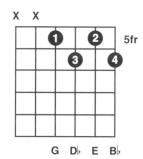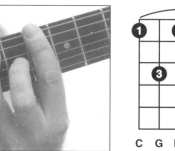

X X

① ② 5fr
③ ④

G D♭ E B♭

① ① ① 8fr
②
③
④

C G B♭ E G D♯

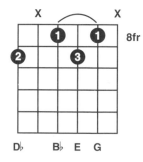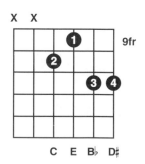

X   X

① ① 8fr
② ③

D♭ B♭ E G

X X

① 9fr
②
③ ④

C E B♭ D♯

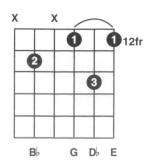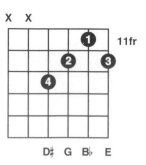

X X

① ① 12fr
②
③

B♭ G D♭ E

X X

① 11fr
② ③
④

D♯ G B♭ E

C7♭5(♯9) (C7-5(+9), Cdom7♭5(♯9))
C dominant seventh, flat fifth, sharp ninth

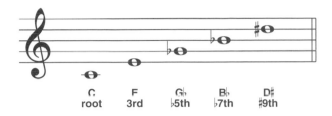

C	F	G♭	B♭	D♯
root	3rd	♭5th	♭7th	♯9th

C11
C eleventh

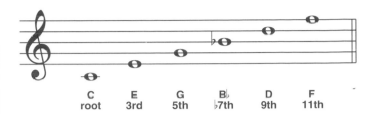

C	E	G	B♭	D	F
root	3rd	5th	♭7th	9th	11th

 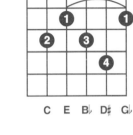

C E B♭ D♯ G♭

 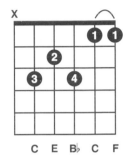

C E B♭ C F

7fr

E B♭ D♯ G♭

 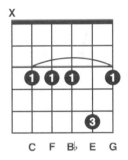

C F B♭ E G

 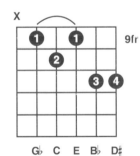

9fr

G♭ C E B♭ D♯

 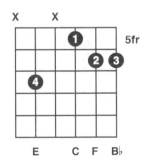

5fr

E C F B♭

 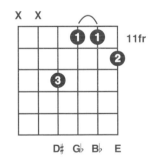

11fr

D♯ G♭ B♭ E

 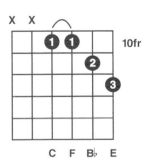

10fr

C F B♭ E

 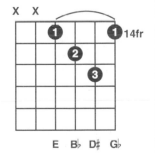

14fr

E B♭ D♯ G♭

 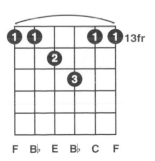

13fr

F B♭ E B♭ C F

C7#11 (C7+11, Cdom7#11)
C dominant seventh, sharp eleventh

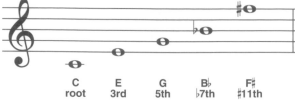

C	E	G	B♭	F#
root	3rd	5th	♭7th	#11th

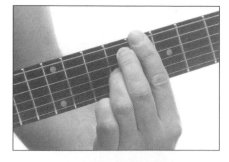

C13 (Cdom13)
C thirteenth

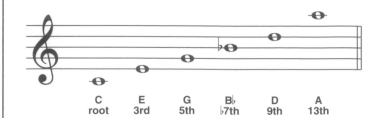

C	E	G	B♭	D	A
root	3rd	5th	♭7th	9th	13th

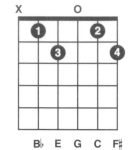
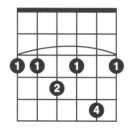
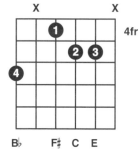
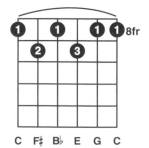
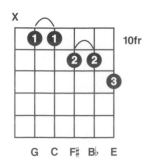
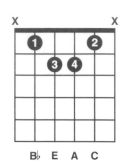
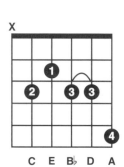
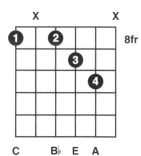
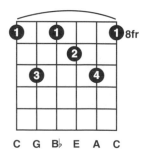
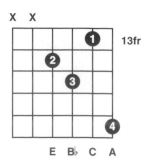

19

C

C13sus4 (C13sus)
C thirteenth, suspended fourth

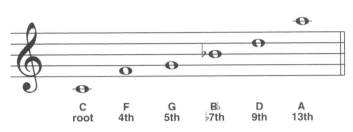

C	F	G	B♭	D	A
root	4th	5th	♭7th	9th	13th

C+ (Caug, C(♯5))
C augmented

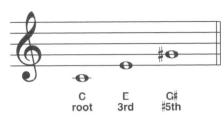

C	E	G♯
root	3rd	♯5th

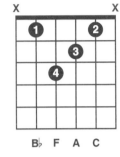
B♭ F A C

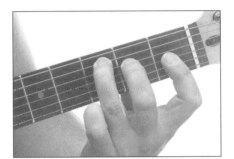
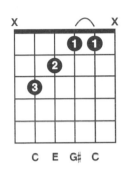
C E G♯ C

C F B♭ D A

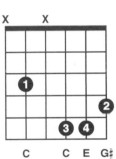
C C E G♯

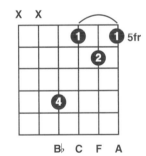
B♭ C F A · 5fr

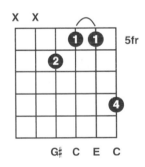
G♯ C E C · 5fr

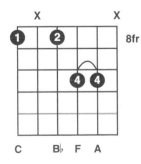
C B♭ F A · 8fr

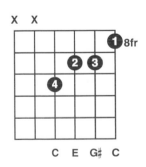
C E G♯ C · 8fr

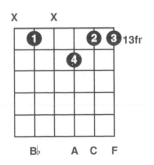
B♭ A C F · 13fr

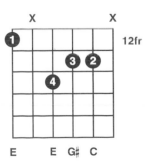
E E G♯ C · 12fr

C+7 (C7♯5)
C dominant seventh, sharp fifth

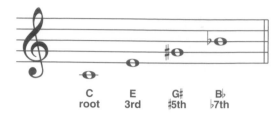

C	E	G♯	B♭
root	3rd	♯5th	♭7th

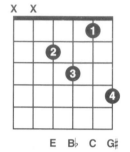

X X
E B♭ C G♯

X
3fr
C G♯ B♭ E G♯

X X
5fr
B♭ G♯ C E

X X
8fr
C B♭ E G♯

X X
10fr
C G♯ B♭ E

C+9 (C9♯5, C9+5)
C ninth, sharp fifth

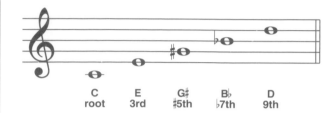

C	E	G♯	B♭	D
root	3rd	♯5th	♭7th	9th

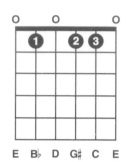

O O O
E B♭ D G♯ C E

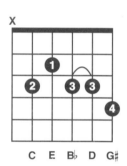

X
C E B♭ D G♯

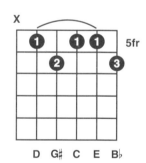

X
5fr
D G♯ C E B♭

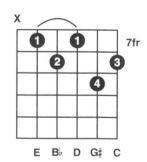

X
7fr
E B♭ D G♯ C

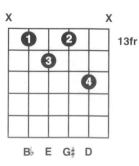

X X
13fr
B♭ E G♯ D

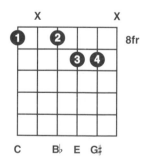
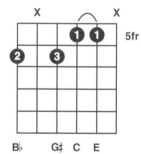
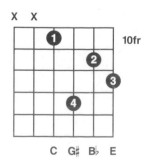

C+7♭9 (C7+5(♭9))

C dominant seventh, sharp fifth, flat ninth

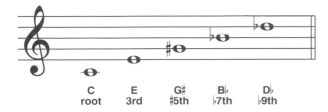

C   E   G#   B♭   D♭
root   3rd   #5th   ♭7th   ♭9th

C+7#9 (C7+5(#9))

C dominant seventh, sharp fifth, sharp ninth

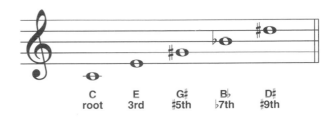

C   E   G#   B♭   D#
root   3rd   #5th   ♭7th   #9th

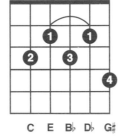

X

C E B♭ D♭ G#

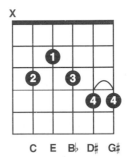

X

C E B♭ D# G#

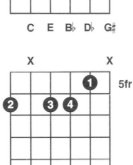

X   X

5fr

B♭   G# D♭ E

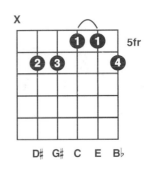

X   X

5fr

D# G# C E B♭

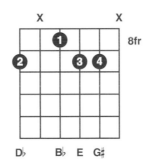

X   X

8fr

D♭   B♭ E G#

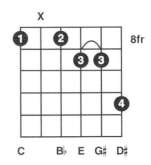

X

8fr

C   B♭ E G# D#

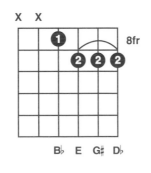

X X

8fr

B♭ E G# D♭

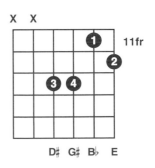

X X

11fr

D# G# B♭ E

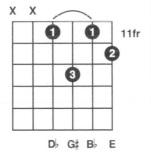

X X

11fr

D♭ G# B♭ E

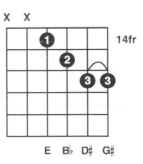

X X

14fr

E B♭ D# G#

C° (C dim)
C diminished

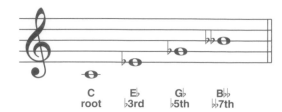

C root • E♭ ♭3rd • G♭ ♭5th

 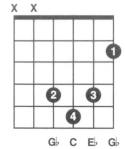

G♭ C E♭ G♭

 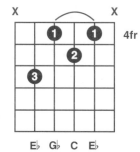

E♭ G♭ C E♭ — 4fr

 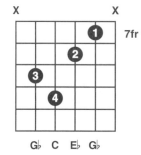

G♭ C E♭ G♭ — 7fr

 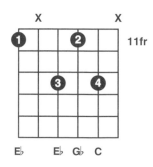

E♭ E♭ G♭ C — 11fr

 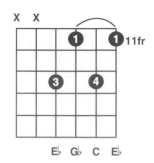

E♭ G♭ C E♭ — 11fr

C°7 (Cdim7)
C diminished seventh

 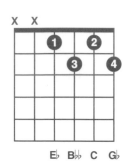

C root • E♭ ♭3rd • G♭ ♭5th • B♭♭ ♭♭7th

E♭ B♭♭ C G♭

 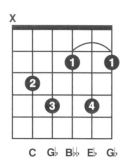

C G♭ B♭♭ E♭ G♭

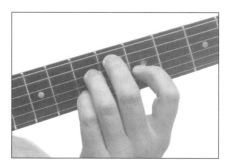 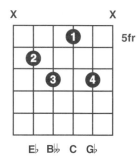

E♭ B♭♭ C G♭ — 5fr

 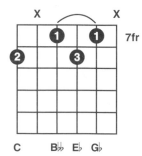

C B♭♭ E♭ G♭ — 7fr

 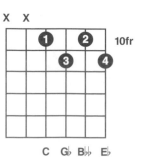

C G♭ B♭♭ E♭ — 10fr

C# (C#maj)
C-sharp major

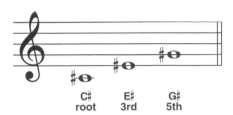

C#   E#   G#
root   3rd   5th

C#5 (C# no 3rd)
C-sharp fifth (power chord)

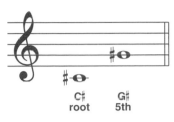

C#   G#
root   5th

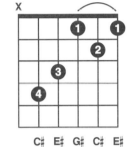

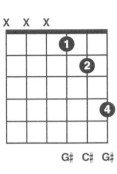

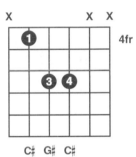

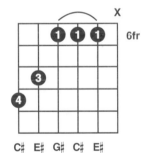

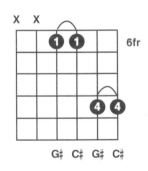

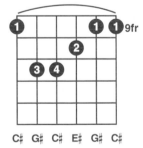

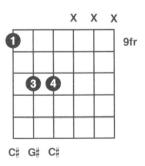

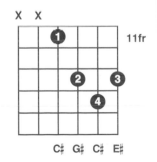

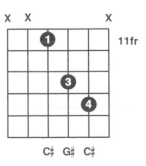

C#

C#sus4 (C#sus)
C-sharp suspended fourth

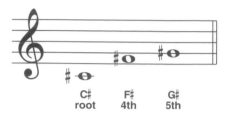

C#	F#	G#
root	4th	5th

X X X

G# C# F#

X

4fr

C# F# C# F# G#

X X 6fr

G# C# F# C#

9fr

C# F# C# F# G# C#

X X 11fr

C# G# C# F#

C#sus2 (C#5add2)
C-sharp suspended second

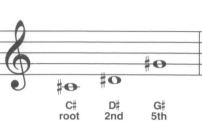

C#	D#	G#
root	2nd	5th

X X X

D# G# C#

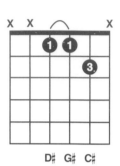

X 4fr

C# G# C# D# G#

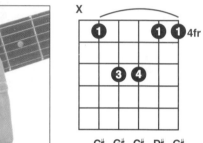

X 6fr

D# G# C# G# C#

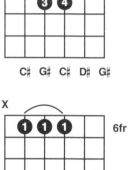

X X X 8fr

C# D# G#

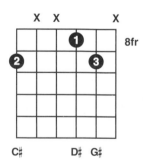

X X 11fr

C# G# C# D#

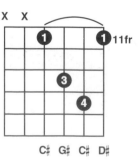

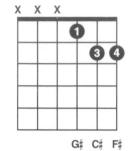

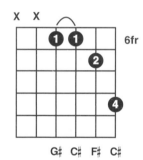

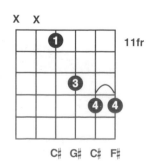

C#add9
C-sharp added ninth

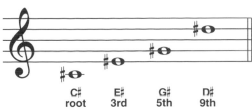

C#	E#	G#	D#
root	3rd	5th	9th

C#

 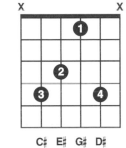

C# E# G# D#

4fr

C# G# D# E#

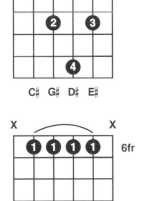

6fr

D# G# C# E#

8fr

E# D# G# C#

9fr

C# E# G# D#

C#6
C-sharp sixth

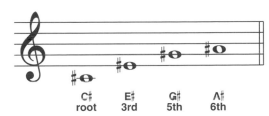

C#	E#	G#	A#
root	3rd	5th	6th

 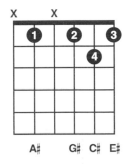

A# G# C# E#

 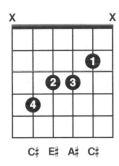

C# E# A# C#

 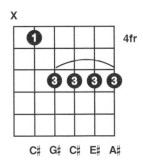

4fr

C# G# C# E# A#

 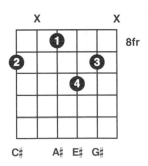

8fr

C# A# E# G#

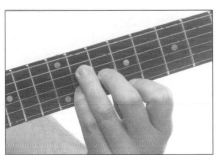 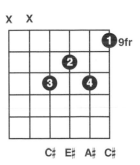

9fr

C# E# A# C#

C#6/9 (C#6add9)
C-sharp sixth, added ninth

C#	E#	G#	A#	D#
root	3rd	5th	6th	9th

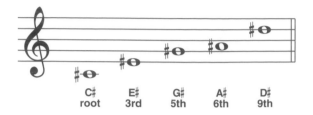

X

① ① ① ① ②

A# D# G# C# E#

X

① ①
② ③ ④

C# E# A# D# G#

① ① ① ① ① 6fr
④

C# D# G# C# E# A#

X X
① ① 8fr
③ ④

E# C# D# A#

X X
① 10fr
② ③ ④

C# E# A# D#

C#maj7 (C#M7)
C-sharp major seventh

C#	E#	G#	B#
root	3rd	5th	7th

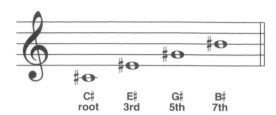

X

① ① ①
③
④

C# E# G# B# E#

X

① ① 4fr
②
③ ④

C# G# B# E# G#

X X

① ① ① 6fr
③

G# C# E# B#

X X
① ② 9fr
③ ④

C# B# E# G#

X X
① 11fr
③ ③ ③

C# G# B# E#

C#maj9 (C#M9)
C-sharp major ninth

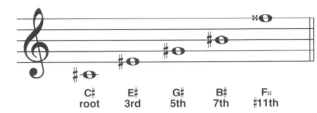

C#	E#	G#	B#	D#
root	3rd	5th	7th	9th

C#maj7#11 (C#M7#11)
C-sharp major seventh, sharp eleventh

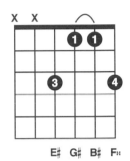

C#	E#	G#	B#	F×
root	3rd	5th	7th	#11th

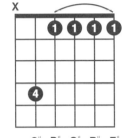

C# D# G# B# E#

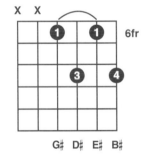

3fr

C# E# B# D#

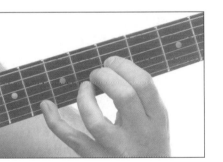

6fr

G# D# E# B#

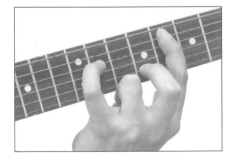
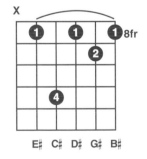

8fr

E# C# D# G# B#

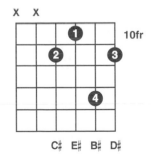

10fr

C# E# B# D#

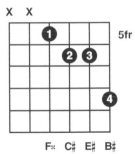

E# G# B# F×

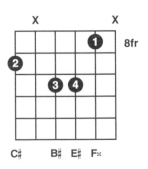

4fr

C# F× B# E# G#

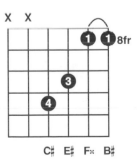

5fr

F× C# E# B#

8fr

C# B# E# F×

8fr

C# E# F× B#

C#maj13 (C#M13)
C-sharp major thirteenth

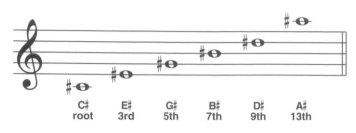

C#	E#	G#	B#	D#	A#
root	3rd	5th	7th	9th	13th

C#m (C#m, C#-)
C-sharp minor

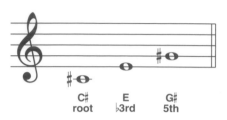

C#	E	G#
root	♭3rd	5th

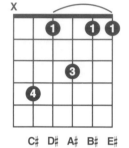

X

C# D# A# B# E#

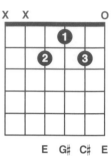

X X O

E G# C# E

X X

4fr

C# B# E# A#

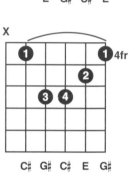

X

4fr

C# G# C# E G#

6fr

B# D# G# C# E# A#

X X

6fr

E G# C# G#

8fr

C# E# A# D# G# B#

9fr

C# G# C# E G# C#

X X

8fr

C# E# A# B#

X X

11fr

C# G# C# E

C#

C#m(add9)
C-sharp minor, added ninth

C#	E	G#	D#
root	♭3rd	5th	9th

C#m6 (C#min6, C#-6)
C-sharp minor sixth

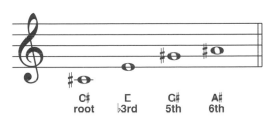

C#	E	G#	A#
root	♭3rd	5th	6th

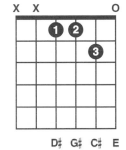
X X O
D# G# C# E

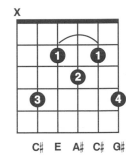
X
C# E A# C# G#

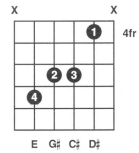
X X 4fr
E G# C# D#

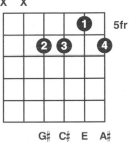
X X 5fr
G# C# E A#

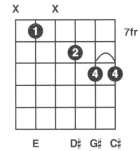
X X 7fr
E D# G# C#

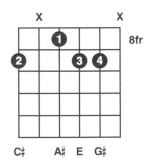
X X 8fr
C# A# E G#

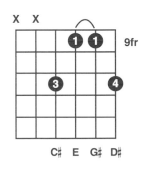
X X 9fr
C# E G# D#

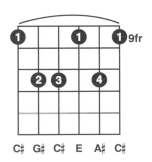
9fr
C# G# C# E A# C#

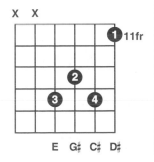
X X 11fr
E G# C# D#

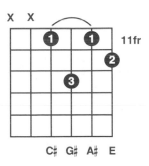
X X 11fr
C# G# A# E

C#m♭6 (C#-(♭6), C#min♭6)
C-sharp minor, flat sixth

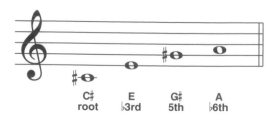

C#	E	G#	A
root	♭3rd	5th	♭6th

C#m6/9
C-sharp minor sixth, added ninth

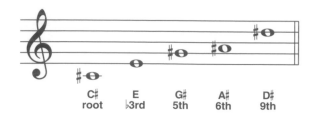

C#	E	G#	A#	D#
root	♭3rd	5th	6th	9th

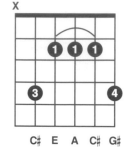

C# E A C# G#

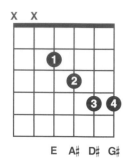

E A# D# G#

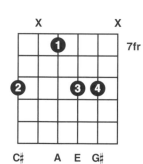

5fr

A G# C# E

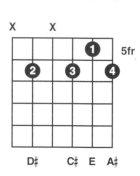

5fr

D# C# E A#

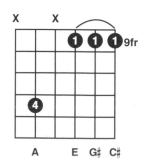

7fr

C# A E G#

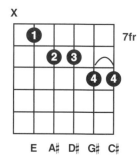

7fr

E A# D# G# C#

9fr

A E G# C#

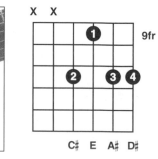

9fr

C# E A# D#

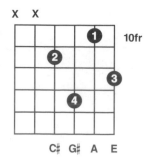

10fr

C# G# A E

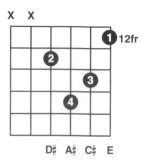

12fr

D# A# C# E

C#m7 (C#min7, C#-7)
C-sharp minor seventh

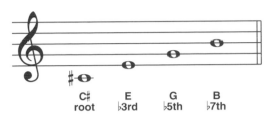

C# root | E ♭3rd | G# 5th | B ♭7th

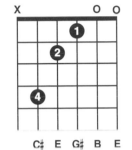

X   O O

① ②
④

C# E G# B E

X

① ① ①   4fr
②
③

C# G# B E G#

X X

①   5fr
② ③
④

G# C# E B

X   X

② ③ ③ ③   9fr

C# B E G#

X X

①   11fr
② ③
④

C# G# B E

C#m7♭5 (C#-7(♭5), C#min7-5)
C-sharp minor seventh, flat fifth

C# root | E ♭3rd | G ♭5th | B ♭7th

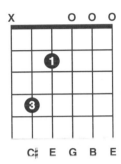

X   O O O

①
③

C# E G B E

X   X

① ①   4fr
② ③

C# G B E

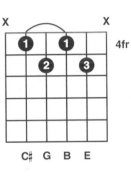

X   X

①   6fr
② ③
④

E C# G B

X   X

①   8fr
② ③ ④

C# B E G

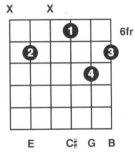

X X

①   11fr
③ ③ ③

C# G B E

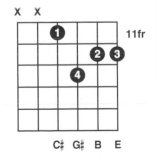
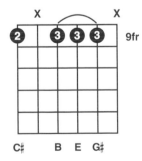

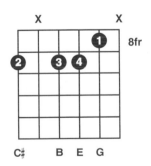
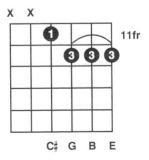
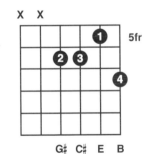

C#m(maj7) (C#m(+7))
C-sharp minor, major seventh

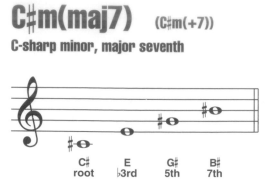

C#	E	G#	B#
root	♭3rd	5th	7th

C# E G# B#

4fr

C# G# B# E G#

9fr

C# B# E G#

9fr

B# E G# C#

11fr

C# G# B# E

C#m9 (C#min9, C#-9)
C-sharp minor ninth

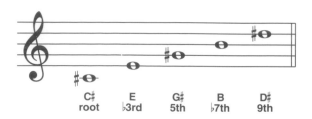

C#	E	G#	B	D#
root	♭3rd	5th	♭7th	9th

C# E B D#

5fr

E D# E B

9fr

C# G# B E G# D#

9fr

C# E B D#

12fr

D# G# B E

C#m9♭5 (C#m8-5, C#min8♭5)
C-sharp minor ninth, flat fifth

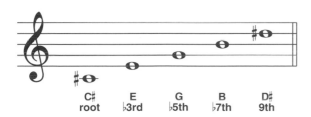

C#	E	G	B	D#
root	♭3rd	♭5th	♭7th	9th

C#m9(maj7) (C#m9+7, C#-9+7)
C-sharp minor ninth, major seventh

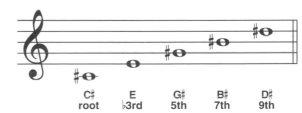

C#	E	G#	B#	D#
root	♭3rd	5th	7th	9th

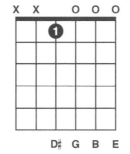
X X O O O
D# G B E

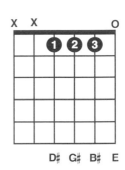
X X O
D# G# B# E

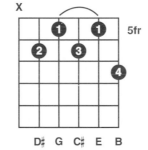
X X
G E B D#

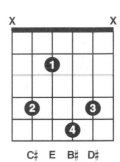
X X
C# E B# D#

X 5fr
D# G C# E B

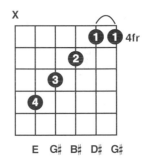
X 4fr
E G# B# D# G#

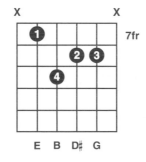
X X 7fr
E B D# G

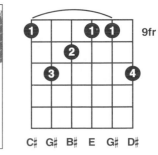
9fr
C# G# B# E G# D#

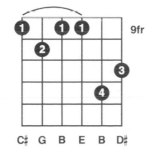
9fr
C# G B E B D#

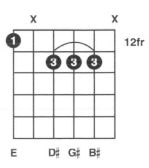
X X 12fr
E D# G# B#

C#m11 (C#-11, C#min11)
C-sharp minor eleventh

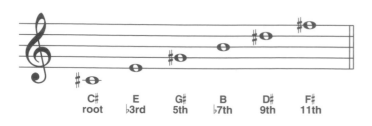

C#	E	G#	B	D#	F#
root	♭3rd	5th	♭7th	9th	11th

X

C# E B D# F#

X

C# F# B E G#

X

E B D# F# C# — 7fr

X X

C# B E F# — 7fr

X X

C# F# B E — 11fr

C#m13 (C#-13, C#min13)
C-sharp minor thirteenth

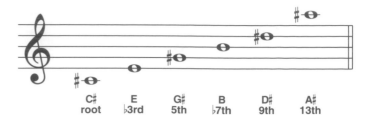

C#	E	G#	B	D#	A#
root	♭3rd	5th	♭7th	9th	13th

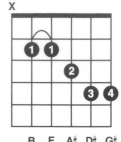

X

B E A# D# G#

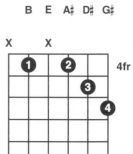

X X

C# B E A# — 4fr

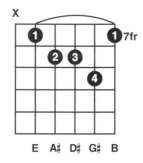

X

E A# D# G# B — 7fr

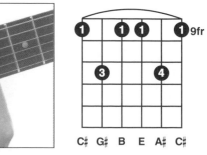

X X

C# G# B E A# C# — 9fr

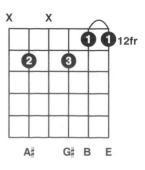

X X

A# G# B E — 12fr

C#7 (C#dom7)
C-sharp dominant seventh

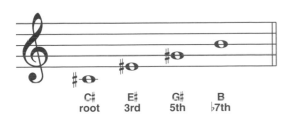

C#	E#	G#	B
root	3rd	5th	♭7th

C#7sus4 (C#7sus)
C-sharp dominant seventh, suspended fourth

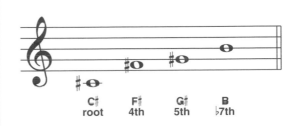

C#	F#	G#	B
root	4th	5th	♭7th

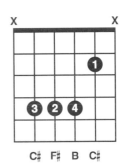

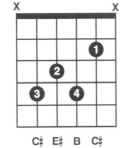
C# E# B C#

C# F# B C#

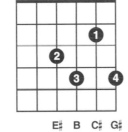
E# B C# G#

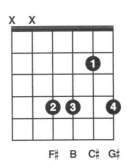
F# B C# G#

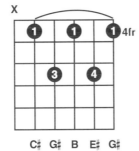
C# G# B E# G#   4fr

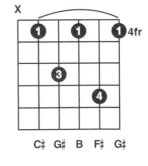
C# G# B F# G#   4fr

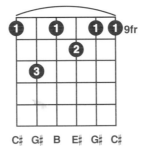
C# G# B E# G# C#   9fr

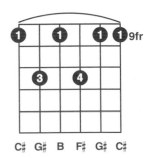
C# G# B F# G# C#   9fr

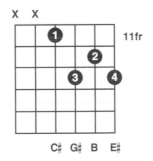
C# G# B E#   11fr

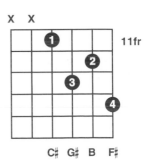
C# G# B F#   11fr

C#7♭5 (C#7-5, C#dom7♭5)
C-sharp dominant seventh, flat fifth

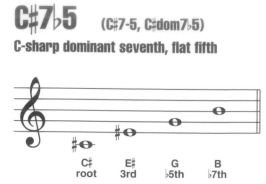

C#	E#	G	B
root	3rd	♭5th	♭7th

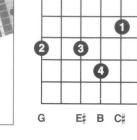

G E# B C#

C# G B E# 4fr

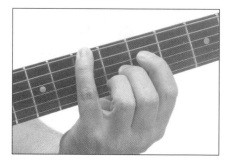
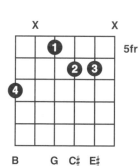

B G C# E# 5fr

C# B E# G 8fr

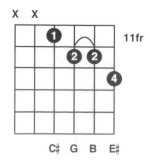

C# G B E# 11fr

C#9
C-sharp ninth

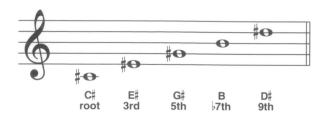

C#	E#	G#	B	D#
root	3rd	5th	♭7th	9th

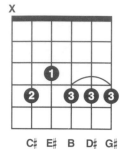

C# E# B D# G#

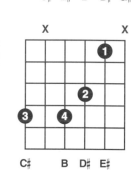

C# B D# E# 6fr

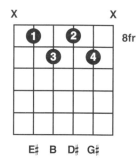

E# B D# G# 8fr

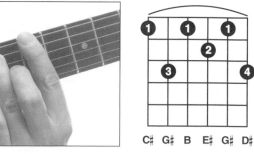

C# G# B E# G# D# 9fr

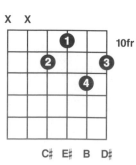

C# E# B D# 10fr

C#9sus4 (C#9sus)
C-sharp ninth, suspended fourth

C#	F#	G#	B	D#
root	4th	5th	♭7th	9th

C#9♭5 (C#9-5, C#dom9♭5)
C-sharp dominant ninth, flat fifth

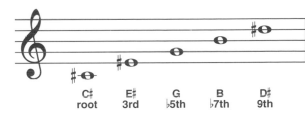

C#	E#	G	B	D#
root	3rd	♭5th	♭7th	9th

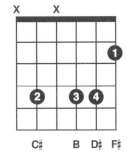
C# B D# F#

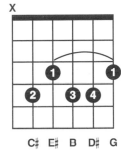
C# E# B D# G

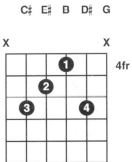
D# G B E# 4fr

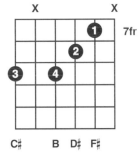
C# B D# F# 7fr

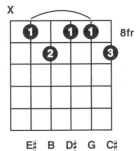
E# B D# G C# 8fr

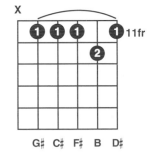
G# C# F# B D# 11fr

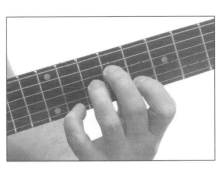
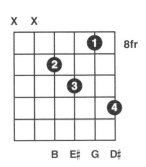
B E# G D# 8fr

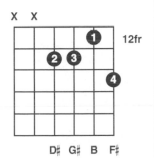
D# G# B F# 12fr

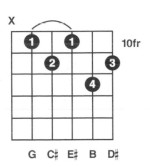
G C# E# B D# 10fr

C#7♭9 (C#7-9, C#dom7♭9)
C-sharp dominant seventh, flat ninth

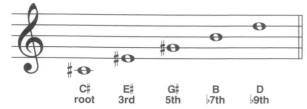

C#	E#	G#	B	D
root	3rd	5th	♭7th	♭9th

X   X

C# E# B D

X   X   4fr

D G# B E#

X X   6fr

G# D E# B

X   X   6fr

C# B D E#

X X   10fr

C# E# B D

C#7#9 (C#7+9, C#dom7#9)
C-sharp dominant seventh, sharp ninth

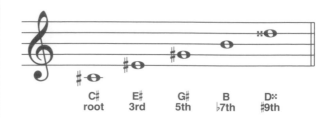

C#	E#	G#	B	D✕
root	3rd	5th	♭7th	#9th

 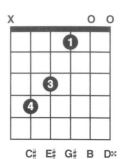

X   O O

C# E# G# B D✕

 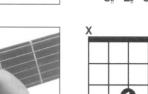 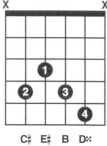

X   X

C# E# B D✕

 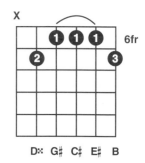

X   6fr

D✕ G# C# E# B

 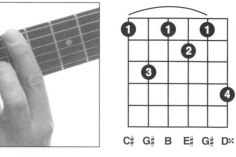

     9fr

C# G# B E# G# D✕

 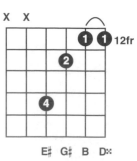

X X   12fr

E# G# B D✕

C#7♭5(#9) (C#7-5(+9), C#dom7♭5(#9))
C-sharp dominant seventh, flat fifth, sharp ninth

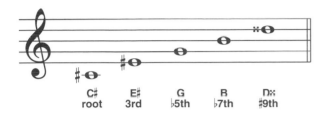

C#	E#	G	B	D𝄪
root	3rd	♭5th	♭7th	#9th

C#11
C-sharp eleventh

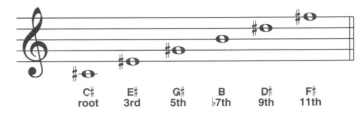

C#	E#	G#	B	D#	F#
root	3rd	5th	♭7th	9th	11th

 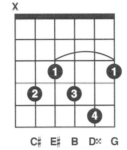

C# E# B D𝄪 G

 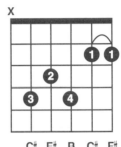

C# E# B C# F#

E# B D𝄪 G — 8fr

 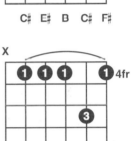

C# F# B E# G# — 4fr

 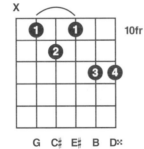

G C# E# B D𝄪 — 10fr

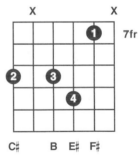 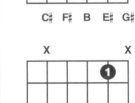

C# B E# F# — 7fr

 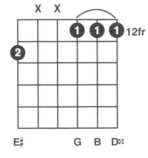

E# G B D𝄪 — 12fr

 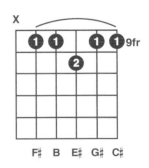

F# B E# G# C# — 9fr

 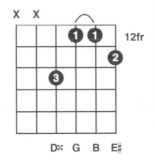

D𝄪 G B E# — 12fr

 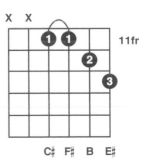

C# F# B E# — 11fr

C#

C#7#11 (C#7+11, C#dom7#11)
C-sharp dominant seventh, sharp eleventh

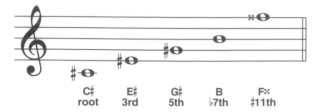

C#	E#	G#	B	F×
root	3rd	5th	♭7th	#11th

C#13 (C#dom13)
C-sharp thirteenth

C#	E#	G#	B	D#	A#
root	3rd	5th	♭7th	9th	13th

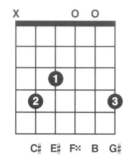
C# E# F× B G#

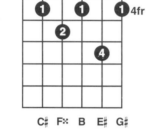
C# F× B E# G# 4fr

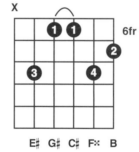
E# G# C# F× B 6fr

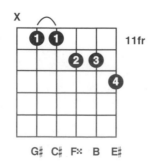
C# F× B E# G# C# 9fr

G# C# F× B E# 11fr

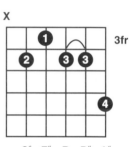
B E# A# C#

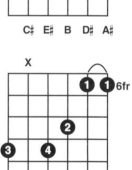

C# E# B D# A# 3fr

C# B D# E# A# 6fr

C# G# B E# A# C# 9fr

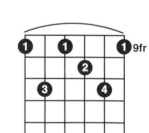
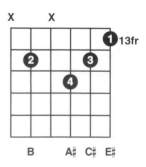

B A# C# E# 13fr

C#13sus4 (C#13sus)
C-sharp thirteenth, suspended fourth

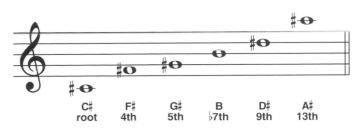

C#	F#	G#	B	D#	A#
root	4th	5th	♭7th	9th	13th

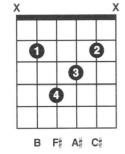

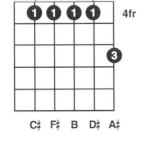

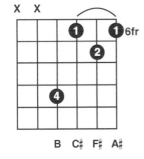

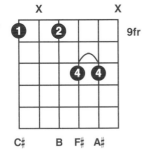

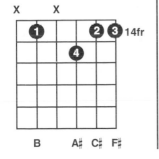

C#+ (C#aug, C#(#5))
C-sharp augmented

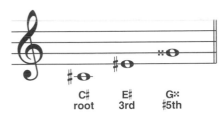

C#	E#	G⁑
root	3rd	#5th

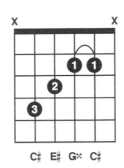

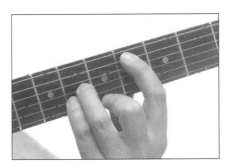
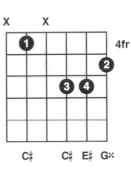

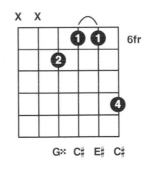

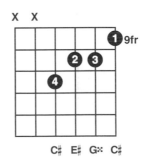

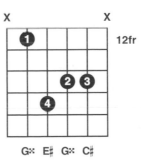

C#+7 (C#7#5)
C-sharp dominant seventh, sharp fifth

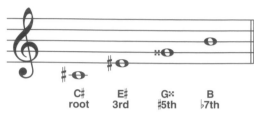

C#	E#	G×	B
root	3rd	#5th	♭7th

C#+9 (C#9#5, C#9+5)
C-sharp ninth, sharp fifth

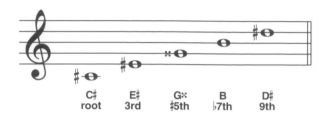

C#	E#	G×	B	D#
root	3rd	#5th	♭7th	9th

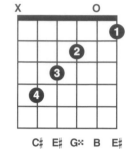
C# E# G× B E#

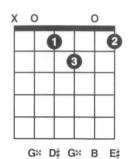
G× D# G× B E#

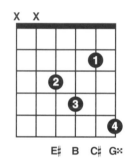
E# B C# G×

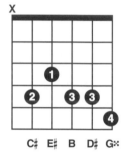
C# E# B D# G×

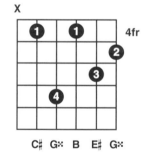
C# G× B E# G× — 4fr

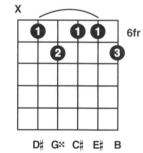
D# G× C# E# B — 6fr

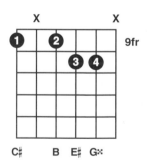
C# B E# G× — 9fr

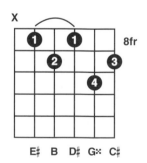
E# B D# G× C# — 8fr

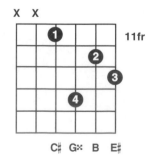
C# G× B E# — 11fr

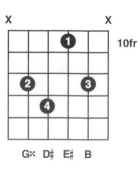
G× D# E# B — 10fr

C#+7♭9 (C#7+5 (♭9))
C-sharp dominant seventh, sharp fifth, flat ninth

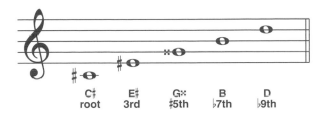

C# E# G𝄪 B D
root 3rd #5th ♭7th ♭9th

C#+7#9 (C#7+5 (#9))
C-sharp dominant seventh, sharp fifth, sharp ninth

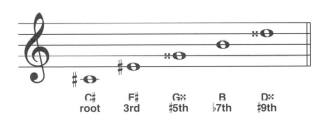

C# F𝄪 G𝄪 B D𝄪
root 3rd #5th ♭7th #9th

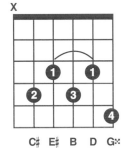

X

C# E# B D G𝄪

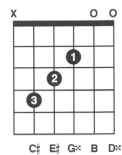

X O O

C# E# G𝄪 B D𝄪

X X

6fr

B G𝄪 D E#

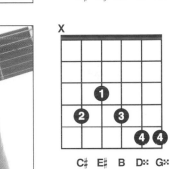

X

C# E# B D𝄪 G𝄪

7fr

C# E# G𝄪 D G𝄪 B

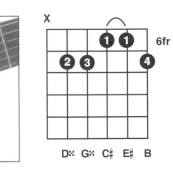

X

6fr

D𝄪 G𝄪 C# E# B

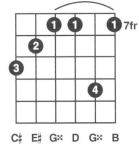

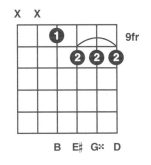

X X

9fr

B E# G𝄪 D

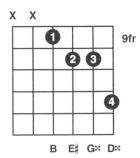

X X

9fr

B E# G𝄪 D𝄪

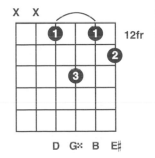

X X

12fr

D G𝄪 B E#

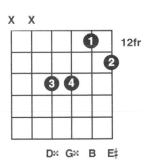

X X

12fr

D𝄪 G𝄪 B E#

C#

C#° (C#dim)
C-sharp diminished

C# E G
root b3rd b5th

C#°7 (C#dim7)
C-sharp diminished seventh

C# E G Bb
root b3rd b5th b7th

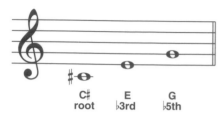
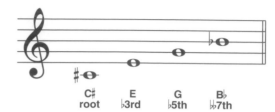

X O O

C# E G C# E

X O O

Bb E G C# E

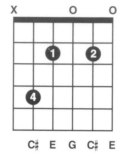
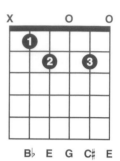

X X

3fr

G C# E G

X X

E Bb C# G

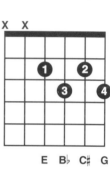

X X
8fr

C# E G C#

X X

C# G Bb E

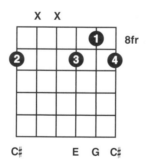
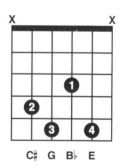

X X
11fr

C# G C# E

X X
8fr

C# Bb E G

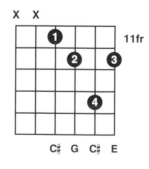
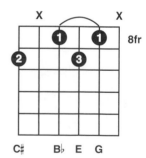

X X
12fr

E E G C#

X X
9fr

E G Bb C#

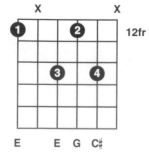
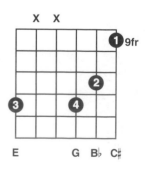

D

D (Dmaj)
D major

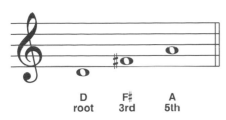

D	F#	A
root	3rd	5th

D5 (D no 3rd)
D fifth (power chord)

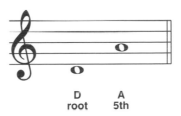

D	A
root	5th

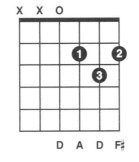

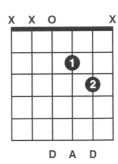

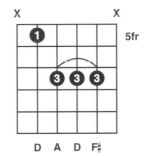

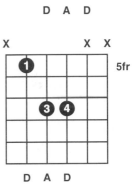

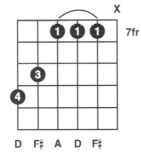

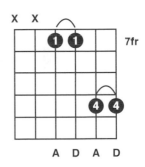

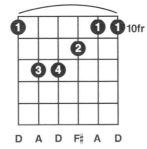

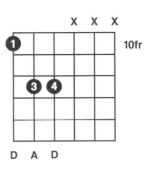

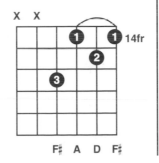

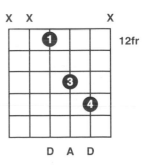

Dsus4 (Dsus)
D suspended fourth

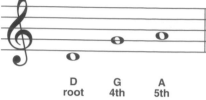

D root   G 4th   A 5th

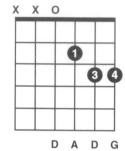

X X O   D A D G

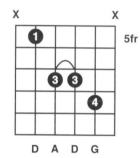

X   X   5fr   D A D G

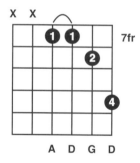

X X   7fr   A D G D

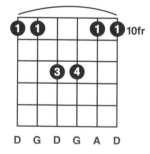

10fr   D G D G A D

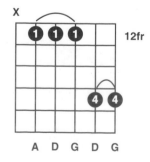

X   12fr   A D G D G

Dsus2 (D5add2)
D suspended second

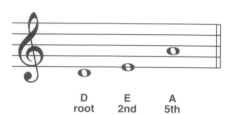

D root   E 2nd   A 5th

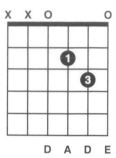

X X O   O   D A D E

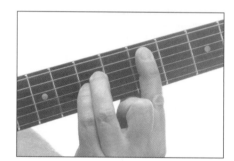
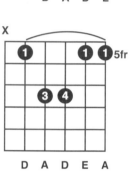

X   5fr   D A D E A

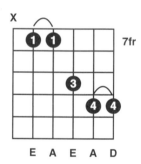

X   7fr   E A E A D

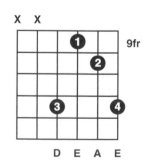

X X   9fr   D E A E

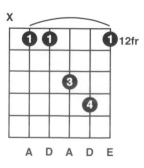

X   12fr   A D A D E

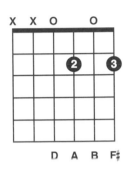

Dadd9

D added ninth

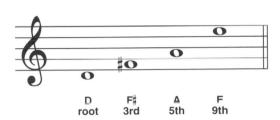

D	F#	A	F
root	3rd	5th	9th

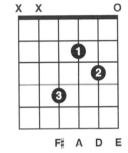

F# A D E

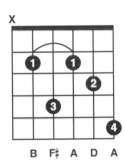

A   F# D E   4fr

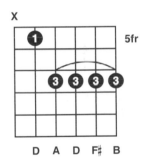

E A D F#   7fr

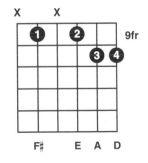

F#   E A D   9fr

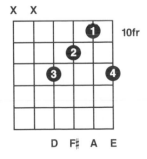

D F# A E   10fr

D6

D sixth

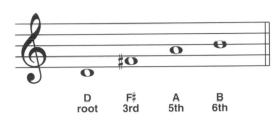

D	F#	A	B
root	3rd	5th	6th

D A B F#

B F# A D A

D A D F# B   5fr

D   B F# A   9fr

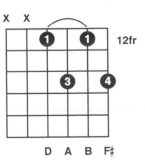

D A B F#   12fr

D6/9 (D6add9)
D sixth, added ninth

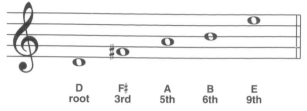

D	F#	A	B	E
root	3rd	5th	6th	9th

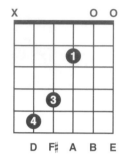

X   O O

D F# A B E

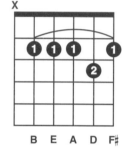

X

B E A D F#

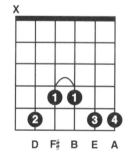

X

D F# B E A

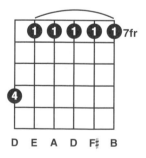

D E A D F# B   7fr

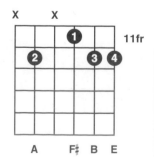

X   X

A   F# B E   11fr

Dmaj7 (DM7)
D major seventh

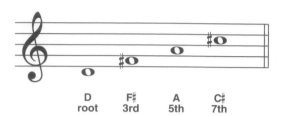

D	F#	A	C#
root	3rd	5th	7th

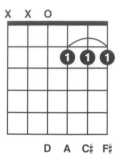

X X O

D A C# F#

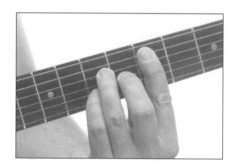
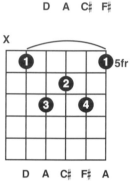

X

D A C# F# A   5fr

X X

A D F# C#   7fr

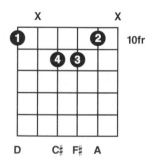

X   X

D C# F# A   10fr

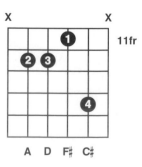

X   X

A D F# C#   11fr

Dmaj9 (DM9)
D major ninth

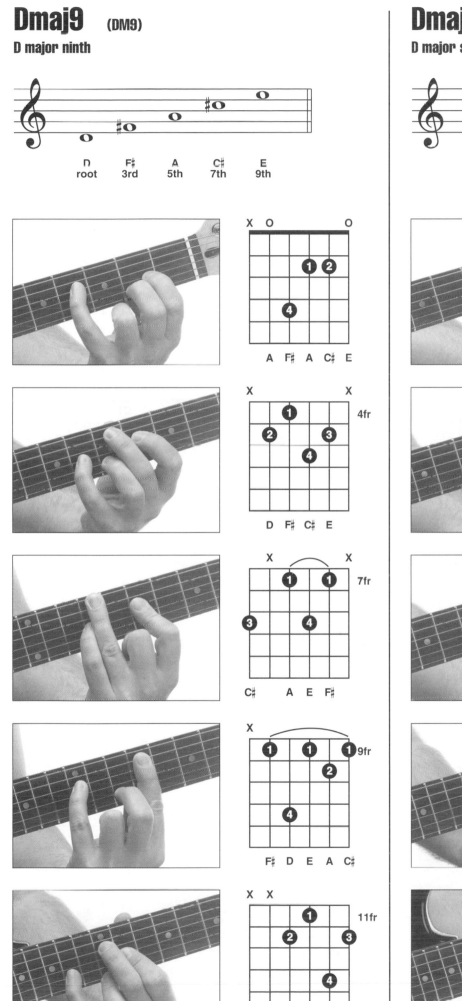

D	F#	A	C#	E
root	3rd	5th	7th	9th

A F# A C# E

D F# C# E   4fr

C# A E F#   7fr

F# D E A C#   9fr

D F# C# E   11fr

Dmaj7♯11 (DM7♯11)
D major seventh, sharp eleventh

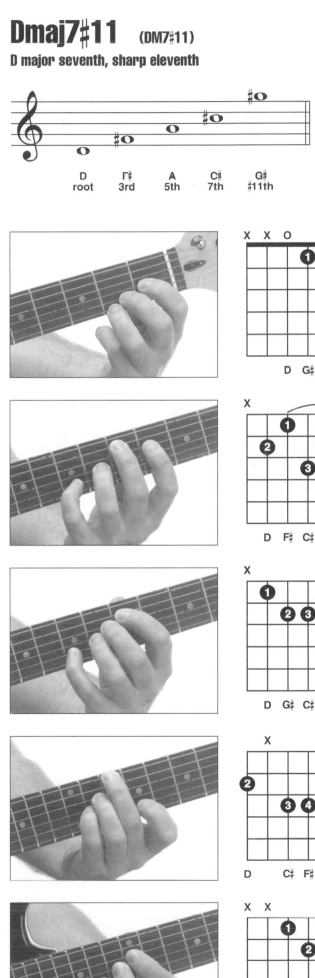

D	F#	A	C#	G#
root	3rd	5th	7th	♯11th

D G# C# F#

D F# C# F# G#   4fr

D G# C# F#   5fr

D C# F# G#   9fr

D G# C# F#   12fr

Dmaj13 (DM13)
D major thirteenth

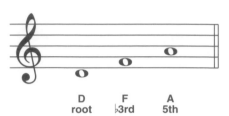

D	F#	A	C#	E	B
root	3rd	5th	7th	9th	13th

Dm (Dmin, D-)
D minor

D	F	A
root	♭3rd	5th

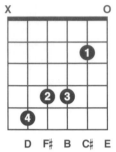 

D F# B C# E

D A D F

 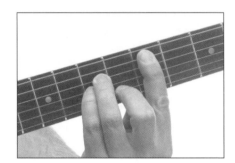

D C# F# B

D A D F A

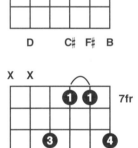 

B D F# C#

A F A D

 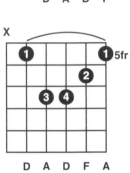

D C# F# B

D A D F A D

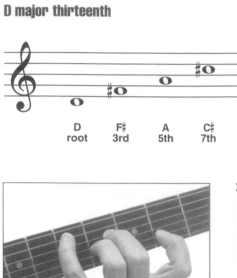 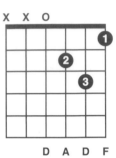

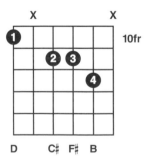 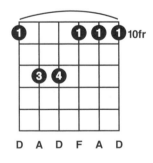

 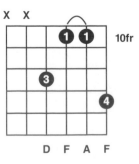

 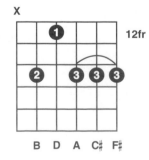

B D A C# F#

D F A F

Dm(add9)
D minor, added ninth

D	F	A	E
root	♭3rd	5th	9th

D

X X   O

F A D E

X   X   5fr

F A D E

X   7fr

F A E A D

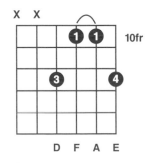

X X   10fr

D F A E

X X   13fr

E A D F

Dm6 (Dmin6, D-6)
D minor sixth

D	F	A	B
root	♭3rd	5th	6th

X X O   O

D A B F

X X

F B D A

X   X   6fr

B A D F

X   X   9fr

D B F A

X X   12fr

D A B F

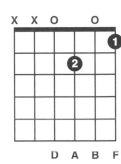
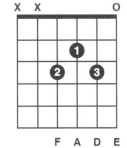
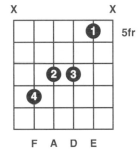
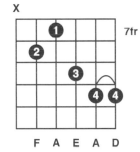
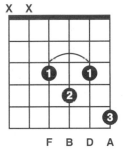
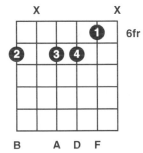
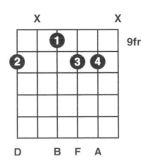
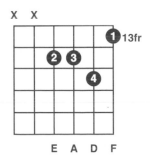

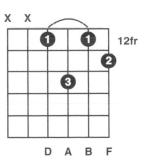
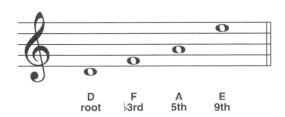
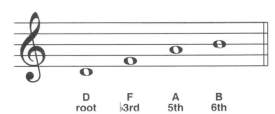

Dm♭6 (D-(♭6), Dmin♭6)
D minor, flat sixth

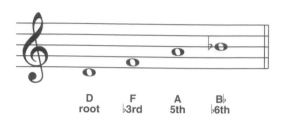

D	F	A	B♭
root	♭3rd	5th	♭6th

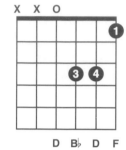

Dm6/9
D minor sixth, added ninth

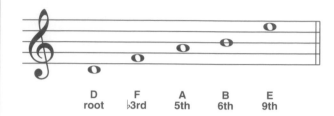

D	F	A	B	E
root	♭3rd	5th	6th	9th

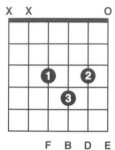

D B♭ D F

F B D E

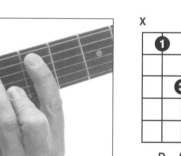
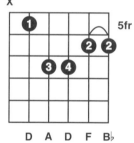
D F B♭ D A

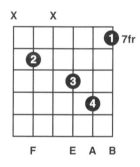
F D E B

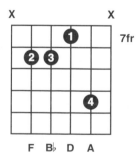
D A D F B♭

F E A B

F B♭ D A

F B E A D

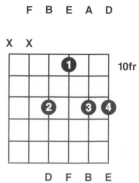
D A D F B♭ D

D F B E

Dm7 (D-7, Dmin7)
D minor seventh

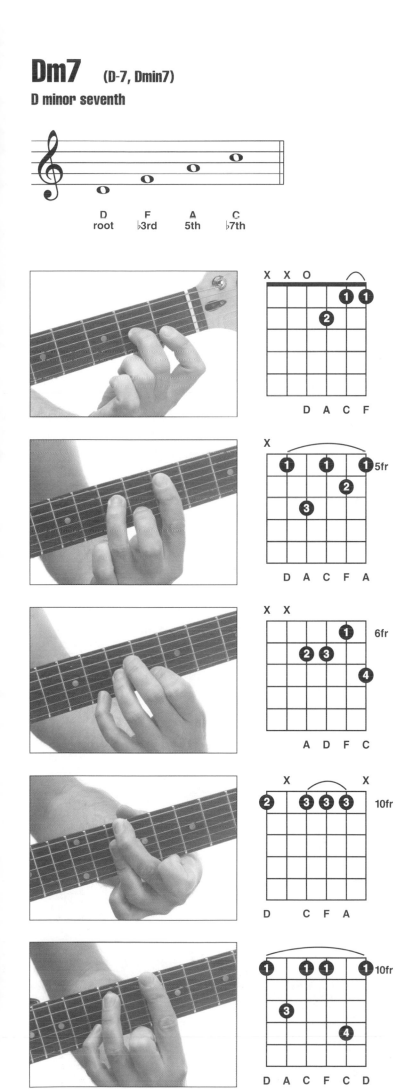

D	F	A	C
root	♭3rd	5th	♭7th

Dm7♭5 (D-7♭5, Dmin7-5)
D minor seventh, flat fifth

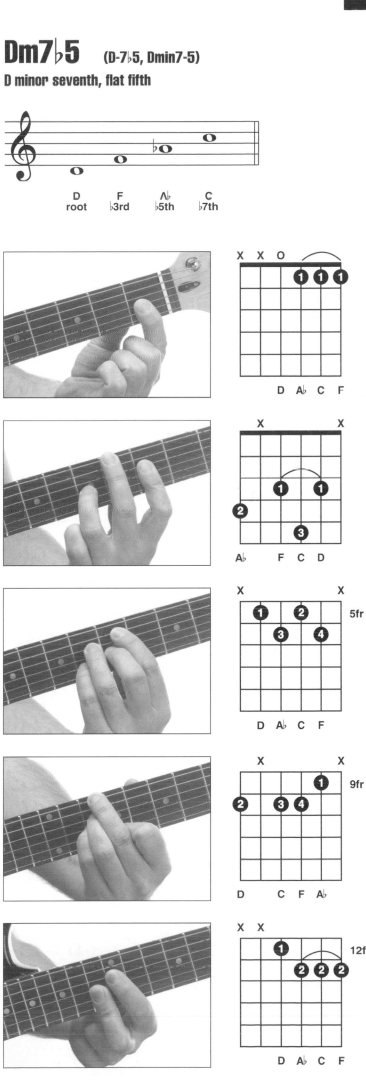

D	F	A♭	C
root	♭3rd	♭5th	♭7th

D

54

Dm(maj7) (D-(+7))
D minor, major seventh

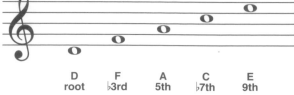

D	F	A	C#
root	♭3rd	5th	7th

X X O

D A C# F

X
5fr

D A C# F A

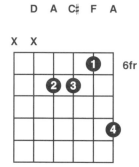
X X
6fr

A D F C#

X X
10fr

D C# F A

X X
10fr

C# F A D

Dm9 (D-9, Dmin9)
D minor ninth

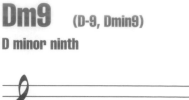

D	F	A	C	E
root	♭3rd	5th	♭7th	9th

X X O

F A C E

X X

D F C E

X X
8fr

F E A C

X X
10fr

C F A E

10fr

D A C F C E

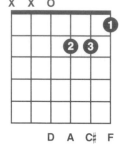
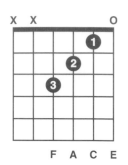
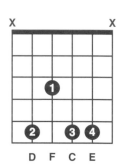
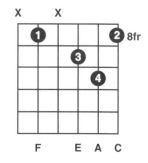
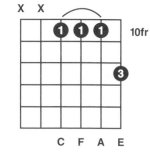
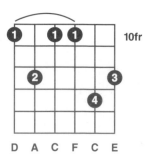
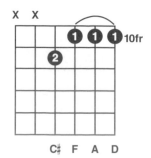
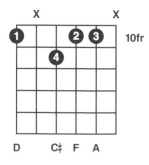

Dm9♭5 (Dm8-5, Dmin8♭5)
D minor ninth, flat fifth

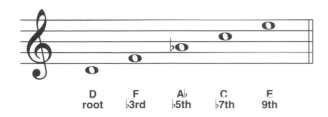

D	F	A♭	C	E
root	♭3rd	♭5th	♭7th	9th

Dm9(maj7) (Dm9+7, D-9+7)
D minor ninth, major seventh

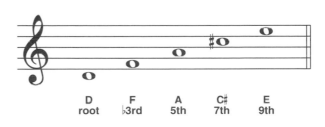

D	F	A	C#	E
root	♭3rd	5th	7th	9th

 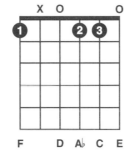
X O   O
F D A♭ C E

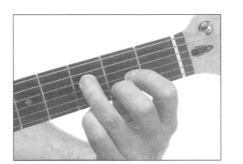 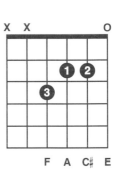
X X   O
F A C# E

 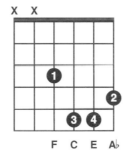
X X
F C E A♭

 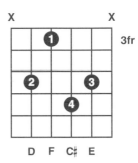 3fr
X   X
D F C# E

 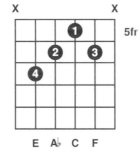 5fr
X   X
E A♭ C F

 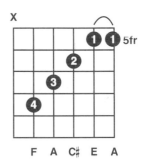 5fr
X
F A C# E A

 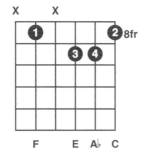 8fr
X X
F   E A♭ C

 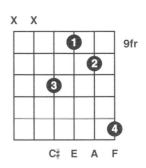 9fr
X X
C# E A F

 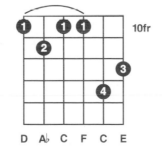 10fr
D A♭ C F C E

 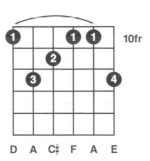 10fr
D A C# F A E

Dm11 (D-11, Dmin11)
D minor eleventh

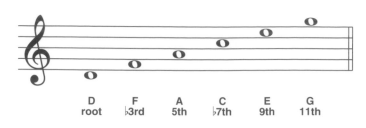

D	F	A	C	E	G
root	♭3rd	5th	♭7th	9th	11th

Dm13 (D-13, Dmin13)
D minor thirteenth

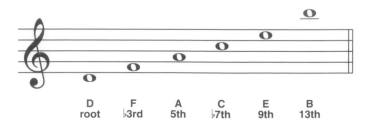

D	F	A	C	E	B
root	♭3rd	5th	♭7th	9th	13th

 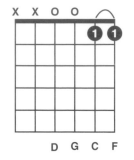
 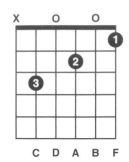

 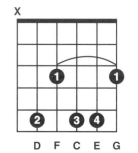
 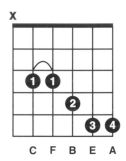

 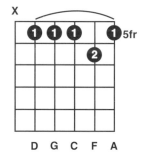
 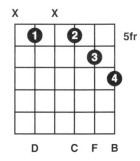

 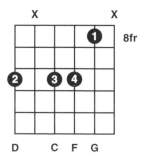
 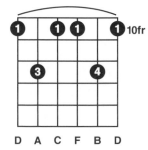

 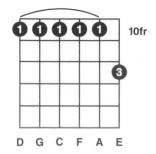
 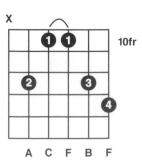

D

D7 (Ddom7)
D dominant seventh

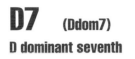
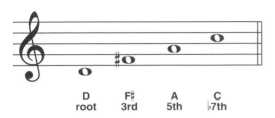

D	F#	A	C
root	3rd	5th	♭7th

D7sus4 (D7sus)
D dominant seventh, suspended fourth

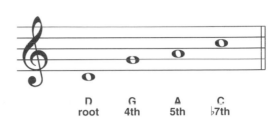

D	G	A	C
root	4th	5th	♭7th

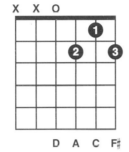

D A C F#

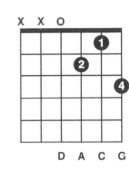

D A C G

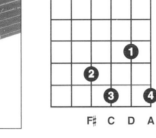

F# C D A

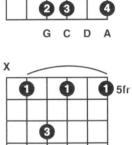

G C D A

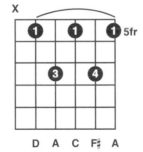

D A C F# A · 5fr

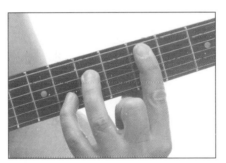

D A C G A · 5fr

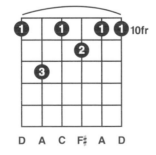

D A C F# A D · 10fr

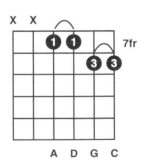

A D G C · 7fr

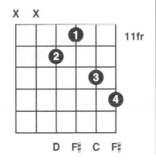

D F# C F# · 11fr

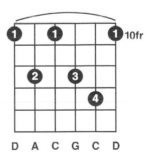

D A C G C D · 10fr

D7♭5 (D7-5, Ddom7♭5)
D dominant seventh, flat fifth

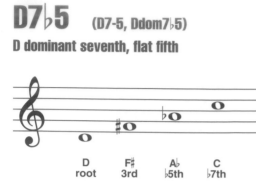

D	F♯	A♭	C
root	3rd	♭5th	♭7th

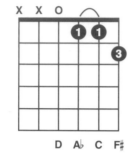

D A♭ C F♯

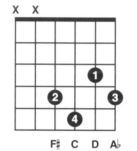

F♯ C D A♭

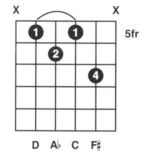

5fr

D A♭ C F♯

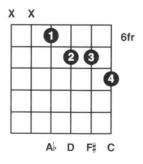

6fr

A♭ D F♯ C

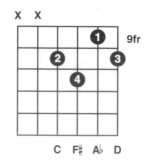

9fr

C F♯ A♭ D

D9
D ninth

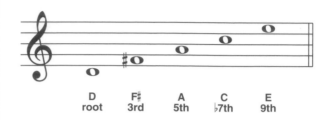

D	F♯	A	C	E
root	3rd	5th	♭7th	9th

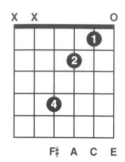

F♯ A C E

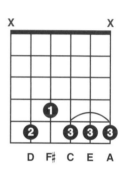

D F♯ C E A

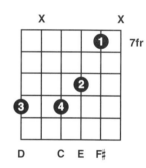

7fr

D C E F♯

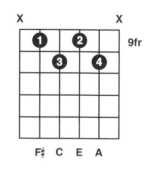

9fr

F♯ C E A

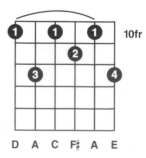

10fr

D A C F♯ A E

D9sus4 (D9sus)
D ninth, suspended fourth

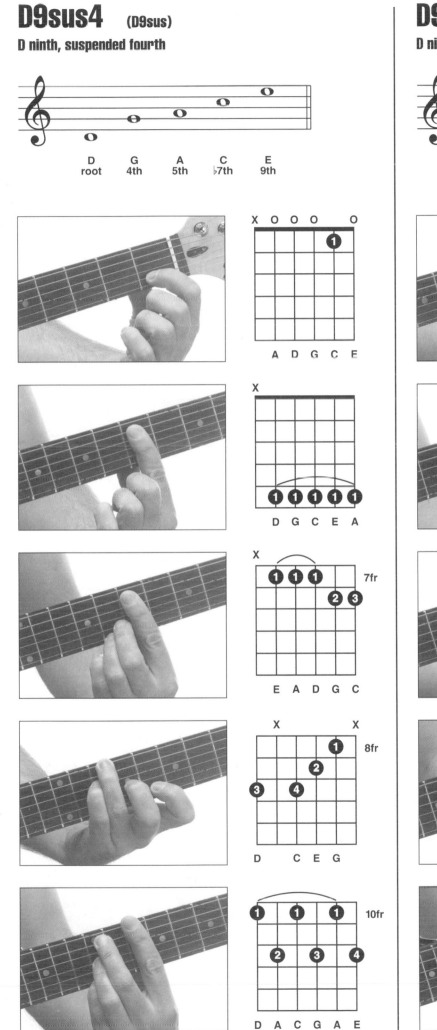

D	G	A	C	E
root	4th	5th	♭7th	9th

X O O O O

A D G C E

X

D G C E A

X 7fr

E A D G C

X X 8fr

D C E G

10fr

D A C G A E

D9♭5 (D9-5, Ddom9♭5)
D ninth, flat fifth

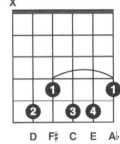

D	F♯	A♭	C	E
root	3rd	♭5th	♭7th	9th

X X

E A♭ C F♯

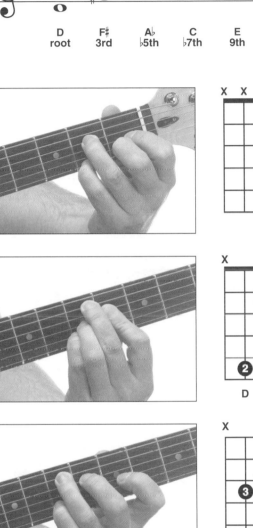

X

D F♯ C E A♭

X X 5fr

E A♭ C F♯

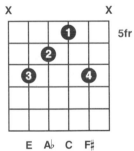

X X 9fr

C F♯ A♭ E

X 11fr

A♭ D F♯ C E

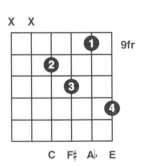
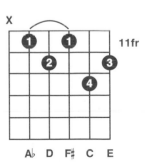

D

D7♭9 (D7-9, Ddom7♭9)
D dominant seventh, flat ninth

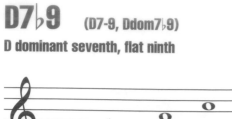

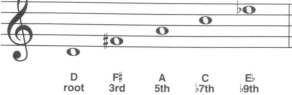

D	F♯	A	C	E♭
root	3rd	5th	♭7th	♭9th

D7♯9 (D7+9, Ddom7♯9)
D dominant seventh, sharp ninth

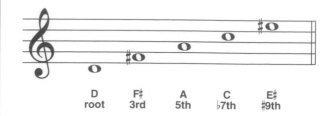

D	F♯	A	C	E♯
root	3rd	5th	♭7th	♯9th

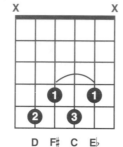

D F♯ C E♭

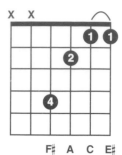

F♯ A C E♯

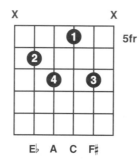

5fr

E♭ A C F♯

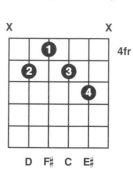

4fr

D F♯ C E♯

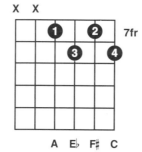

7fr

A E♭ F♯ C

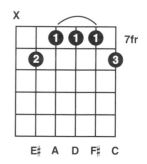

7fr

E♯ A D F♯ C

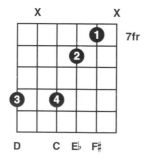

7fr

D C E♭ F♯

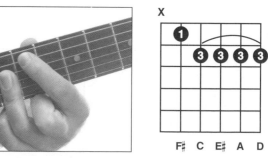

9fr

F♯ C E♯ A D

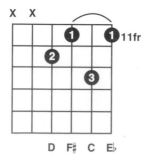

11fr

D F♯ C E♭

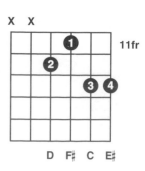

11fr

D F♯ C E♯

D7♭5(♯9) (D7-5(+9), Ddom7♭5(♯9))
D dominant seventh, flat fifth, sharp ninth

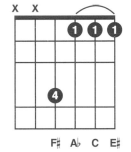

D	F♯	A♭	C	E♯
root	3rd	♭5th	♭7th	♯9th

D11
D eleventh

D	F♯	A	C	E	G
root	3rd	5th	♭7th	9th	11th

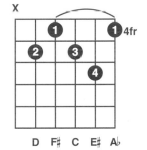

F♯ A♭ C E♯

D G C F♯

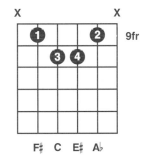

4fr

D F♯ C E♯ A♭

X

9fr

F♯ C E♯ A♭

5fr

D G C F♯ A

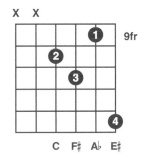

9fr

C F♯ A♭ E♯

7fr

F♯ D G C

13fr

E♯ A♭ C F♯

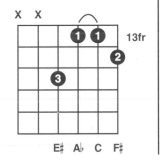

8fr

D C F♯ G

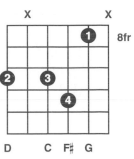

D7#11 (D7+11, Ddom7#11)
D dominant seventh, sharp eleventh

D	F#	A	C	G#
root	3rd	5th	♭7th	#11th

X X O
D G# C F#

X X 3fr
F# C D G#

5fr
A D G# C F# A

X 7fr
C F# A D G#

10fr
D G# C F# A D

D13 (Ddom13)
D thirteenth

D	F#	A	C	E	B
root	3rd	5th	♭7th	9th	13th

X O O
A D B C F#

X 3fr
C F# B D A

X 4fr
D F# C E B

X 7fr
D C E F# B

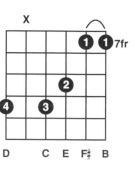
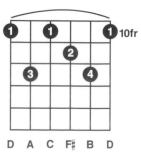

10fr
D A C F# B D

D13sus4 (D13sus)
D thirteenth, suspended fourth

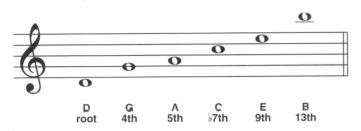

D	G	A	C	E	B
root	4th	5th	♭7th	9th	13th

D+ (Daug, D(♯5))
D augmented

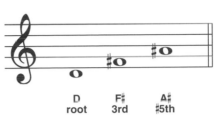

D	F♯	A♯
root	3rd	♯5th

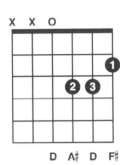

D

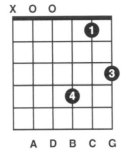

A D B C G

D A♯ D F♯

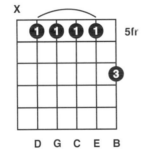

3fr

C G B D

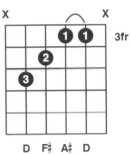

3fr

D F♯ A♯ D

5fr

D G C E B

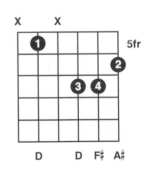

5fr

D D F♯ A♯

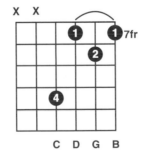

7fr

C D G B

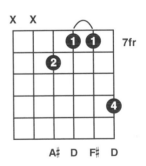

7fr

A♯ D F♯ D

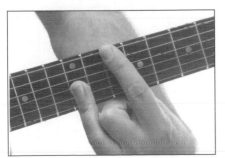
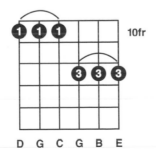

10fr

D G C G B E

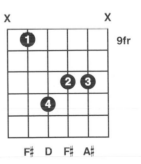

9fr

F♯ D F♯ A♯

D+7 (D7#5)
D dominant seventh, sharp fifth

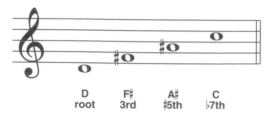

D	F#	A#	C
root	3rd	#5th	♭7th

X X O

D A# C F#

X X   3fr

F# C D A#

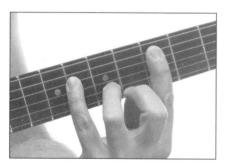

X   5fr

D A# C F# A#

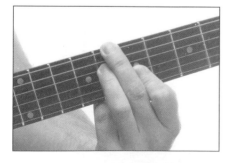

X   X   7fr

C A# D F#

X   X   10fr

D C F# A#

D+9 (D9#5, D9+5)
D ninth, sharp fifth

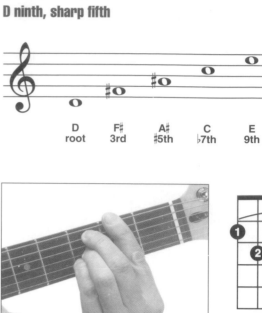

D	F#	A#	C	E
root	3rd	#5th	♭7th	9th

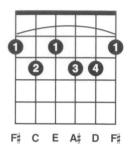

F# C E A# D F#

X   4fr

D F# C E A#

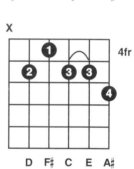

X X   7fr

A# E F# C

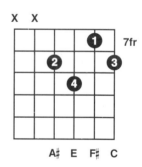

X   9fr

F# C E A# D

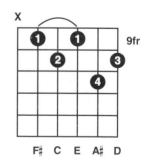

X   10fr

D C F# A# E

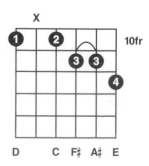

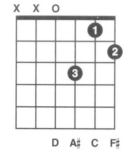
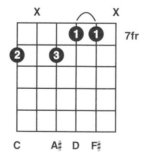
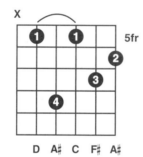
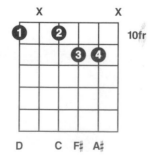

D+7♭9 (D7+5(♭9))

D dominant seventh, sharp fifth, flat ninth

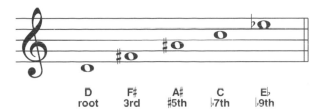

D	F#	A#	C	E♭
root	3rd	#5th	♭7th	♭9th

D+7♯9 (D7+5(♯9))

D dominant seventh, sharp fifth, sharp ninth

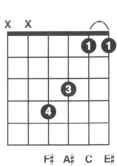

D	F#	A#	C	E#
root	3rd	#5th	♭7th	#9th

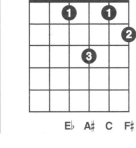

E♭ A# C F#

F# A# C E#

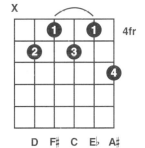

4fr

D F# C E♭ A#

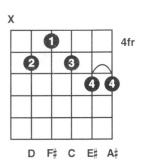

4fr

D F# C E# A#

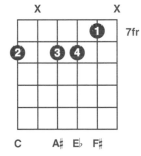

7fr

C A# E♭ F#

7fr

E# A# D F# C

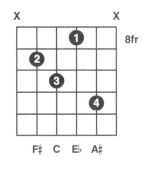

8fr

F# C E♭ A#

10fr

D C F# A# E#

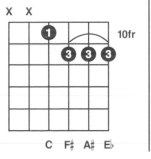

10fr

C F# A# E♭

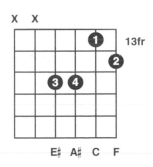

13fr

E# A# C F

D° (D dim)
D diminished

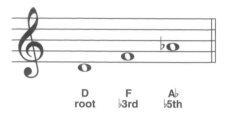

D	F	A♭
root	♭3rd	♭5th

D°7 (Ddim7)
D diminished seventh

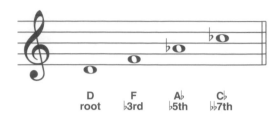

D	F	A♭	C♭
root	♭3rd	♭5th	♭♭7th

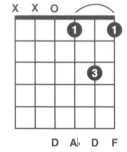
D A♭ D F

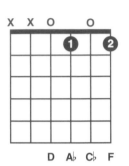
D A♭ C♭ F

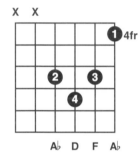
A♭ D F A♭ 4fr

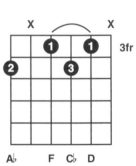
A♭ F C♭ D 3fr

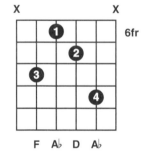
F A♭ D A♭ 6fr

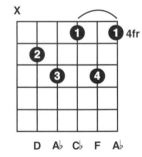
D A♭ C♭ F A♭ 4fr

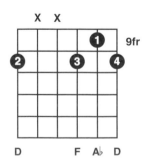
D F A♭ D 9fr

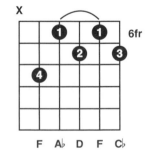
F A♭ D F C♭ 6fr

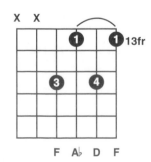
F A♭ D F 13fr

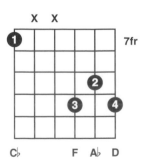
C♭ F A♭ D 7fr

E♭ (E♭maj)
E-flat major

E♭   G   B♭
root   3rd   5th

E♭5 (E♭ no 3rd)
E-flat fifth (power chord)

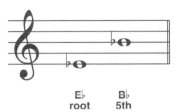

E♭   B♭
root   5th

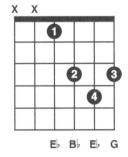
E♭ B♭ E♭ G

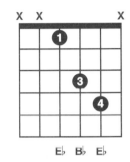
E♭ B♭ E♭

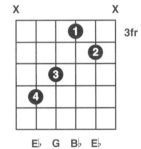
3fr
E♭ G B♭ E♭

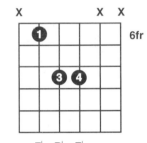
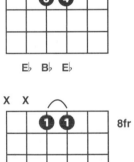
6fr
E♭ B♭ E♭

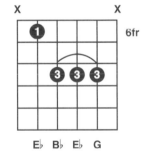
6fr
E♭ B♭ E♭ G

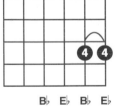
8fr
B♭ E♭ B♭ E♭

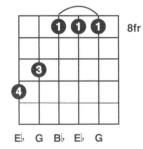
8fr
E♭ G B♭ E♭ G

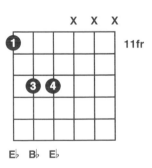
11fr
E♭ B♭ E♭

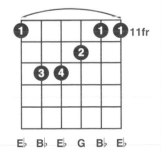
11fr
E♭ B♭ E♭ G B♭ E♭

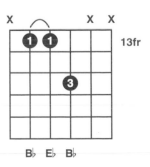
13fr
B♭ E♭ B♭

E♭

E♭sus4 (E♭sus)
E-flat suspended fourth

E♭	A♭	B♭
root	4th	5th

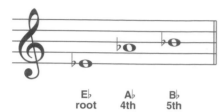 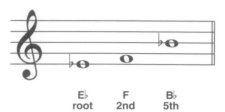

X   X

A♭   E♭   B♭   E♭

 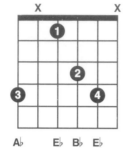

X   X   6fr

E♭   B♭   E♭   A♭

 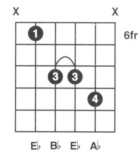

X   X   8fr

B♭   E♭   A♭   E♭

 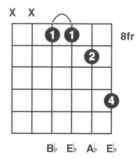

11fr

E♭   A♭   E♭   A♭   B♭   E♭

 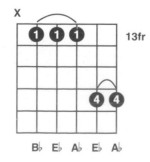

X   13fr

B♭   E♭   A♭   E♭   A♭

E♭sus2 (E♭5add2)
E-flat suspended second

E♭	F	B♭
root	2nd	5th

 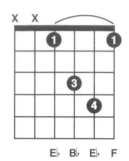

X   X

E♭   B♭   E♭   F

 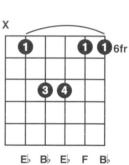

X   6fr

E♭   B♭   E♭   F   B♭

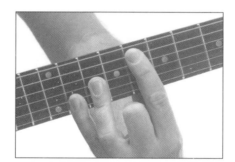 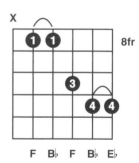

X   8fr

F   B♭   F   B♭   E♭

 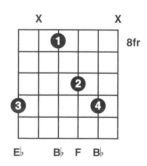

X   X   8fr

E♭   B♭   F   B♭

 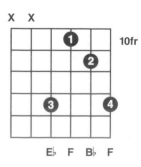

X   X   10fr

E♭   F   B♭   F

E♭add9

E-flat added ninth

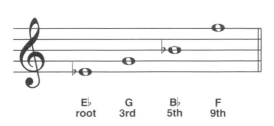

E♭	G	B♭	F
root	3rd	5th	9th

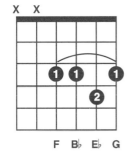

F B♭ E♭ G

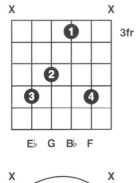

3fr

E♭ G B♭ F

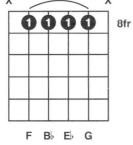

8fr

F B♭ E♭ G

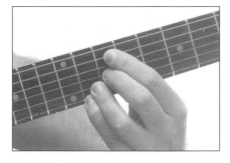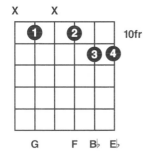

10fr

G   F B♭ E♭

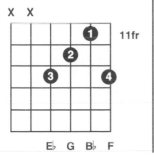

11fr

E♭ G B♭ F

E♭6

E-flat sixth

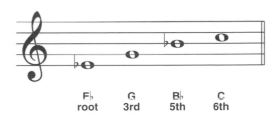

E♭	G	B♭	C
root	3rd	5th	6th

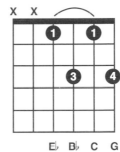

E♭ B♭ C G

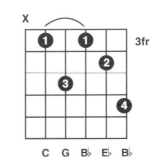

3fr

C G B♭ E♭ B♭

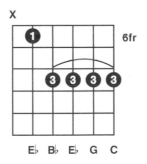

6fr

E♭ B♭ E♭ G C

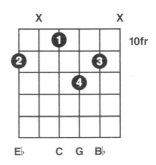

10fr

E♭   C G B♭

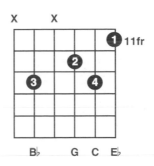

11fr

B♭   G C E♭

E♭

E♭6/9 (E♭6add9)
E-flat sixth, added ninth

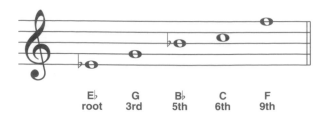

E♭	G	B♭	C	F
root	3rd	5th	6th	9th

E♭maj7 (E♭M7)
E-flat major seventh

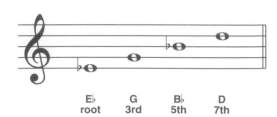

E♭	G	B♭	D
root	3rd	5th	7th

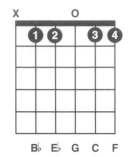

X   O

B♭ E♭ G C F

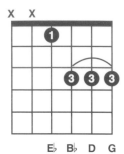

X X

E♭ B♭ D G

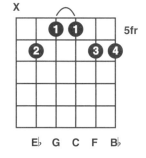

X

C F B♭ E♭ G

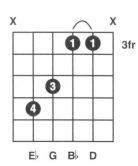

X   X

3fr

E♭ G B♭ D

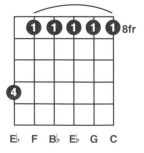

X

5fr

E♭ G C F B♭

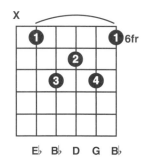

X

6fr

E♭ B♭ D G B♭

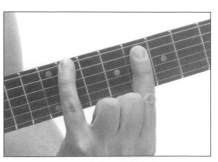

X

8fr

E♭ F B♭ E♭ G C

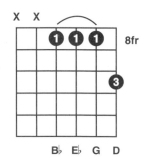

X X

8fr

B♭ E♭ G D

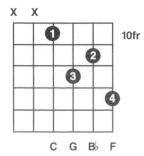

X X

10fr

C G B♭ F

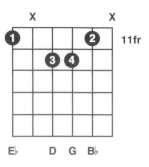

X   X

11fr

E♭   D G B♭

E♭maj9 (E♭M9)
E-flat major ninth

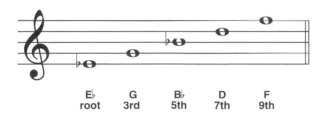

E♭	G	B♭	D	F
root	3rd	5th	7th	9th

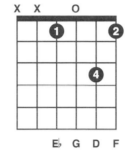

E♭ G D F

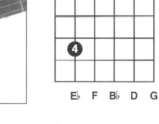

E♭ F B♭ D G

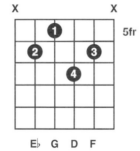

5fr — E♭ G D F

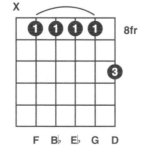

8fr — F B♭ E♭ G D

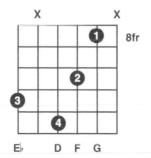

8fr — E♭ D F G

E♭maj7♯11 (E♭M7♯11)
E-flat major seventh, sharp eleventh

E♭	G	B♭	D	A
root	3rd	5th	7th	♯11th

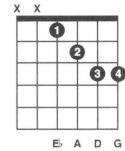

E♭ A D G

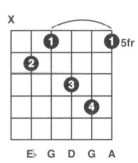

5fr — E♭ G D G A

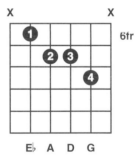

6fr — E♭ A D G

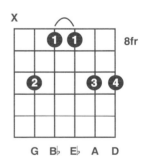

8fr — G B♭ E♭ A D

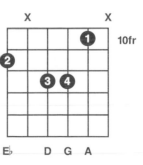

10fr — E♭ D G A

E♭maj13 (E♭M13)
E-flat major thirteenth

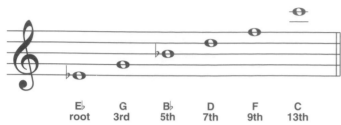

E♭	G	B♭	D	F	C
root	3rd	5th	7th	9th	13th

E♭m (E♭min, E♭-)
E-flat minor

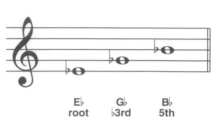

E♭	G♭	B♭
root	♭3rd	5th

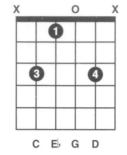
X O X

C E♭ G D

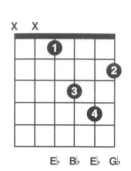
X X

E♭ B♭ E♭ G♭

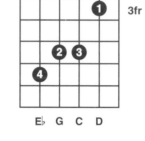
X X

3fr

E♭ G C D

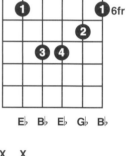
X

6fr

E♭ B♭ E♭ G♭ B♭

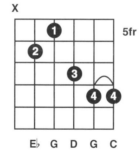
X

5fr

E♭ G D G C

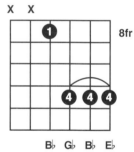
X X

8fr

B♭ G♭ B♭ E♭

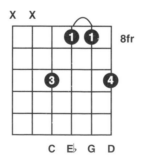
X X

8fr

C E♭ G D

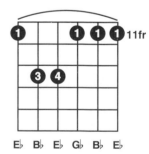
11fr

E♭ B♭ E♭ G♭ B♭ E♭

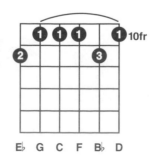
10fr

E♭ G C F B♭ D

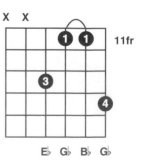
X X

11fr

E♭ G♭ B♭ G♭

E♭m(add9)
E-flat minor, added ninth

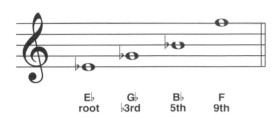

E♭	G♭	B♭	F
root	♭3rd	5th	9th

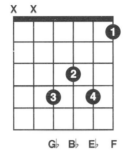

G♭ B♭ E♭ F

6fr

F E♭ G♭ B♭

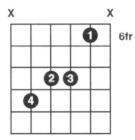

6fr

G♭ B♭ E♭ F

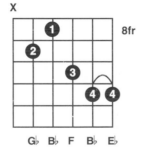

8fr

G♭ B♭ F B♭ E♭

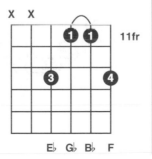

11fr

E♭ G♭ B♭ F

E♭m6 (E♭min6, E♭-6)
E-flat minor sixth

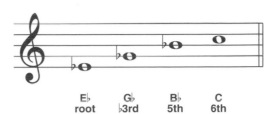

E♭	G♭	B♭	C
root	♭3rd	5th	6th

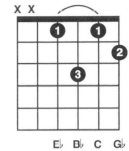

E♭ B♭ C G♭

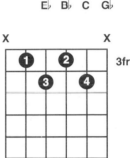

3fr

C G♭ B♭ E♭

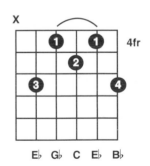

4fr

E♭ G♭ C E♭ B♭

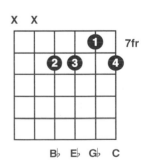

7fr

B♭ E♭ G♭ C

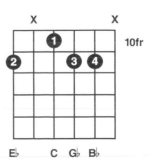

10fr

E♭ C G♭ B♭

E♭m♭6 (E♭-(♭6), E♭min♭6)
E-flat minor, flat sixth

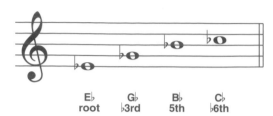

E♭	G♭	B♭	C♭
root	♭3rd	5th	♭6th

E♭m6/9
E-flat minor sixth, added ninth

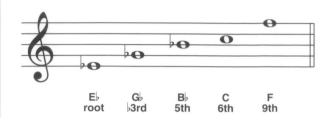

E♭	G♭	B♭	C	F
root	♭3rd	5th	6th	9th

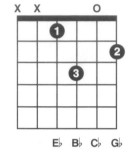

X X · O
E♭ B♭ C♭ G♭

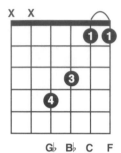

X X
G♭ B♭ C F

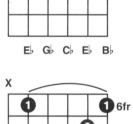

X · 4fr
E♭ G♭ C♭ E♭ B♭

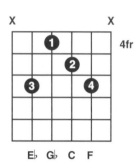

X X 4fr
E♭ G♭ C F

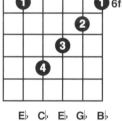

X 6fr
E♭ C♭ E♭ G♭ B♭

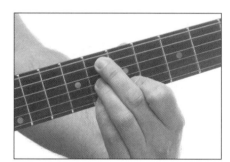
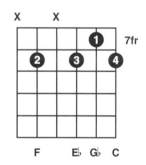

X X 7fr
F E♭ G♭ C

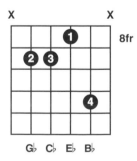

X X 8fr
G♭ C♭ E♭ B♭

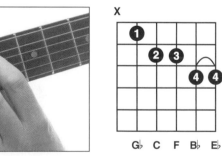

X 9fr
G♭ C F B♭ E♭

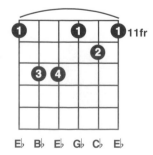

11fr
E♭ B♭ E♭ G♭ C♭ E♭

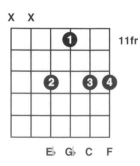

X X 11fr
E♭ G♭ C F

E♭m7 (E♭min7, E♭-7)
E-flat minor seventh

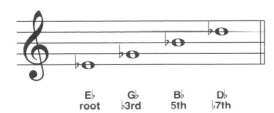

E♭	G♭	B♭	D♭
root	♭3rd	5th	♭7th

X X

E♭ B♭ D♭ G♭

X
4fr

E♭ G♭ D♭ E♭ B♭

X
6fr

E♭ B♭ D♭ G♭ B♭

X X
11fr

E♭ D♭ G♭ B♭

11fr

E♭ B♭ D♭ G♭ D♭ E♭

E♭m7♭5 (E♭-7♭5, E♭min7-5)
E-flat minor seventh, flat fifth

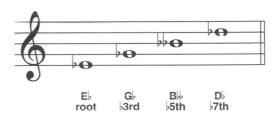

E♭	G♭	B♭♭	D♭
root	♭3rd	♭5th	♭7th

X X

E♭ B♭♭ D♭ G♭

X X
5fr

E♭ D♭ G♭ B♭♭

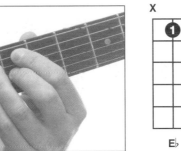

X X
6fr

E♭ B♭♭ D♭ G♭

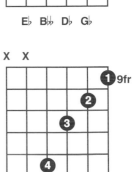

X X
9fr

E♭ G♭ B♭♭ D♭

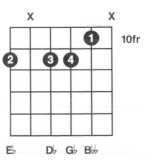

X X
10fr

E♭ D♭ G♭ B♭♭

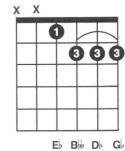
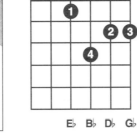
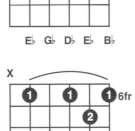
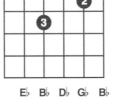
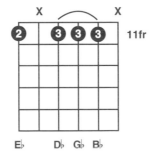

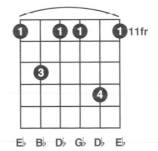

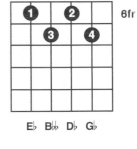
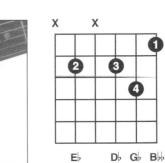

E♭

E♭m(maj7) (E♭-(+7))
E-flat minor, major seventh

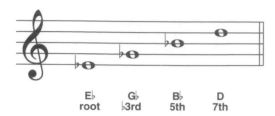

E♭	G♭	B♭	D
root	♭3rd	5th	7th

E♭ B♭ D G♭

E♭ G♭ B♭ D — 3fr

E♭ B♭ D G♭ B♭ — 6fr

B♭ E♭ G♭ D — 7fr

E♭ D G♭ B♭ — 11fr

E♭m9 (E♭min9, E♭-9)
E-flat minor ninth

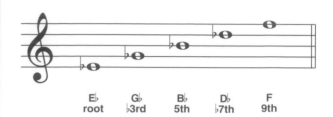

E♭	G♭	B♭	D♭	F
root	♭3rd	5th	♭7th	9th

G♭ B♭ D♭ F

E♭ G♭ D♭ F — 4fr

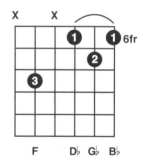

F D♭ G♭ B♭ — 6fr

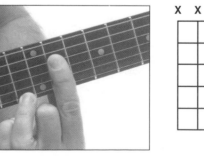

D♭ G♭ B♭ F — 11fr

E♭ B♭ D♭ G♭ D♭ F — 11fr

E♭m9♭5 (E♭m9-5, E♭min9♭5)

E-flat minor ninth, flat fifth

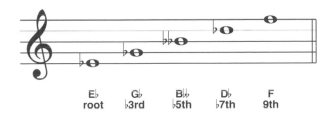

E♭	G♭	B♭♭	D♭	F
root	♭3rd	♭5th	♭7th	9th

 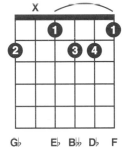

G♭   E♭ B♭♭ D♭   F

 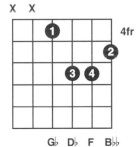

4fr

G♭ D♭ F B♭♭

 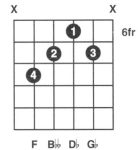

6fr

F B♭♭ D♭ G♭

 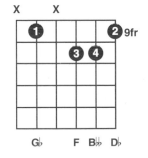

9fr

G♭   F B♭♭ D♭

 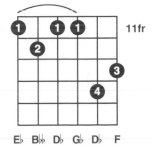

11fr

E♭ B♭♭ D♭ G♭ D♭ F

E♭m9(maj7) (E♭m9+7, E♭-9+7)

E-flat minor ninth, major seventh

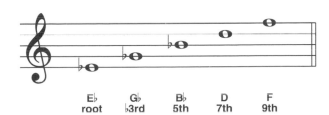

E♭	G♭	B♭	D	F
root	♭3rd	5th	7th	9th

 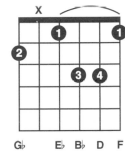

G♭   E♭ B♭ D   F

 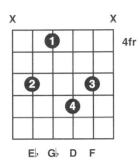

4fr

E♭ G♭ D F

 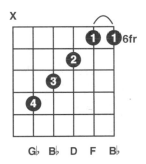

6fr

G♭ B♭ D F B♭

 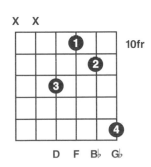

10fr

D F B♭ G♭

 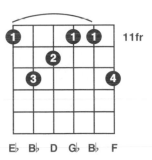

11fr

E♭ B♭ D G♭ B♭ F

E♭m11 (E♭-11, E♭min11)
E-flat minor eleventh

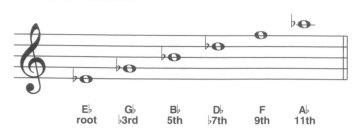

E♭	G♭	B♭	D♭	F	A♭
root	♭3rd	5th	♭7th	9th	11th

E♭m13 (E♭-13, E♭min13)
E-flat minor thirteenth

E♭	G♭	B♭	D♭	F	C
root	♭3rd	5th	♭7th	9th	13th

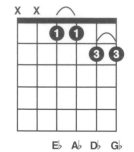
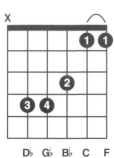

E♭ A♭ D♭ G♭

D♭ G♭ B♭ C F

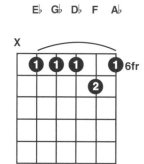
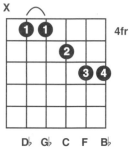

E♭ G♭ D♭ F A♭ (4fr)

D♭ G♭ C F B♭ (4fr)

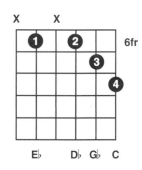

E♭ A♭ D♭ G♭ B♭ (6fr)

E♭ D♭ G♭ C (6fr)

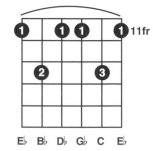

E♭ D♭ G♭ A♭ (9fr)

E♭ B♭ D♭ G♭ C E♭ (11fr)

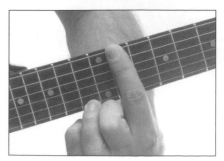

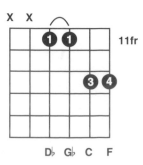

E♭ A♭ D♭ G♭ B♭ F (11fr)

D♭ G♭ C F (11fr)

E♭7 (E♭dom7)
E-flat dominant seventh

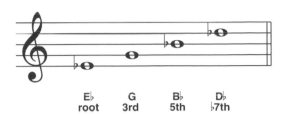

E♭	G	B♭	D♭
root	3rd	5th	♭7th

X X

E♭ B♭ D♭ G

X X

3fr

D♭ B♭ E♭ G

X X

4fr

E♭ G D♭ E♭

X

6fr

E♭ B♭ D♭ G B♭

11fr

E♭ B♭ D♭ G D♭ E♭

E♭7sus4 (E♭7sus)
E-flat dominant seventh, suspended fourth

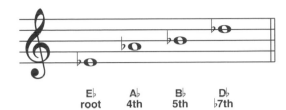

E♭	A♭	B♭	D♭
root	4th	5th	♭7th

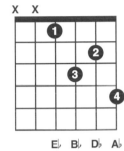

X X

E♭ B♭ D♭ A♭

X X

4fr

A♭ D♭ E♭ B♭

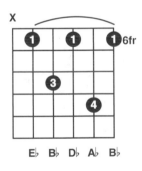

X

6fr

E♭ B♭ D♭ A♭ B♭

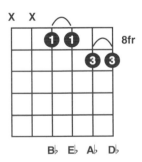

X X

8fr

B♭ E♭ A♭ D♭

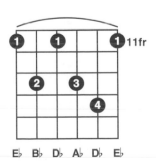

11fr

E♭ B♭ D♭ A♭ D♭ E♭

E♭

E♭7♭5 (E♭7-5, E♭dom7♭5)
E-flat dominant seventh, flat fifth

E♭	G	B♭♭	D♭
root	3rd	♭5th	♭7th

 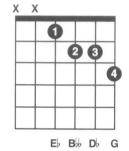

E♭ B♭♭ D♭ G

 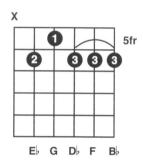

4fr
G D♭ E♭ B♭♭

6fr
E♭ B♭♭ D♭ G

7fr
B♭♭ E♭ G D♭

10fr
E♭ D♭ G B♭♭

E♭9
E-flat ninth

E♭	G	B♭	D♭	F
root	3rd	5th	♭7th	9th

 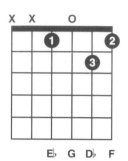

E♭ G D♭ F

 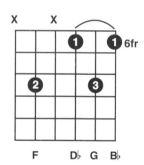

5fr
E♭ G D♭ F B♭

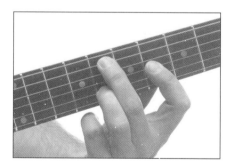

6fr
F D♭ G B♭

 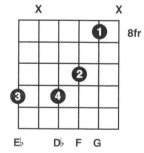

8fr
E♭ D♭ F G

 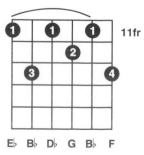

11fr
E♭ B♭ D♭ G B♭ F

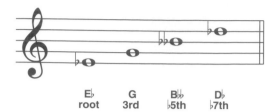 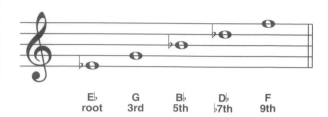 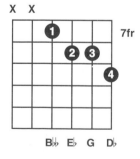 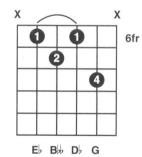 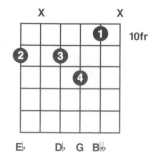

E♭9sus4 (E♭9sus)
E-flat ninth, suspended fourth

E♭	A♭	B♭	D♭	F
root	4th	5th	♭7th	9th

E♭9♭5 (E♭9-5, E♭dom9♭5)
E-flat ninth, flat fifth

E♭	G	B♭♭	D♭	F
root	3rd	♭5th	♭7th	9th

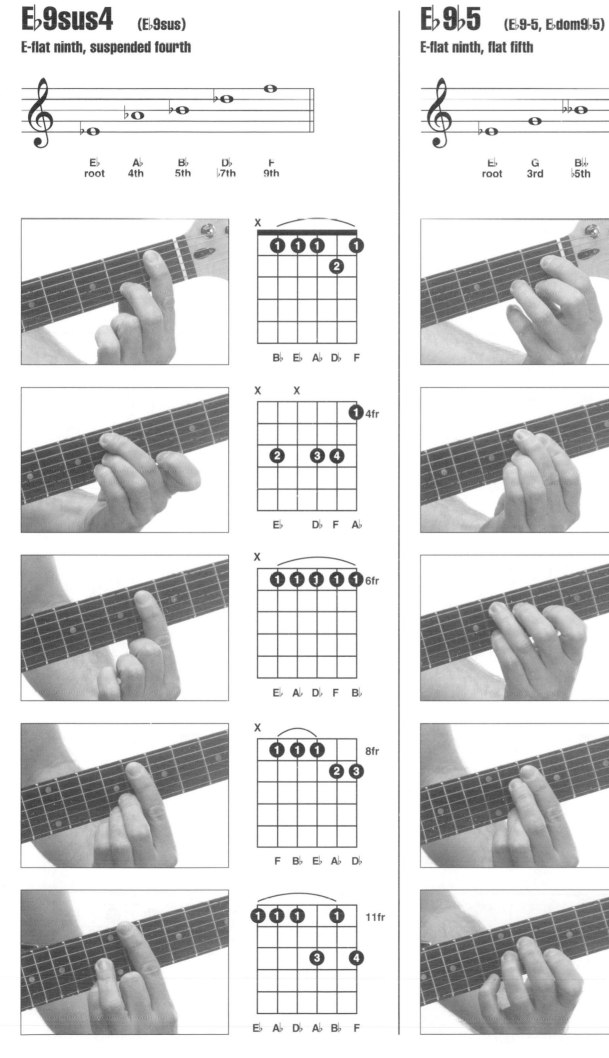

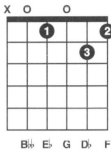
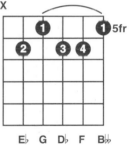
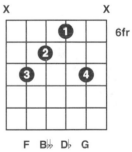
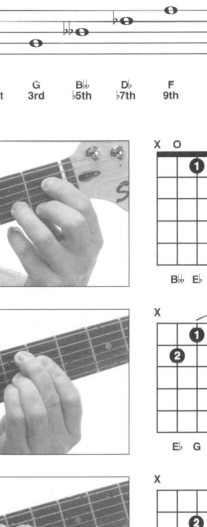
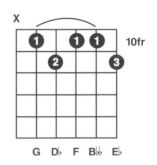
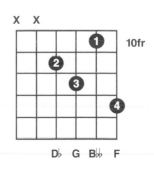

E♭7♭9 (E♭7-9, E♭dom7♭9)
E-flat dominant seventh, flat ninth

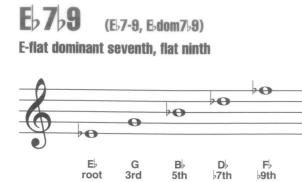

E♭	G	B♭	D♭	F♭
root	3rd	5th	♭7th	♭9th

X X O O
E♭ G D♭ F♭

X X
D♭ B♭ F♭ G

X X 5fr
E♭ G D♭ F♭

X X 8fr
B♭ F♭ G D♭

X X 8fr
E♭ D♭ F♭ G

E♭7♯9 (E♭7+9, E♭dom7♯9)
E-flat dominant seventh, sharp ninth

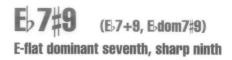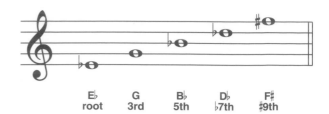

E♭	G	B♭	D♭	F♯
root	3rd	5th	♭7th	♯9th

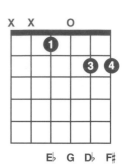
X X O
E♭ G D♭ F♯

X X
F♯ B♭ D♭ G

X X 5fr
E♭ G D♭ F♯

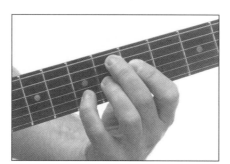
X 10fr
G D♭ F♯ B♭ E♭

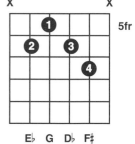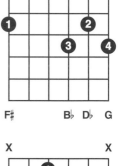

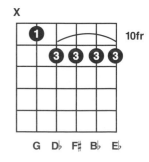

11fr
E♭ B♭ D♭ G B♭ F♯

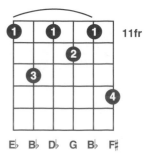

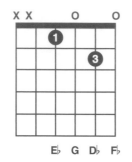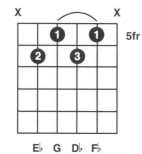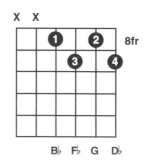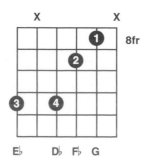

E♭7♭5(♯9) (E♭7-5(+9), E♭dom7♭5(♯9))
E-flat dominant seventh, flat fifth, sharp ninth

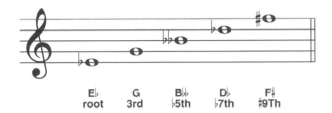

E♭	G	B♭♭	D♭	F♯
root	3rd	♭5th	♭7th	♯9Th

E♭11
E-flat eleventh

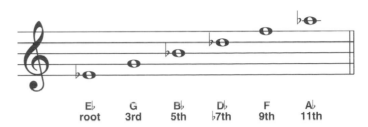

E♭	G	B♭	D♭	F	A♭
root	3rd	5th	♭7th	9th	11th

E♭

X O O

B♭♭ E♭ G D♭ F♯

X X

E♭ A♭ D♭ G

X   5fr

E♭ G D♭ F♯ B♭♭

4fr

A♭ D♭ G D♭ E♭ A♭

X   X   6fr

F♯ B♭♭ D♭ G

X   4fr

E♭ G D♭ E♭ A♭

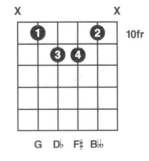

X   X   10fr

G D♭ F♯ B♭♭

X   6fr

E♭ A♭ D♭ G B♭

X X   14fr

G   B♭♭ D♭ F♯

X X   8fr

G   E♭ A♭ D♭

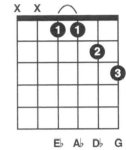
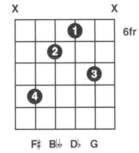
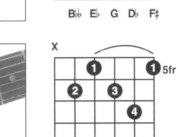
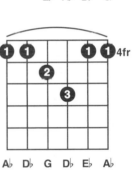
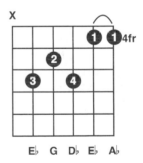
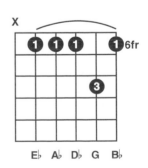
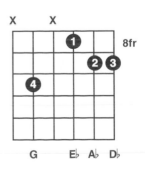

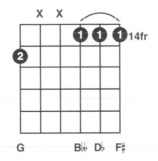

E♭7#11 (E♭7+11, E♭dom7#11)
E-flat dominant seventh, sharp eleventh

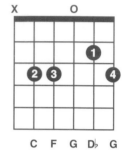

E♭	G	B♭	D♭	A
root	3rd	5th	♭7th	#11th

E♭13 (E♭dom13)
E-flat dominant thirteenth

E♭	G	B♭	D♭	F	C
root	3rd	5th	♭7th	9th	13th

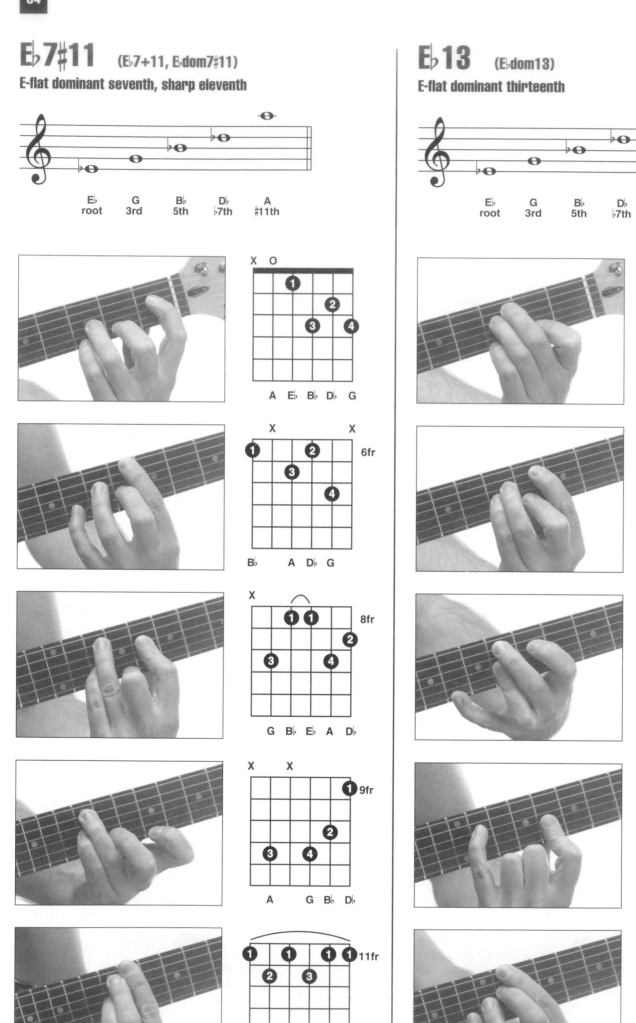

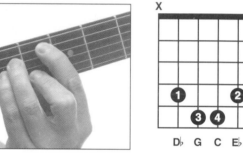

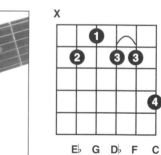

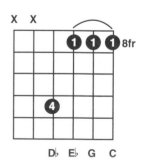

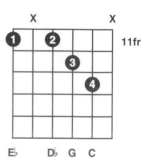

E♭13sus4 (E♭13sus)
E-flat thirteenth, suspended fourth

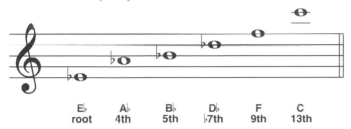

E♭ root	A♭ 4th	B♭ 5th	D♭ ♭7th	F 9th	C 13th

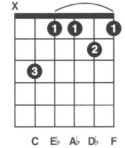

C E♭ A♭ D♭ F

D♭ C E♭ A♭

E♭ A♭ D♭ F C   6fr

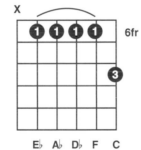

D♭ E♭ A♭ C   8fr

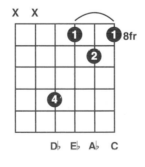

E♭ D♭ A♭ C   11fr

E♭+ (E♭aug, E♭(♯5))
E-flat augmented

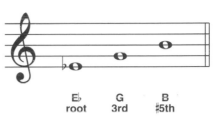

E♭ root	G 3rd	B ♯5th

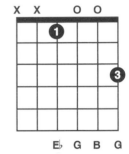

E♭ G B G

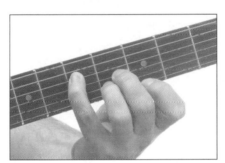

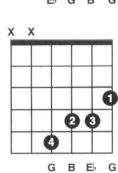

G B E♭ G

E♭ G B E♭   4fr

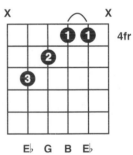

E♭ E♭ G B   6fr

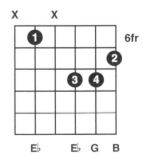

B E♭ G E♭   8fr

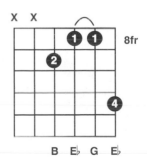

E♭

E♭+7 (E♭7♯5)
E-flat dominant seventh, sharp fifth

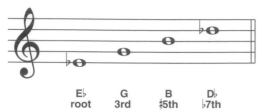

E♭	G	B	D♭
root	3rd	♯5th	♭7th

X · · O · ·

B E♭ G D♭ G

X · · · · X

2fr

E♭ G B D♭

X · · · · ·

6fr

E♭ B D♭ G B

· · X · · X

8fr

D♭ B E♭ G

X · · · · ·

11fr

E♭ D♭ G B

E♭+9 (E♭9♯5, E♭9+5)
E-flat ninth, sharp fifth

E♭	G	B	D♭	F
root	3rd	♯5th	♭7th	9th

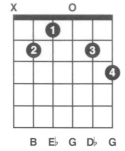
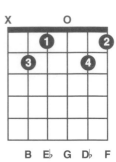

X · · O · ·

B E♭ G D♭ F

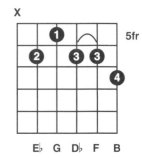

G D♭ F B E♭ G

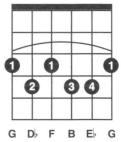

X · · · · ·

5fr

E♭ G D♭ F B

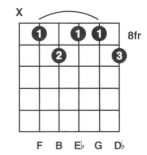

X · · · · ·

8fr

F B E♭ G D♭

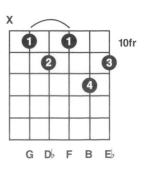

X · · · · ·

10fr

G D♭ F B E♭

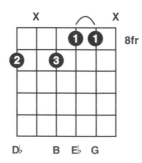
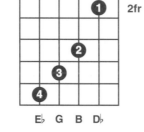
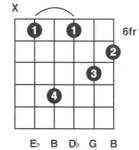
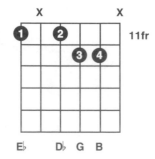

E♭+7♭9 (E♭7+5(♭9))

E-flat dominant seventh, sharp fifth, flat ninth

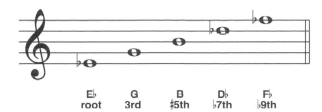

E♭	G	B	D♭	F♭
root	3rd	#5th	♭7th	♭9th

E♭+7♯9 (E♭7+5(♯9))

E-flat dominant seventh, sharp fifth, sharp ninth

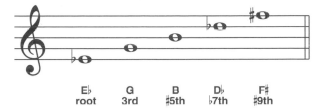

E♭	G	B	D♭	F♯
root	3rd	#5th	♭7th	#9th

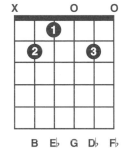

B E♭ G D♭ F♭

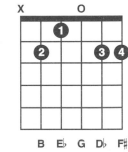

B E♭ G D♭ F♯

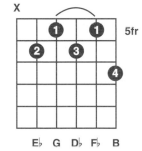

F♭ B D♭ G

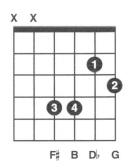

F♯ B D♭ G

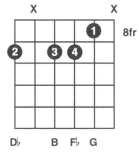

5fr

E♭ G D♭ F♭ B

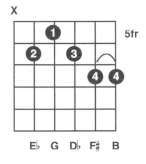

5fr

E♭ G D♭ F♯ B

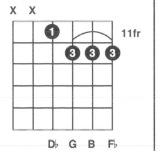

8fr

D♭ B F♭ G

8fr

F♯ B E♭ G D♭

11fr

D♭ G B F♭

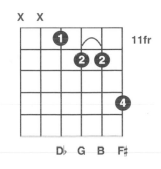

11fr

D♭ G B F♯

E♭° (E♭dim)
E-flat diminished

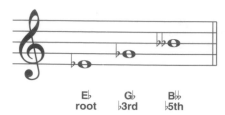

E♭   G♭   B♭♭
root   ♭3rd   ♭5th

E♭°7 (E♭dim7)
E-flat diminished seventh

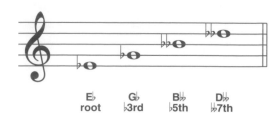

E♭   G♭   B♭♭   D♭♭
root   ♭3rd   ♭5th   ♭♭7th

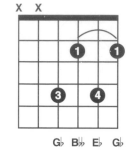

X X

G♭ B♭♭ E♭ G♭

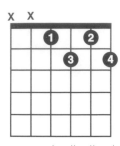

X X

E♭ B♭♭ D♭♭ G♭

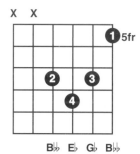

X X   5fr

B♭♭ E♭ G♭ B♭♭

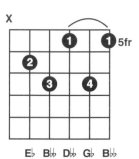

X   5fr

E♭ B♭♭ D♭♭ G♭ B♭♭

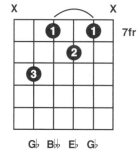

X   X   7fr

G♭ B♭♭ E♭ G♭

X   X   8fr

G♭   E♭ B♭♭ D♭♭

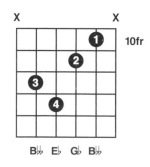

X   X   10fr

B♭♭ E♭ G♭ B♭♭

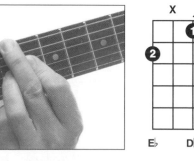
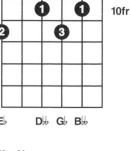

X   X   10fr

E♭   D♭♭ G♭ B♭♭

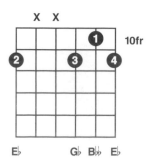

X X   10fr

E♭   G♭ B♭♭ E♭

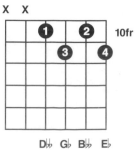

X X   10fr

D♭♭ G♭ B♭♭ E♭

E (Emaj)
E major

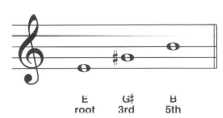

E — root
G# — 3rd
B — 5th

E5 (E no 3rd)
E fifth (power chord)

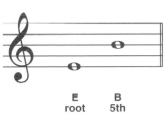

E — root
B — 5th

 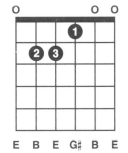

E B E G# B E

 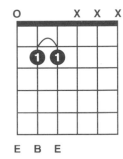

E B E

 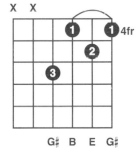

4fr

G# B E G#

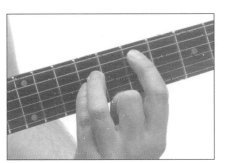 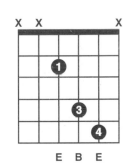

E B E

 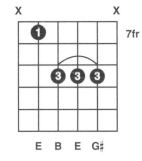

7fr

E B E G#

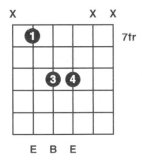

7fr

E B E

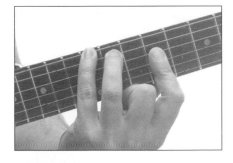 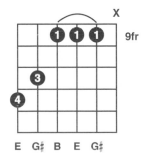

9fr

E G# B E G#

 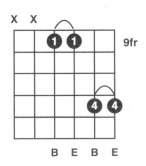

9fr

B E B E

 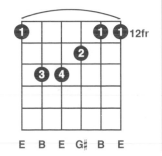

12fr

E B E G# B E

 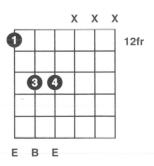

12fr

E B E

E

Esus4 (Esus)
E suspended fourth

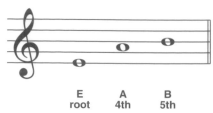

E A B
root 4th 5th

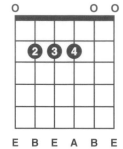

O   O O

E B E A B E

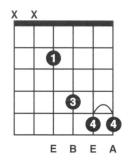

X X

①

③

④④

E B E A

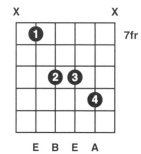

X   X

①   7fr

② ③

④

E B E A

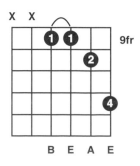

X X

① ①   9fr

②

④

B E A E

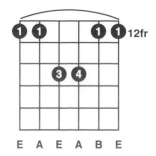

① ① ① ①12fr

③ ④

E A E A B E

Esus2 (E5add2)
E suspended second

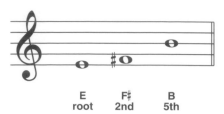

E F# B
root 2nd 5th

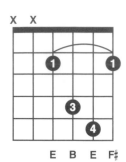

X X

①   ①

③

④

E B E F#

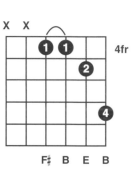

X X

① ①   4fr

②

④

F# B E B

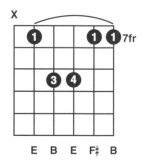

X

①   ① ①7fr

③ ④

E B E F# B

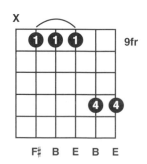

X

① ① ①   9fr

④ ④

F# B E B E

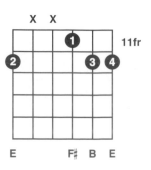

X X

①   11fr

②   ③ ④

E F# B E

Eadd9
E added ninth

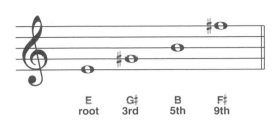

E	G#	B	F#
root	3rd	5th	9th

O O
2 3 1 4

E B E G# B F#

X X
1 1 1
2

F# B E G#

X X
1
2 3
4

6fr

B G# E F#

X X
1 1 1 1

9fr

F# B E G#

X X
1 2
3 4

11fr

G# F# B E

E6
E sixth

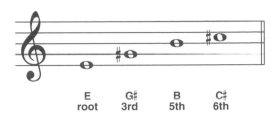

E	G#	B	C#
root	3rd	5th	6th

O O
2 3 1 4

E B E G# C# E

X X
1 1
3 4

E B C# G#

X X
1
2 3
4

6fr

E C# G# B

X
1
3 3 3 3

7fr

E B E G# C#

X X
1
2 3
4

11fr

E C# G# B

E6/9 (E6add9)
E sixth, added ninth

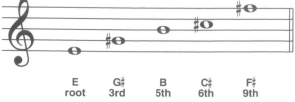

E	G#	B	C#	F#
root	3rd	5th	6th	9th

 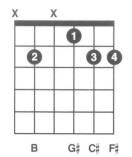

B G# C# F#

 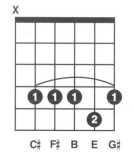

C# F# B E G#

 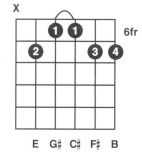

E G# C# F# B — 6fr

 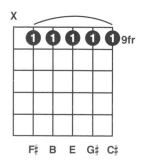

F# B E G# C# — 9fr

 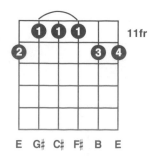

E G# C# F# B E — 11fr

Emaj7 (EM7)
E major seventh

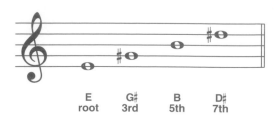

E	G#	B	D#
root	3rd	5th	7th

 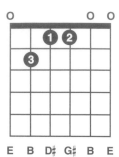

E B D# G# B E

   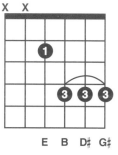

E B D# G#

 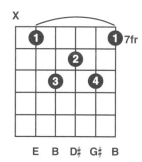

E B D# G# B — 7fr

 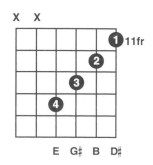

E G# B D# — 11fr

 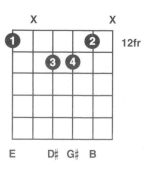

E D# G# B — 12fr

Emaj9 (EM9)
E major ninth

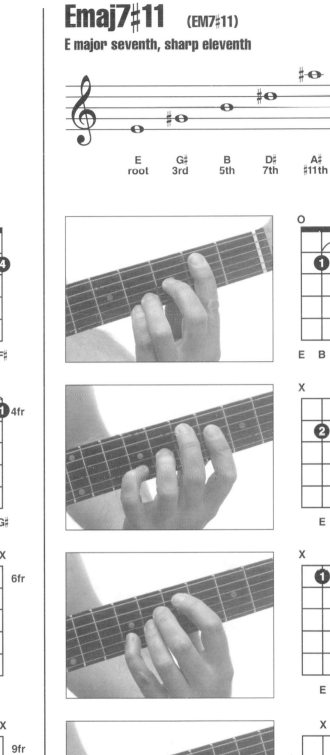

E	G#	B	D#	F#
root	3rd	5th	7th	9th

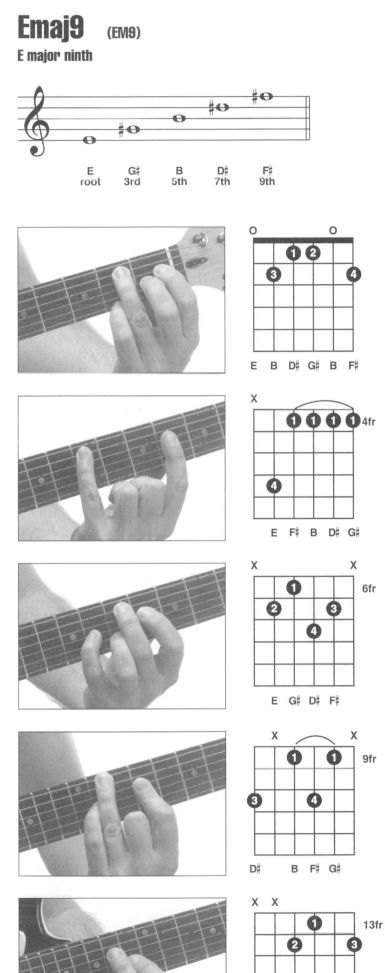

E B D# G# B F#

E F# B D# G#   4fr

E G# D# F#   6fr

D# B F# G#   9fr

E G# D# F#   13fr

Emaj7#11 (EM7#11)
E major seventh, sharp eleventh

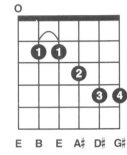

E	G#	B	D#	A#
root	3rd	5th	7th	#11th

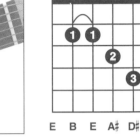

E B E A# D# G#

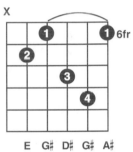

E G# D# G# A#   6fr

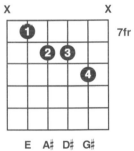

E A# D# G#   7fr

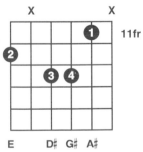

E D# G# A#   11fr

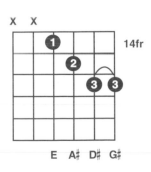

E A# D# G#   14fr

E

Emaj13 (EM13)
E major thirteenth

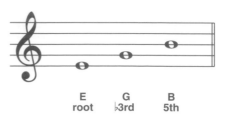

E	G#	B	D#	F#	C#
root	3rd	5th	7th	9th	13th

Em (Emin, E-)
E minor

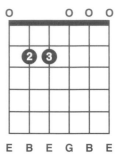

E	G	B
root	♭3rd	5th

E B D# G# C# F#

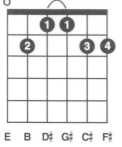

E B E G B E

4fr

E G# C# D#

E B E G

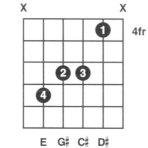

7fr

E D# G# C#

7fr

E B E G B

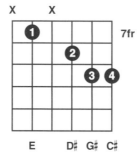

9fr

C# E G# D#

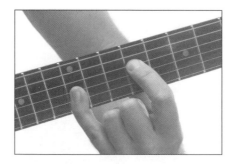

9fr

B G B E

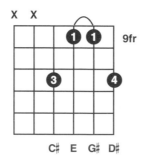

11fr

E G# C# F# B D#

12fr

E B E G B E

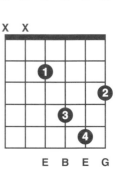

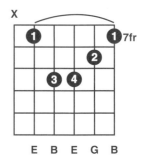

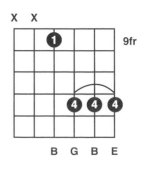

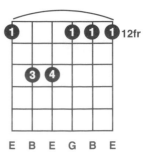

Em(add9)
E minor, added ninth

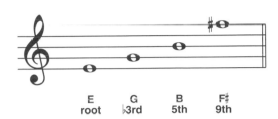

E   G   B   F#
root   ♭3rd   5th   9th

 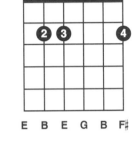

O   O   O

② ③   ④

E   B   E   G   B   F#

 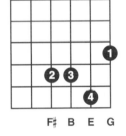

X   X

① ② ③ ④

F#   B   E   G

 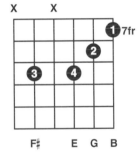

X   X

①7fr ② ③ ④

F#   E   G   B

 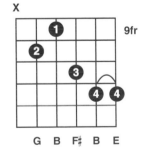

X

①9fr ② ③ ④ ④

G   B   F#   B   E

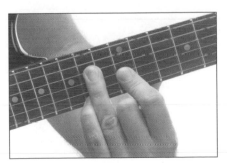 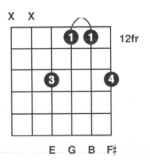

X   X

① ①12fr ③ ④

E   G   B   F#

Em6 (Emin6, E-6)
E minor sixth

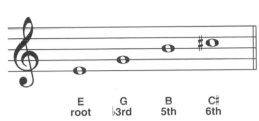

E   G   B   C#
root   ♭3rd   5th   6th

 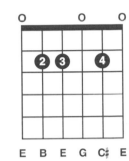

O   O   O

② ③   ④

E   B   E   G   C#   E

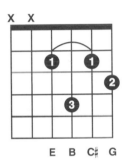

X   X

① ① ② ③

E   B   C#   G

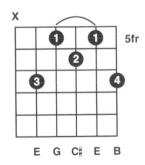

X

① ①5fr ② ③ ④

E   G   C#   E   B

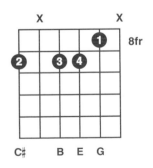

X   X

①8fr ② ③ ④

C#   B   E   G

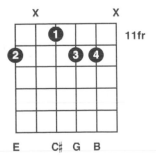

X   X

①11fr ② ③ ④

E   C#   G   B

E

Em♭6 (E-(♭6), Emin♭6)
E minor, flat sixth

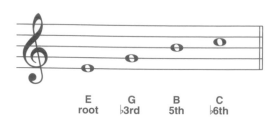

E	G	B	C
root	♭3rd	5th	♭6th

Em6/9
E minor sixth, added ninth

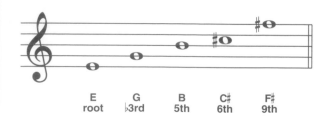

E	G	B	C♯	F♯
root	♭3rd	5th	6th	9th

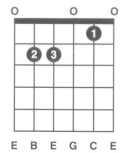

E B E G C E

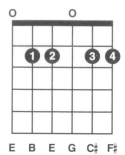

E B E G C♯ F♯

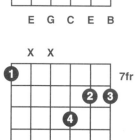

5fr

E G C E B

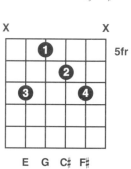

5fr

E G C♯ F♯

7fr

B E G C

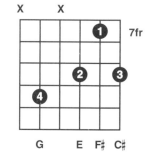

7fr

G E F♯ C♯

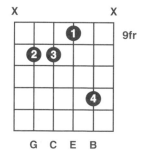

9fr

G C E B

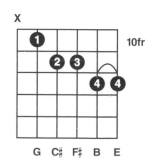

10fr

G C♯ F♯ B E

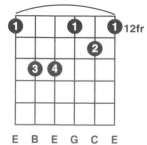

12fr

E B E G C E

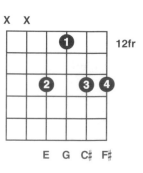

12fr

E G C♯ F♯

Em7 (Emin7, E-7)
E minor seventh

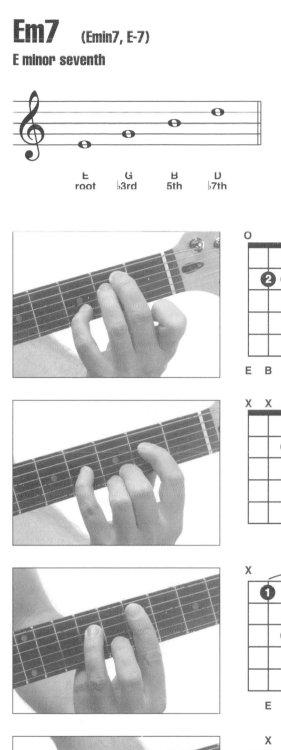

E root · G ♭3rd · B 5th · D ♭7th

O O O

E B E G D E

X X

E B D G

X 7fr

E B D G B

X X 12fr

E D G B

12fr

E B D G B E

Em7♭5 (E-7♭5, Emin7-5)
E minor seventh, flat fifth

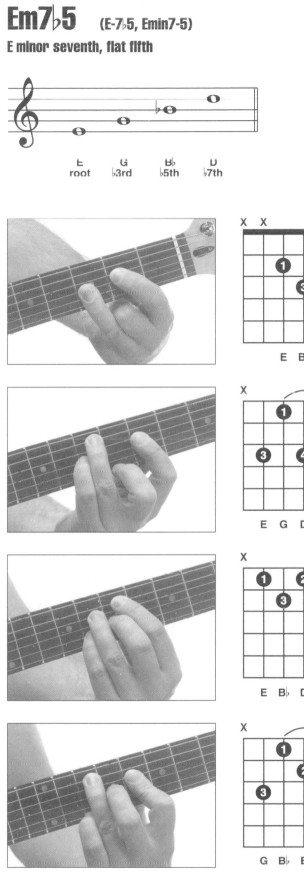

E root · G ♭3rd · B♭ ♭5th · D ♭7th

X X

E B♭ D G

X 5fr

E G D E B♭

X X 7fr

E B♭ D G

X 8fr

G B♭ E G D

X X 11fr

E D G B♭

E

Em(maj7) (E-(+7))
E minor, major seventh

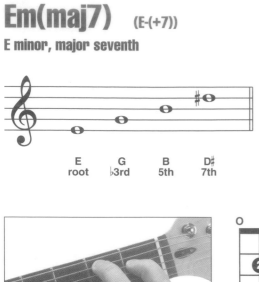

E	G	B	D#
root	♭3rd	5th	7th

O   O O O

E B D# G B E

X X

E B D# G

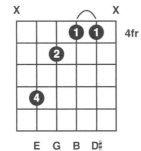

X   X   4fr

E G B D#

X   7fr

E B D# G B

X   X   12fr

E D# G B

Em9 (Emin9, E-9)
E minor ninth

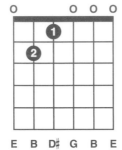

E	G	B	D	F#
root	♭3rd	5th	♭7th	9th

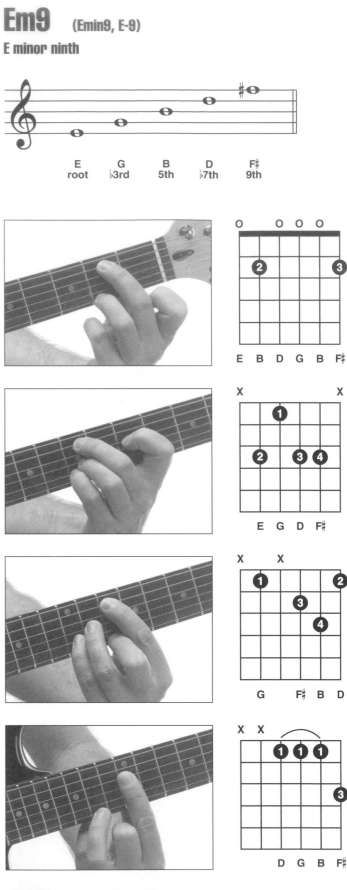

O   O O O

E B D G B F#

X   X   5fr

E G D F#

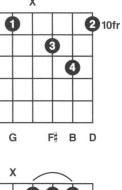

X   X   10fr

G F# B D

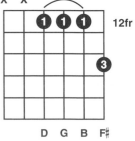

X X   12fr

D G B F#

12fr

E B D G D F#

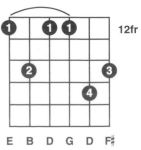

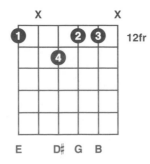

Em9♭5 (Em9-5, Emin9♭5)
E minor ninth, flat fifth

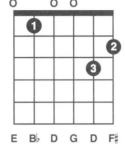

E	G	B♭	D	F#
root	♭3rd	♭5th	♭7th	9th

E B♭ D G D F#

G   F# B♭ D

G D F# B♭

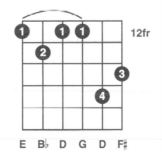

F# B♭ D G

E B♭ D G D F#

Em9(maj7) (Em8+7, E-8+7)
E minor ninth, major seventh

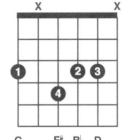

E	G	B	D#	F#
root	♭3rd	5th	7th	9th

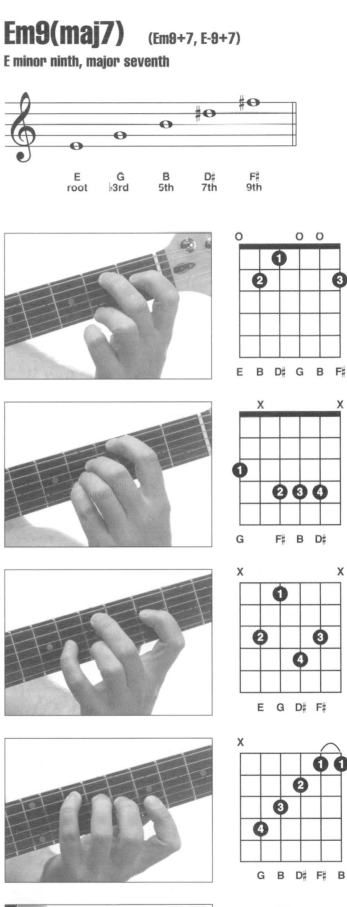

E B D# G B F#

G   F# B D#

E G D# F#

G B D# F# B

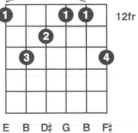

E B D# G B F#

Em11 (E-11, Emin11)
E minor eleventh

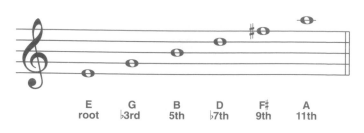

E	G	B	D	F#	A
root	b3rd	5th	b7th	9th	11th

O O O O O

E A D G B F#

X   5fr

E G D F# A

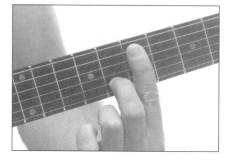

X   7fr

E A D G B

X   X   10fr

E   D G A

X X   14fr

E A D G

Em13 (E-13, Emin13)
E minor thirteenth

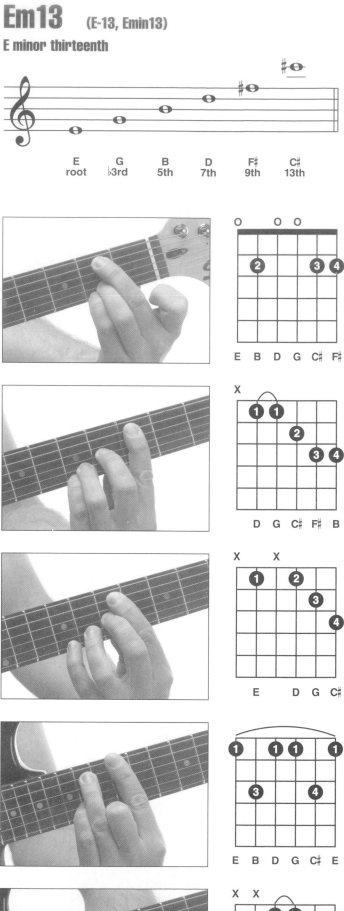

E	G	B	D	F#	C#
root	b3rd	5th	7th	9th	13th

O   O   O

E B D G C# F#

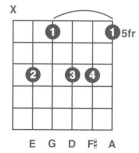

X   5fr

D G C# F# B

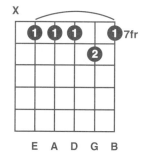

X   X   7fr

E   D G C#

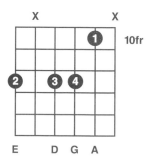

12fr

E B D G C# E

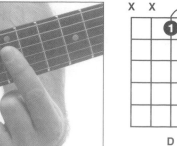

X X   12fr

D G C# F#

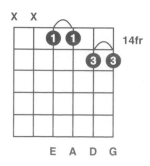
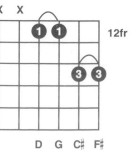
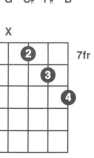

E7 (Edom7)
E dominant seventh

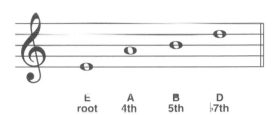

E	G#	B	D
root	3rd	5th	♭7th

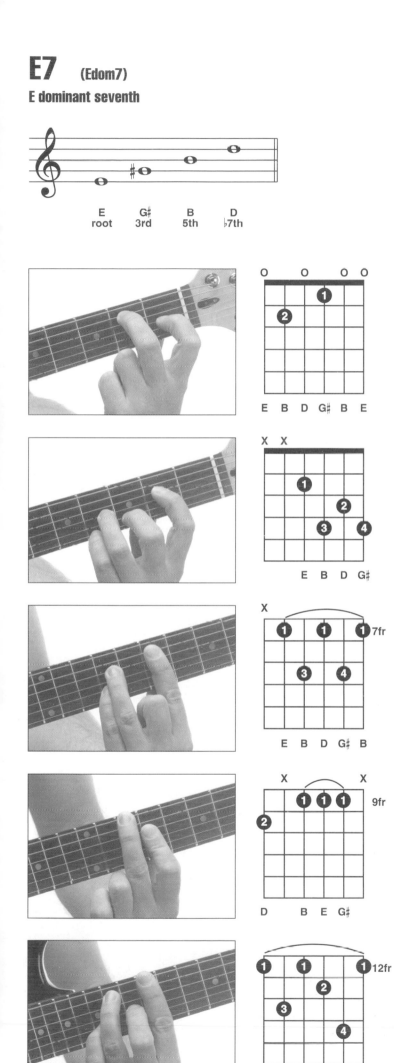

E7sus4 (E7sus)
E dominant seventh, suspended fourth

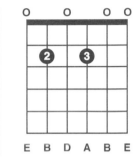

E	A	B	D
root	4th	5th	♭7th

O O O O
E B D G# B E

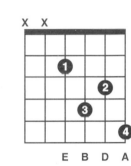

X X
E B D G#

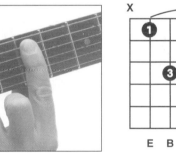
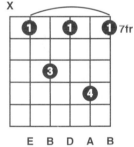

7fr
E B D G# B

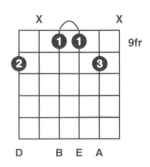

9fr
D B E G#

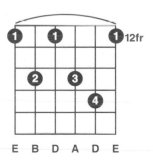

12fr
E B D G# D E

O O O O
E B D A B E

X X
E B D A

7fr
E B D A B

9fr
D B E A

12fr
E B D A D E

E

E7♭5 (E7-5, Edom7♭5)
E dominant seventh, flat fifth

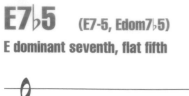

E	G#	B♭	D
root	3rd	♭5th	♭7th

E9
E ninth

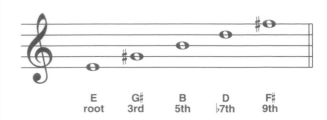

E	G#	B	D	F#
root	3rd	5th	♭7th	9th

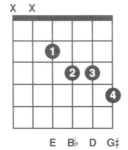

X X

E B♭ D G#

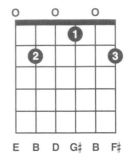

O O O

E B D G# B F#

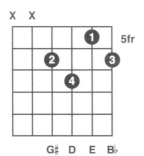

X X 5fr

G# D E B♭

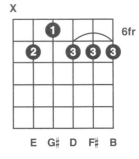

X 6fr

E G# D F# B

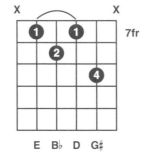

X X 7fr

E B♭ D G#

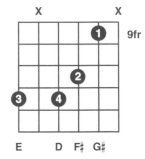

X X 9fr

E D F# G#

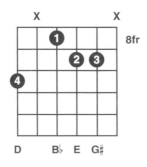

X X 8fr

D B♭ E G#

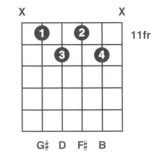

X X 11fr

G# D F# B

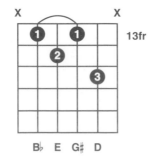

X X 13fr

B♭ E G# D

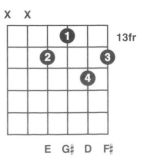

X X 13fr

E G# D F#

E9sus4 (E9sus)
E ninth, suspended fourth

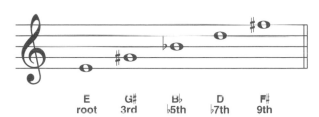

E	A	B	D	F#
root	4th	5th	♭7th	9th

E9♭5 (E9-5, Edom9♭5)
E ninth, flat fifth

E	G#	B♭	D	F#
root	3rd	♭5th	♭7th	9th

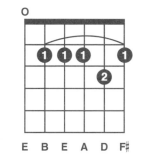

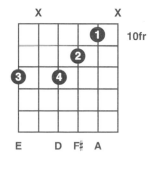

E B E A D F#

X X
E D F# A 5fr

X
E A D F# B 7fr

X X
E D F# A 10fr

X X
E A D F# 14fr

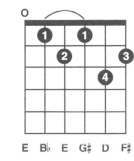

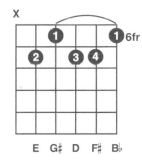

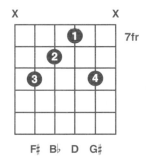

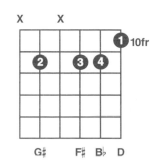

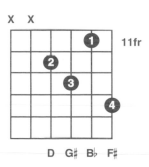

E B♭ E G# D F#

X
E G# D F# B♭ 6fr

X X
F# B♭ D G# 7fr

X X
G# F# B♭ D 10fr

X X
D G# B♭ F# 11fr

E

E7♭9 (E7-9, Edom7♭9)
E dominant seventh, flat ninth

E	G♯	B	D	F
root	3rd	5th	♭7th	♭9th

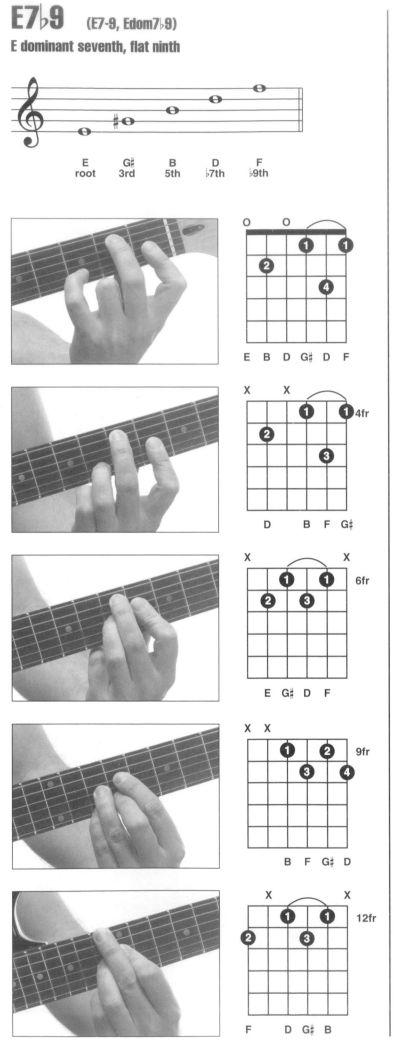

E B D G♯ D F

D B F G♯   4fr

E G♯ D F   6fr

B F G♯ D   9fr

F D G♯ B   12fr

E7♯9 (E7+9, Edom7♯9)
E dominant seventh, sharp ninth

E	G♯	B	D	F𝄪
root	3rd	5th	♭7th	♯9th

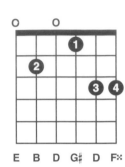

E B D G♯ D F𝄪

F𝄪 B D G♯

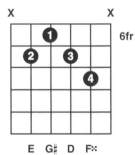

E G♯ D F𝄪   6fr

G♯ D F𝄪 B E   11fr

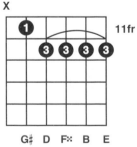

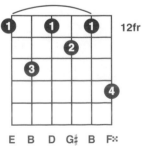

E B D G♯ B F𝄪   12fr

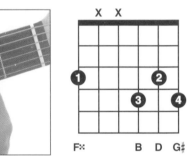

E7♭5(♯9) (E7-5(+9), Edom7♭5(♯9))

E dominant seventh, flat fifth, sharp ninth

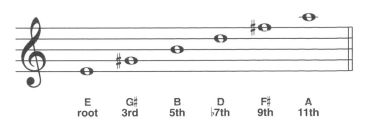

E	G♯	B♭	D	F𝄪
root	3rd	♭5th	♭7th	♯9th

E B♭ E G♯ D F𝄪

F𝄪 B♭ D G♯

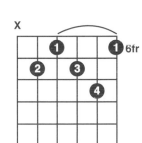

E G♯ D F𝄪 B♭ — 6fr

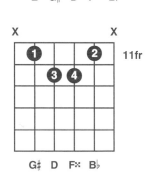

G♯ D F𝄪 B♭ — 11fr

B♭ E G♯ D F𝄪 — 13fr

E11

E eleventh

E	G♯	B	D	F♯	A
root	3rd	5th	♭7th	9th	11th

E A E G♯ D F♯

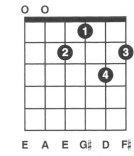

E A D G♯

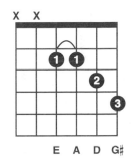

E G♯ D E A — 5fr

E A D G♯ B — 7fr

A G♯ B D — 10fr

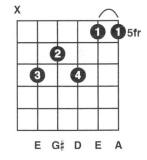

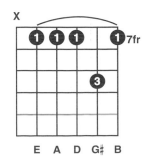

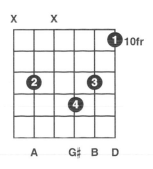

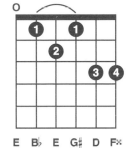

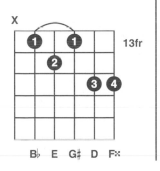

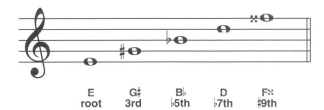

E

E7#11 (E7+11, Edom7#11)
E dominant seventh, sharp eleventh

E	G#	B	D	F#	A#
root	3rd	5th	b7th	9th	#11th

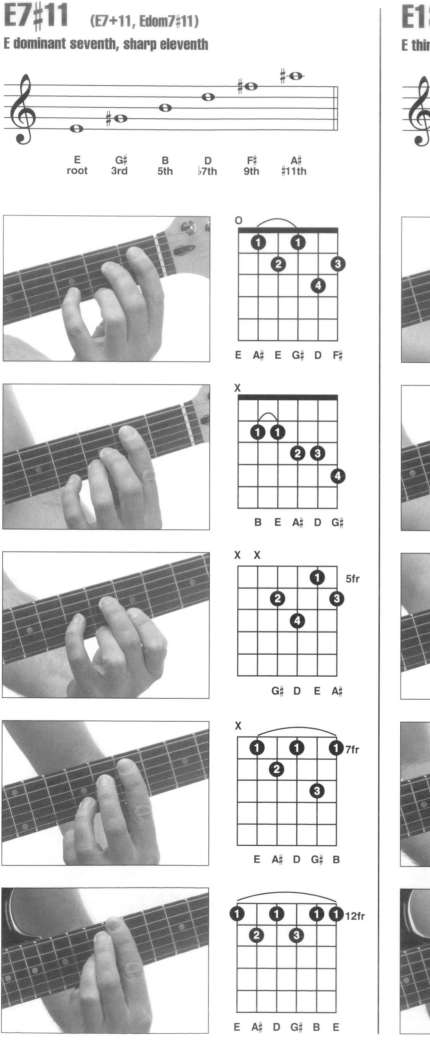

E13 (Edom13)
E thirteenth

E	G#	B	D	F#	C#
root	3rd	5th	b7th	9th	13th

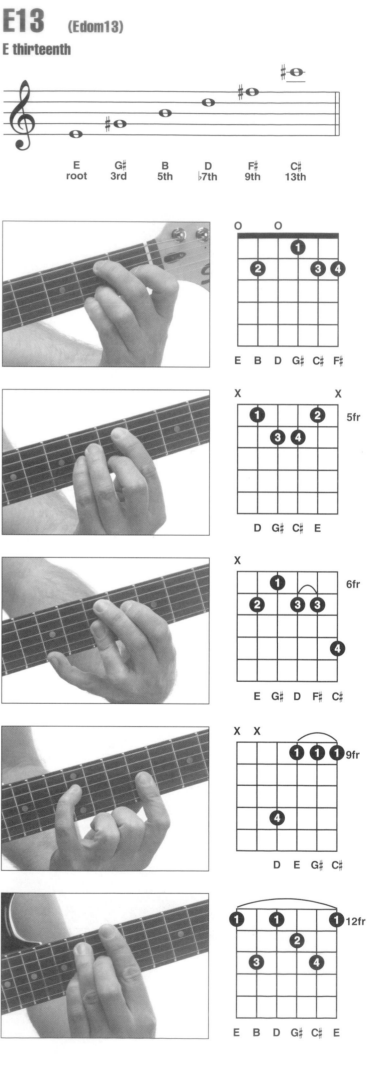

E13sus4 (E13sus)
E thirteenth, suspended fourth

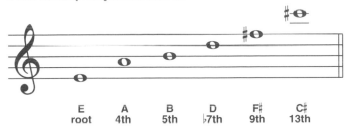

E	A	B	D	F#	C#
root	4th	5th	♭7th	9th	13th

E+ (Eaug, E(#5))
E augmented

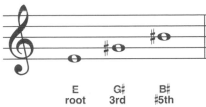

E	G#	B#
root	3rd	#5th

E

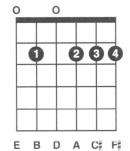

E B D A C# F#

X X O — E G# B# E

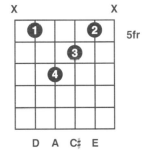

5fr — D A C# E

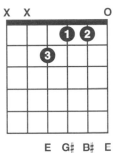

X X — G# B# E G#

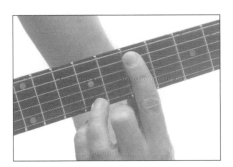
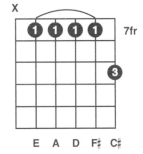

7fr — E A D F# C#

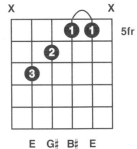

X X — 5fr — E G# B# E

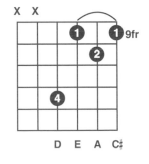

9fr — D E A C#

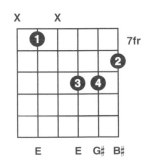

X X — 7fr — E E G# B#

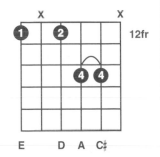

12fr — E D A C#

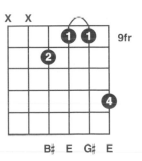

X X — 9fr — B# E G# E

E+7 (E7♯5)
E seventh, sharp fifth

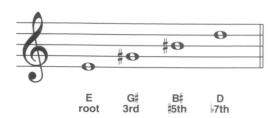

E	G♯	B♯	D
root	3rd	♯5th	♭7th

X X O   O

D G♯ B♯ E

X X

E B♯ D G♯

X   7fr

E B♯ D G♯ B♯

X   X   9fr

D B♯ E G♯

X   X   12fr

E D G♯ B♯

E+9 (E9♯5, E9+5)
E ninth, sharp fifth

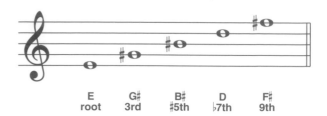

E	G♯	B♯	D	F♯
root	3rd	♯5th	♭7th	9th

X X O

D G♯ B♯ F♯

X X

F♯ B♯ D G♯

X   6fr

E G♯ D F♯ B♯

X   9fr

F♯ B♯ E G♯ D

X   11fr

G♯ D F♯ B♯ E

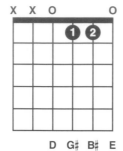
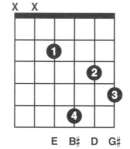
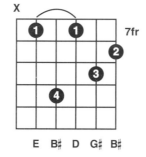
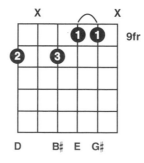
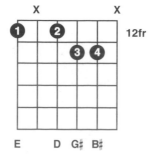

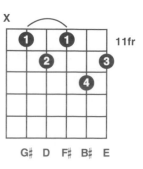
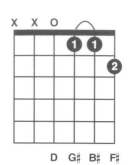
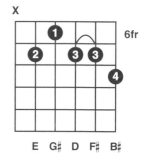
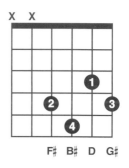
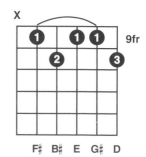

E+7♭9 (E7+5(♭9))
E dominant seventh, sharp fifth, flat ninth

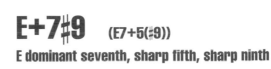

E	G#	B#	D	F
root	3rd	#5th	♭7th	♭9th

 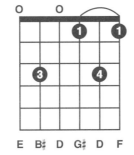

E B# D G# D F

 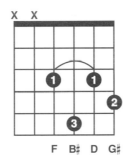

F B# D G#

 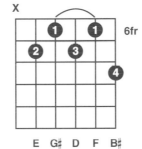

E G# D F B# — 6fr

 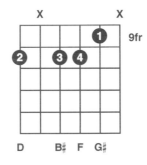

D B# F G# — 9fr

 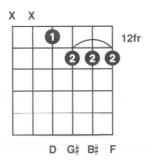

D G# B# F — 12fr

E+7#9 (E7+5(#9))
E dominant seventh, sharp fifth, sharp ninth

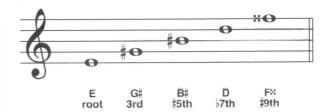

E	G#	B#	D	F𝄪
root	3rd	#5th	♭7th	#9th

 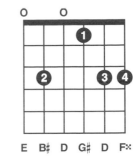

E B# D G# D F𝄪

 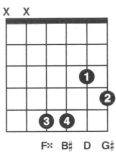

F𝄪 B# D G#

 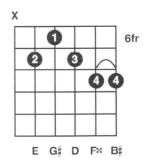

E G# D F𝄪 B# — 6fr

 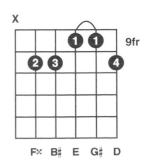

F𝄪 B# E G# D — 9fr

 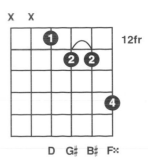

D G# B# F𝄪 — 12fr

110

E° (Edim)
E diminished

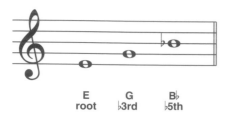

E — root
G — ♭3rd
B♭ — ♭5th

E°7 (Edim7)
E diminished seventh

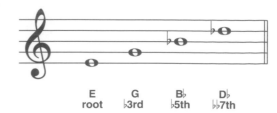

E — root
G — ♭3rd
B♭ — ♭5th
D♭ — ♭♭7th

X X
E B♭ E G

O   O   O
E B♭ E G D♭ E

X X

3fr

G B♭ E B♭

X X

E B♭ D♭ G

X   X

7fr

E B♭ E G

X

6fr

E B♭ D♭ G B♭

X X

10fr

G   G B♭ E

X   X

11fr

E   D♭ G B♭

X   X

11fr

B♭ E G B♭

X X

14fr

E B♭ D♭ G

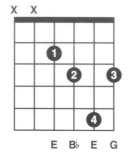
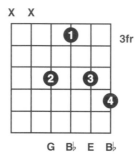
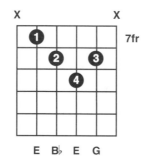
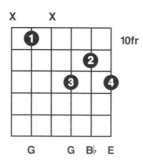
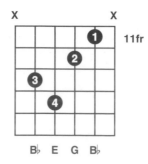
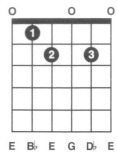
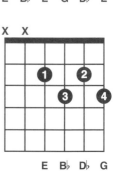
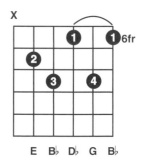
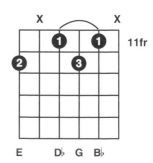
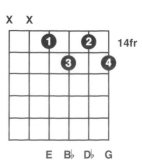

F (Fmaj)
F major

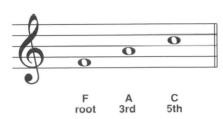

F   A   C
root 3rd 5th

F5 (F no 3rd)
F fifth (power chord)

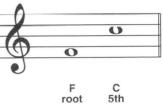

F   C
root 5th

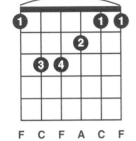

F C F A C F

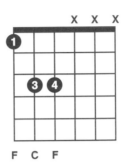

F C F

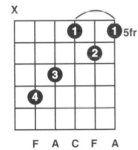

5fr

F A C F A

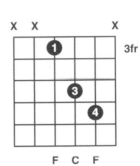

3fr

F C F

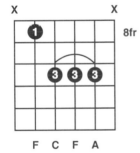

8fr

F C F A

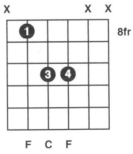

8fr

F C F

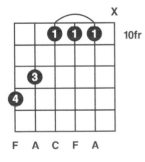
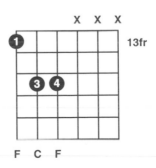

10fr

F A C F A

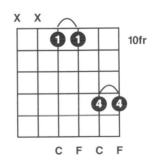

10fr

C F C F

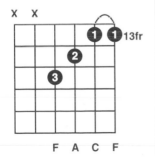

13fr

F A C F

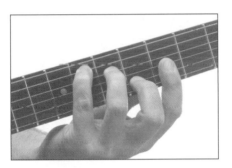

13fr

F C F

F

Fsus4 (Fsus)
F suspended fourth

F	B♭	C
root	4th	5th

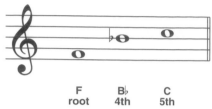
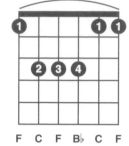

F C F B♭ C F

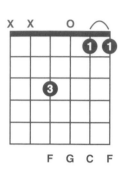

3fr

F C F B♭

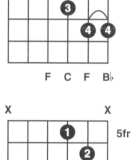

5fr

F B♭ C F

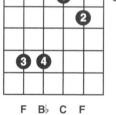

8fr

F C F B♭

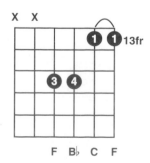

13fr

F B♭ C F

Fsus2 (F5add2)
F suspended second

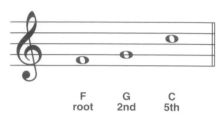

F	G	C
root	2nd	5th

X X O

F G C F

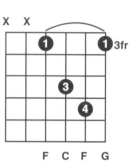

3fr

F C F G

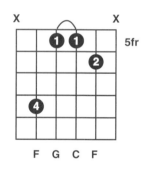

5fr

F G C F

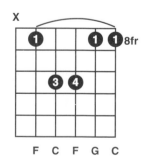

8fr

F C F G C

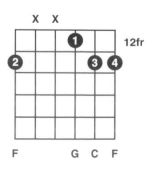

12fr

F G C F

Fadd9
F added ninth

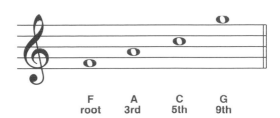

F	A	C	G
root	3rd	5th	9th

F6
F sixth

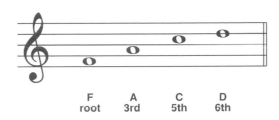

F	A	C	D
root	3rd	5th	6th

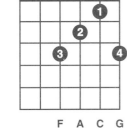
X X
F A C G

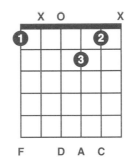
X O X
F D A C

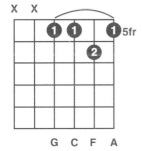
X X 5fr
G C F A

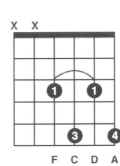
X X
F C D A

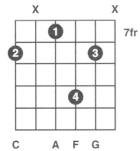
X X 7fr
C A F G

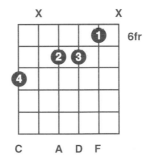
X X 6fr
C A D F

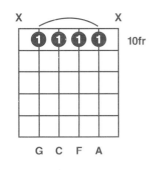
X X 10fr
G C F A

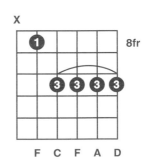
X 8fr
F C F A D

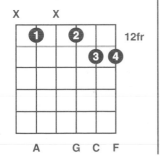
X X 12fr
A G C F

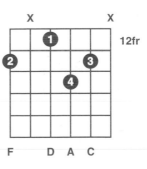
X X 12fr
F D A C

F6/9 (F6add9)
F sixth, added ninth

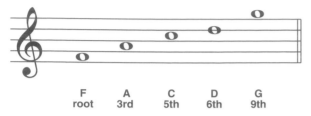

F	A	C	D	G
root	3rd	5th	6th	9th

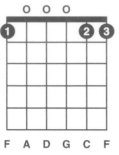

O O O

F A D G C F

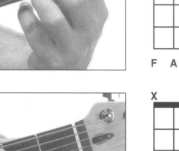

X

C F A D G

X

D G C F A 5fr

X

F A D G C 7fr

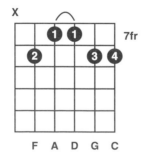

X

F G C F A D 10fr

Fmaj7 (FM7)
F major seventh

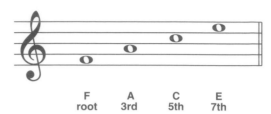

F	A	C	E
root	3rd	5th	7th

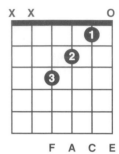

X X O

F A C E

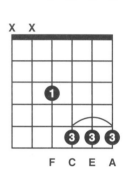

X X

F C E A

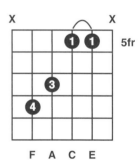

X X

F A C E 5fr

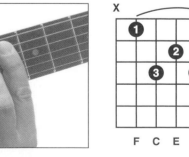

X

F C E A C 8fr

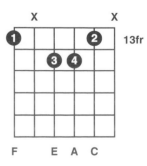

X X

F E A C 13fr

Fmaj9 (FM9)

F major ninth

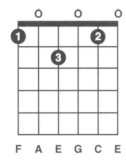

F	A	C	E	G
root	3rd	5th	7th	9th

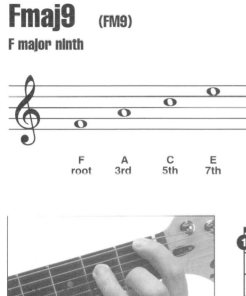

F A E G C E

F A E G

F G C E A   5fr

F A E G   7fr

F E G A   10fr

Fmaj7#11 (FM7#11)

F major seventh, sharp eleventh

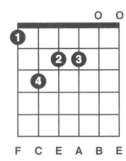

F	A	C	E	B
root	3rd	5th	7th	#11th

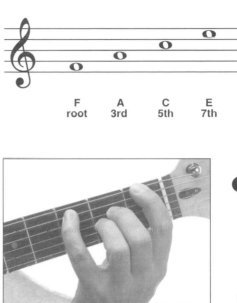

F C E A B E

F B E A

F A E A B   7fr

F B E A C   8fr

F E A B   12fr

F

Fmaj13 (FM13)
F major thirteenth

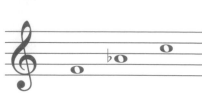

F	A	C	E	G	D
root	3rd	5th	7th	9th	13th

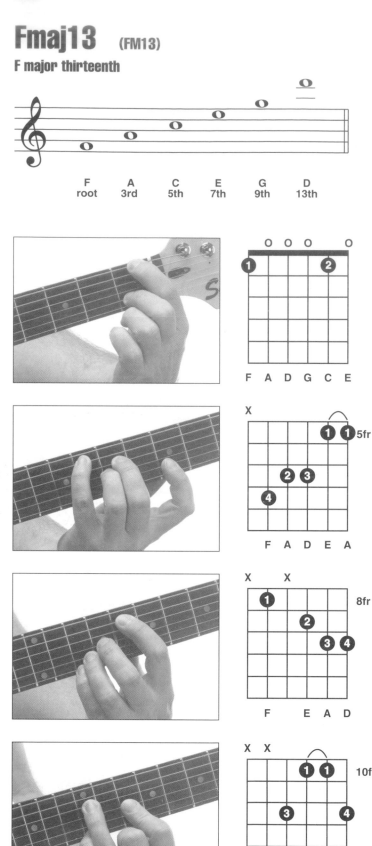

O O O   O

F A D G C E

X   5fr

F A D E A

X X   8fr

F   E A D

X X   10fr

D F A E

X   X   13fr

F   E A D

Fm (Fmin, F-)
F minor

F	A♭	C
root	♭3rd	5th

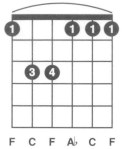

F C F A♭ C F

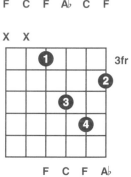

X X   3fr

F C F A♭

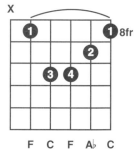

X   8fr

F C F A♭ C

X   X   9fr

A♭ C F A♭

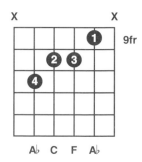

X X   10fr

C A♭ C F

Fm(add 9)
F minor, added ninth

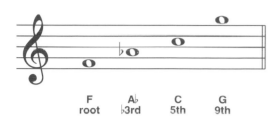

F	A♭	C	G
root	♭3rd	5th	9th

Fm6
(Fmin6, F-6)
F minor sixth

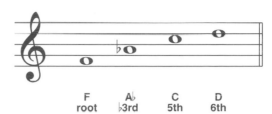

F	A♭	C	D
root	♭3rd	5th	6th

 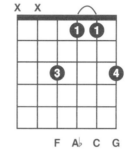

F A♭ C G

 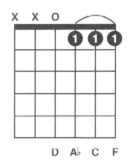

D A♭ C F

 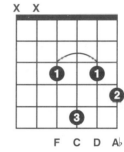

4fr — A♭ G C F

F C D A♭

 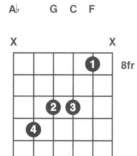 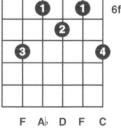

8fr — A♭ C F G

6fr — F A♭ D F C

 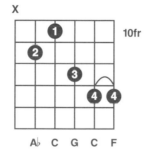 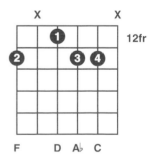

10fr — A♭ C G C F

12fr — F D A♭ C

 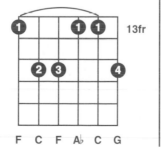 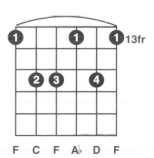

13fr — F C F A♭ C G

13fr — F C F A♭ D F

Fm♭6 (F-(♭6), Fmin♭6)
F minor, flat sixth

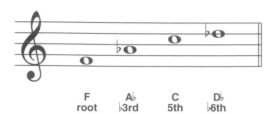

F	A♭	C	D♭
root	♭3rd	5th	♭6th

F C F A♭ D♭ F

4fr
D♭ C F A♭

6fr
F A♭ D♭ F C

8fr
F C F A♭ D♭

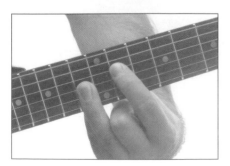
11fr
D♭ A♭ C F

Fm6/9
F minor sixth, added ninth

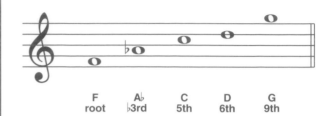

F	A♭	C	D	G
root	♭3rd	5th	6th	9th

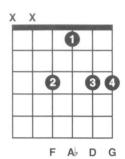
F A♭ D G

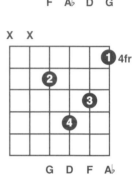
4fr
G D F A♭

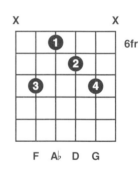
6fr
F A♭ D G

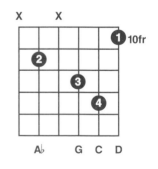
10fr
A♭ G C D

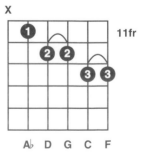
11fr
A♭ D G C F

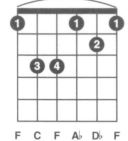
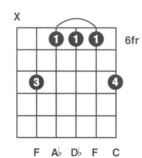
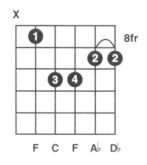
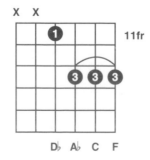

Fm7 (F-7, Fmin7)
F minor seventh

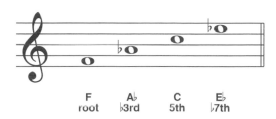

F	A♭	C	E♭
root	♭3rd	5th	♭7th

F C E♭ A♭ C F

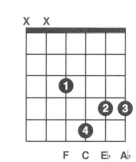

F C E♭ A♭

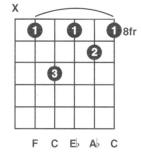

F C E♭ A♭ C 8fr

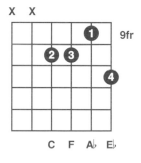

C F A♭ E♭ 9fr

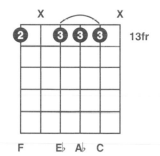

F E♭ A♭ C 13fr

Fm7♭5 (F-7♭5, Fmin7-5)
F minor seventh, flat fifth

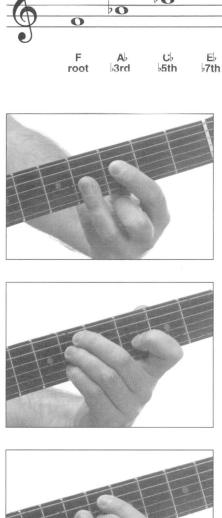

F	A♭	C♭	E♭
root	♭3rd	♭5th	♭7th

F C♭ E♭ A♭

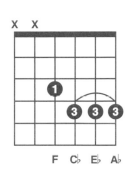

E♭ A♭ C♭ F 4fr

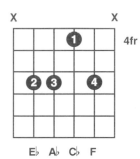

F C♭ E♭ A♭ 8fr

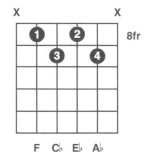

A♭ F C♭ E♭ 10fr

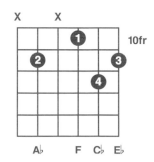

F E♭ A♭ C♭ 12fr

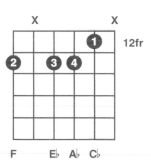

Fm(maj7) (Fm(+7))
F minor, major seventh

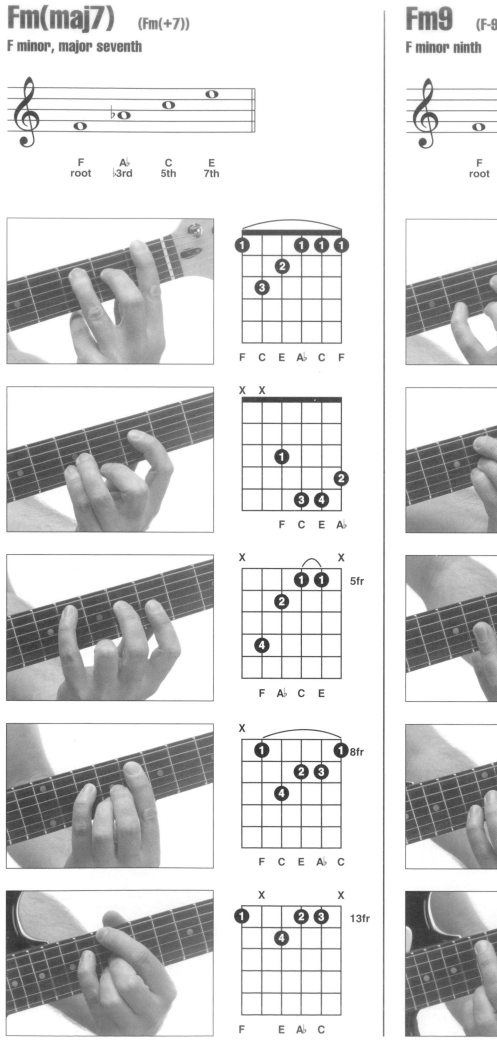

F	A♭	C	E
root	♭3rd	5th	7th

Fm9 (F-9, Fmin9)
F minor ninth

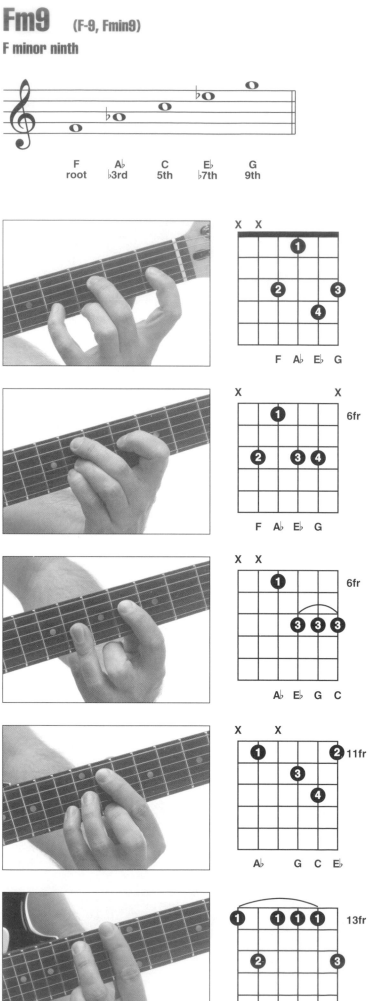

F	A♭	C	E♭	G
root	♭3rd	5th	♭7th	9th

Fm9♭5 (Fm9-5, Fmin9♭5)
F minor ninth, flat fifth

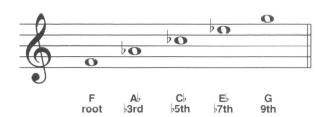

F	A♭	C♭	E♭	G
root	♭3rd	♭5th	♭7th	9th

Fm9(maj7) (Fm9+7, F-9+7)
F minor ninth, major seventh

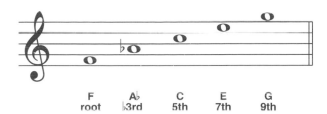

F	A♭	C	E	G
root	♭3rd	5th	7th	9th

 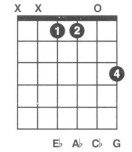

E♭ A♭ C♭ G

 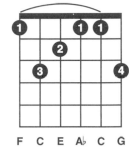

F C E A♭ C G

 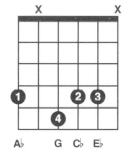

A♭ G C♭ E♭

 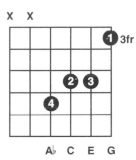

A♭ C E G (3fr)

 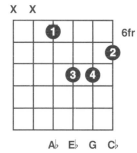

A♭ E♭ G C♭ (6fr)

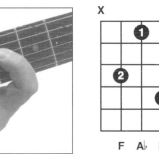 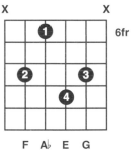

F A♭ E G (6fr)

 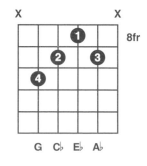

G C♭ E♭ A♭ (8fr)

 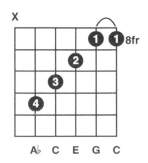

A♭ C E G C (8fr)

 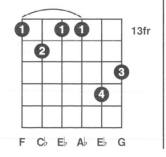

F C♭ E♭ A♭ E♭ G (13fr)

 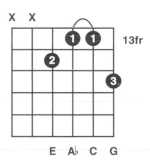

E A♭ C G (13fr)

Fm11 (F-11, Fmin11)
F minor eleventh

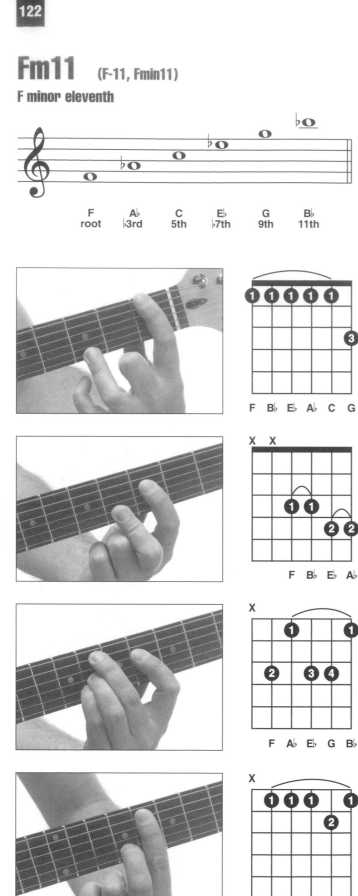

F	A♭	C	E♭	G	B♭
root	♭3rd	5th	♭7th	9th	11th

F B♭ E♭ A♭ C G

F B♭ E♭ A♭

F A♭ E♭ G B♭

F B♭ E♭ A♭ C

F E♭ A♭ B♭

Fm13 (F-13, Fmin13)
F minor thirteenth

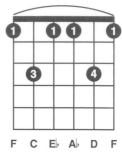
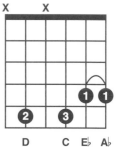
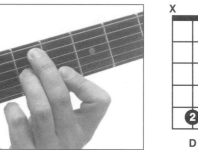
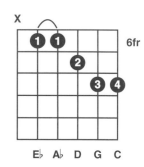
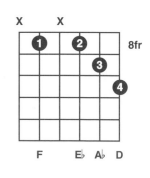
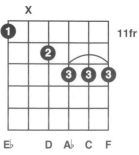

F	A♭	C	E♭	G	D
root	♭3rd	5th	♭7th	9th	13th

F C E♭ A♭ D F

D C E♭ A♭

E♭ A♭ D G C

F E♭ A♭ D

E♭ D A♭ C F

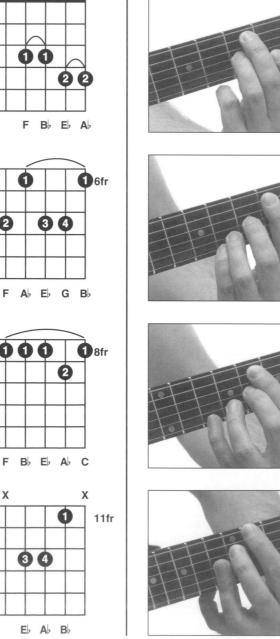

F7 (Fdom7)
F dominant seventh

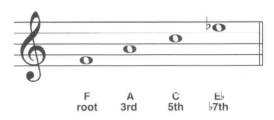

F	A	C	E♭
root	3rd	5th	♭7th

F C E♭ A C F

 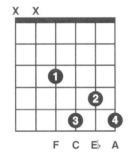

X X
F C E♭ A

 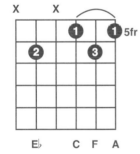

X X 5fr
E♭ C F A

 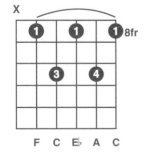

X 8fr
F C E♭ A C

 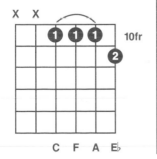

X X 10fr
C F A E♭

F7sus4 (F7sus)
F dominant seventh, suspended fourth

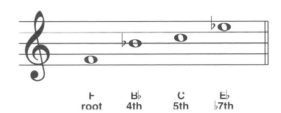

F	B♭	C	E♭
root	4th	5th	♭7th

 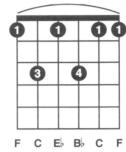

F C E♭ B♭ C F

 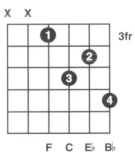

X X 3fr
F C E♭ B♭

 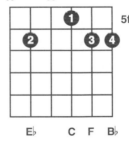

X X 5fr
E♭ C F B♭

 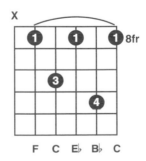

X 8fr
F C E♭ B♭ C

F

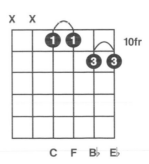

X X 10fr
C F B♭ E♭

F7♭5 (F7-5, Fdom7♭5)
F dominant seventh, flat fifth

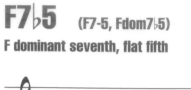

F	A	C♭	E♭
root	3rd	♭5th	♭7th

F9
F ninth

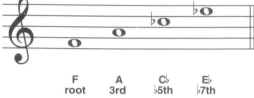

F	A	C	E♭	G
root	3rd	5th	♭7th	9th

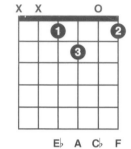

X X   O

E♭ A C♭ F

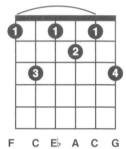

F C E♭ A C G

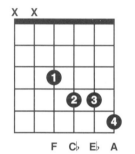

X X

F C♭ E♭ A

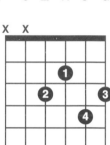

X X

F A E♭ G

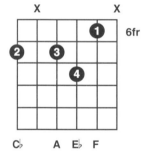

X   X

6fr

C♭ A E♭ F

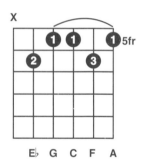

X

5fr

E♭ G C F A

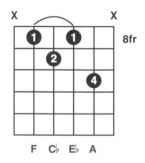

X   X

8fr

F C♭ E♭ A

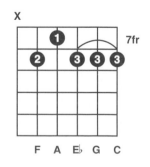

X

7fr

F A E♭ G C

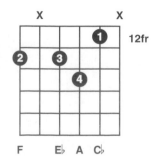

X   X

12fr

F E♭ A C♭

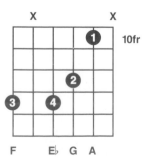

X   X

10fr

F E♭ G A

F9sus4 (F9sus)
F ninth, suspended fourth

F	Bb	C	Eb	G
root	4th	5th	b7th	9th

F C Eb Bb C G

F Bb Eb G

Eb G C F Bb — 5fr

F Bb Eb G C — 8fr

F Eb G Bb — 11fr

F9b5 (F9-5, Fdom9b5)
F ninth, flat fifth

F	A	Cb	Eb	G
root	3rd	b5th	b7th	9th

X X O

Eb A Cb G

X X

A G Cb Eb

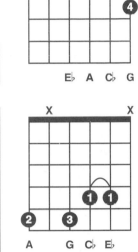

X 7fr

F A Eb G Cb

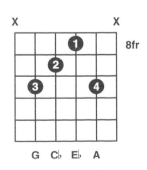

X X 8fr

G Cb Eb A

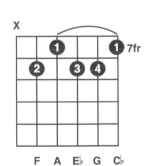

X 12fr

A Eb G Cb F

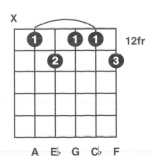

F

F7♭9 (F7-9, Fdom7♭9)
F dominant seventh, flat ninth

F	A	C	E♭	G♭
root	3rd	5th	♭7th	♭9th

F7♯9 (F7+9, Fdom7♯9)
F dominant seventh, sharp ninth

F	A	C	E♭	G♯
root	3rd	5th	♭7th	♯9th

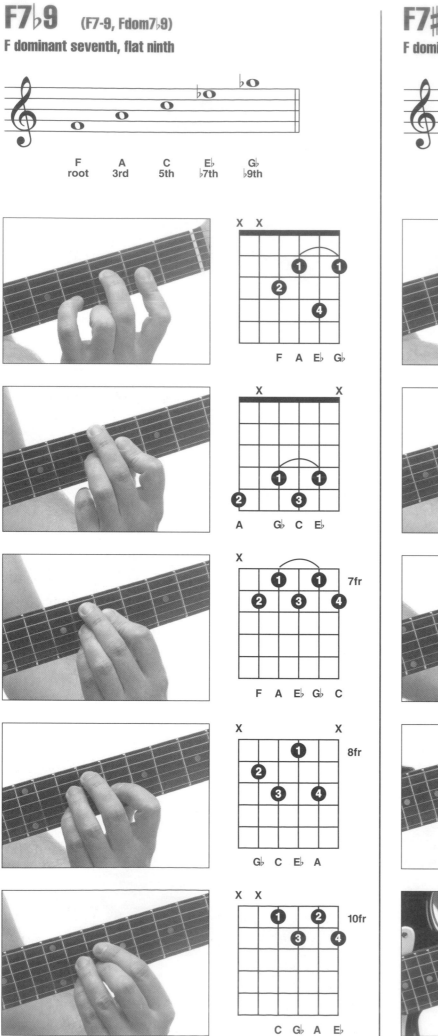

F A E♭ G♭

A G♭ C E♭

F A E♭ G♭ C 7fr

G♭ C E♭ A 8fr

C G♭ A E♭ 10fr

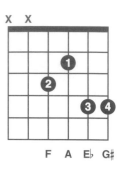

F A E♭ G♯

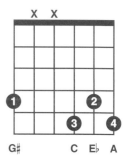

G♯ C E♭ A

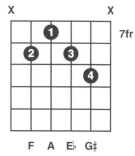

F A E♭ G♯ 7fr

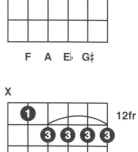

A E♭ G♯ C F 12fr

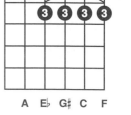

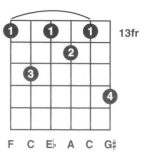

F C E♭ A C G♯ 13fr

F7♭5(♯9) (F7-5 (+8), Fdom7♭5(♯9))
F dominant seventh, flat fifth, sharp ninth

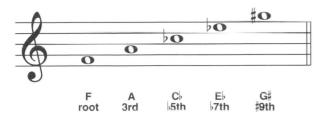

F	A	C♭	E♭	G♯
root	3rd	♭5th	♭7th	♯9th

F11
F eleventh

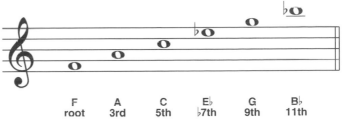

F	A	C	E♭	G	B♭
root	3rd	5th	♭7th	9th	11th

 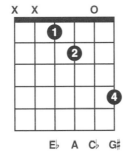

E♭ A C♭ G♯

 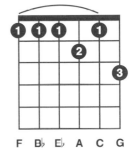

F B♭ E♭ A C G

 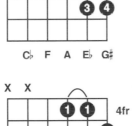

C♭ F A E♭ G♯

 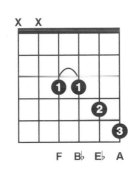

F B♭ E♭ A

 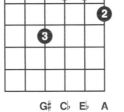

G♯ C♭ E♭ A

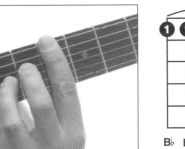 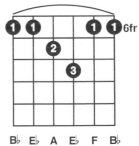

B♭ E♭ A E♭ F B♭

 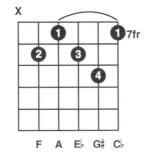

F A E♭ G♯ C♭

 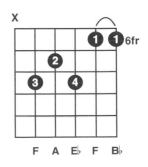

F A E♭ F B♭

 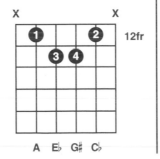

A E♭ G♯ C♭

 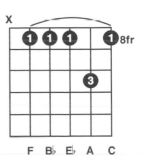

F B♭ E♭ A C

F

F7♯11   (F7+11, Fdom7♯11)
F dominant seventh, sharp eleventh

F	A	C	E♭	B
root	3rd	5th	♭7th	♯11th

F13   (Fdom13)
F thirteenth

F	A	C	E♭	G	D
root	3rd	5th	♭7th	9th	13th

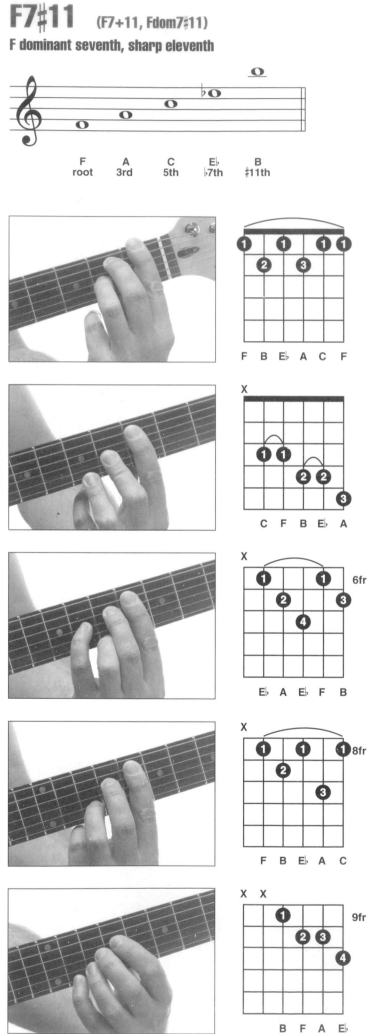

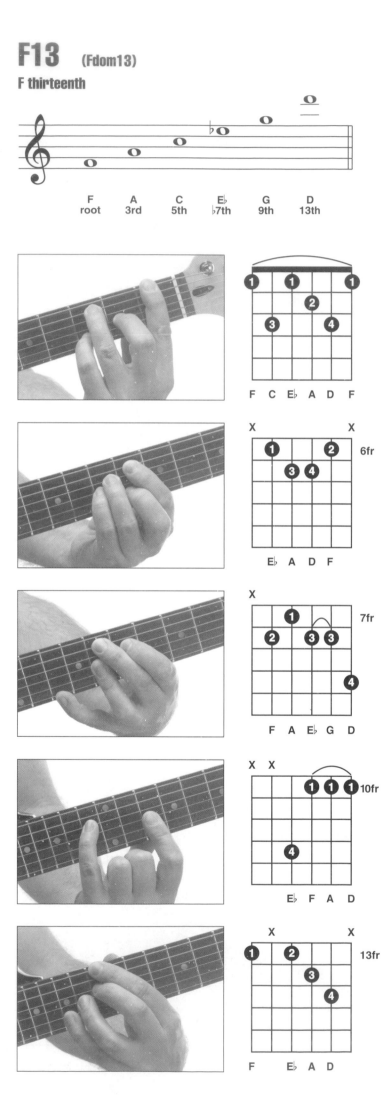

F13sus4 (F13sus)
F thirteenth, suspended fourth

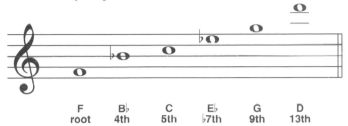

F	B♭	C	E♭	G	D
root	4th	5th	♭7th	9th	13th

F+ (Faug, F(♯5))
F augmented

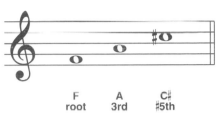

F	A	C♯
root	3rd	♯5th

F C E♭ B♭ D F

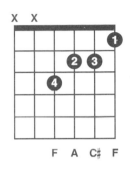
F A C♯ F

D F B♭ E♭ G

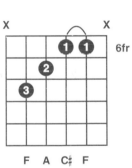
C♯ C♯ F A (4fr)

E♭ D F B♭ (6fr)

F A C♯ F (6fr)

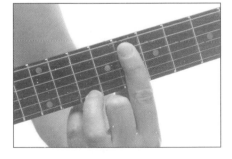
F B♭ E♭ G D (8fr)

C♯ C♯ F A (9fr)

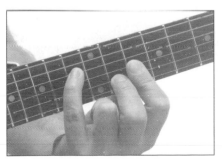
E♭ F B♭ D (10fr)

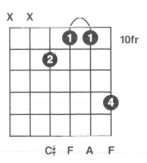
C♯ F A F (10fr)

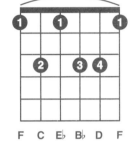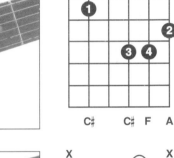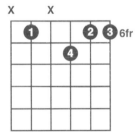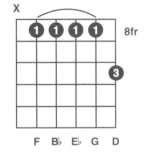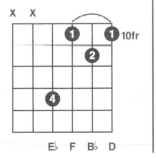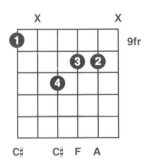

F+7 (F7#5)
F dominant seventh, sharp fifth

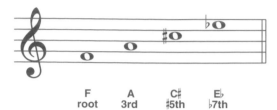

F	A	C#	E♭
root	3rd	#5th	♭7th

F+9 (F9#5, F9+5)
F ninth, sharp fifth

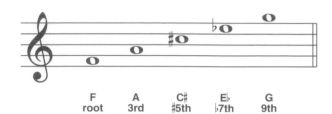

F	A	C#	E♭	G
root	3rd	#5th	♭7th	9th

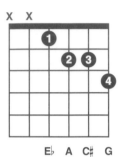
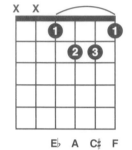
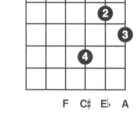

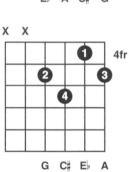

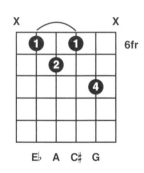
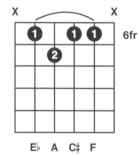

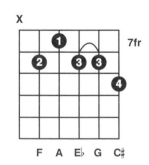
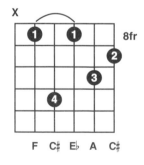

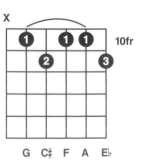
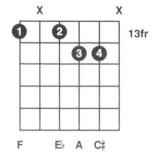

F+7♭9 (F7+5(♭9))
F dominant seventh, sharp fifth, flat ninth

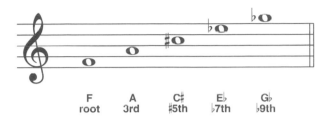

F root | A 3rd | C# #5th | E♭ ♭7th | G♭ ♭9th

Eb A C# Gb

Gb C# Eb A 4fr

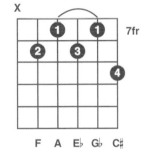
F A Eb Gb C# 7fr

Eb C# Gb A 10fr

F Eb A C# Gb 13fr

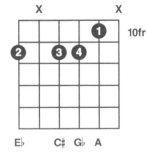
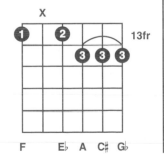

F+7#9 (F7+5(#9))
F dominant seventh, sharp fifth, sharp ninth

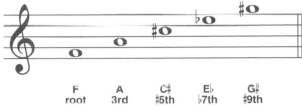

F root | A 3rd | C# #5th | E♭ ♭7th | G# #9th

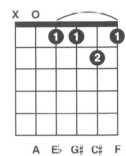
A Eb G# C# F

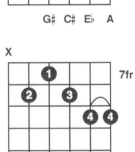
G# C# Eb A 4fr

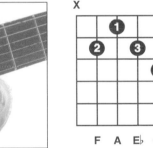
F A Eb G# C# 7fr

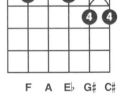
G# C# F A Eb 10fr

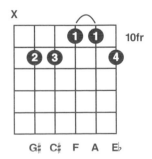
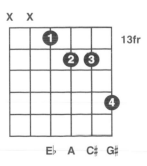
Eb A C# G# 13fr

F

F° (Fdim)
F diminished

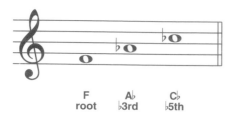

F A♭ C♭
root ♭3rd ♭5th

F°7 (Fdim7)
F diminished seventh

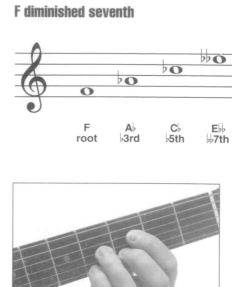

F A♭ C♭ E♭♭
root ♭3rd ♭5th ♭♭7th

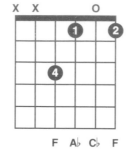

X X   O
F A♭ C♭ F

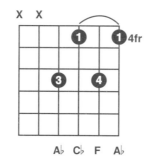

X   X
4fr
A♭   A♭ C♭ F

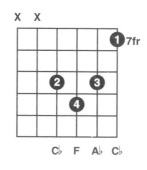

X X
4fr
A♭ C♭ F A♭

X X
7fr
C♭ F A♭ C♭

X   X
9fr
A♭ C♭ F A♭

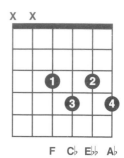

X X
F C♭ E♭♭ A♭

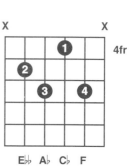

X   X
4fr
E♭♭ A♭ C♭ F

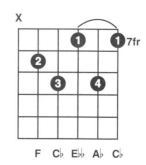

X
7fr
F C♭ E♭♭ A♭ C♭

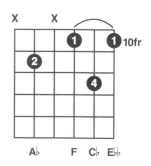

X   X
10fr
A♭   F C♭ E♭♭

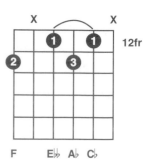

X   X
12fr
F   E♭♭ A♭ C♭

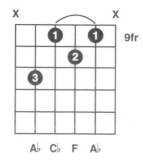

F# (F#maj)
F-sharp major

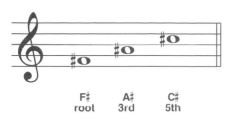

F#   A#   C#
root 3rd 5th

F#5 (F# no 3rd)
F-sharp fifth (power chord)

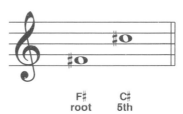

F#   C#
root 5th

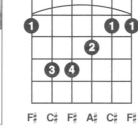

F# C# F# A# C# F#

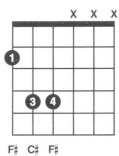

X X X

F# C# F#

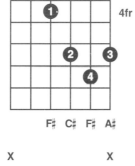

4fr

F# C# F# A#

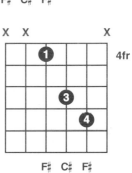

X X X

4fr

F# C# F#

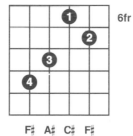

6fr

F# A# C# F#

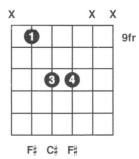

X X X

9fr

F# C# F#

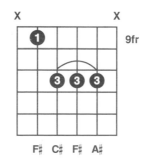

9fr

F# C# F# A#

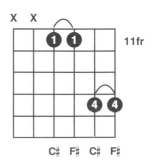

X X

11fr

C# F# C# F#

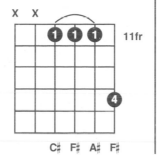

11fr

C# F# A# F#

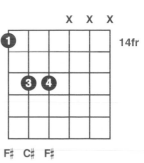

X X X

14fr

F# C# F#

F#

F#sus4 (F#sus)
F-sharp suspended fourth

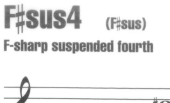

	F#	B	C#
	root	4th	5th

F# C# F# B C# F#

X X ... 4fr

F# C# F# B

X X ... 6fr

F# B C# F#

X X ... 9fr

F# C# F# B

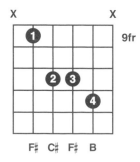

X X ... 11fr

C# F# B F#

F#sus2 (F#5add2)
F-sharp suspended second

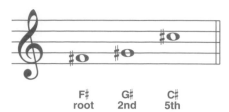

	F#	G#	C#
	root	2nd	5th

 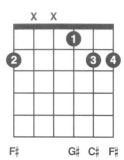

X X

F# G# C# F#

 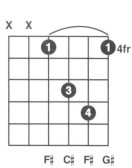

X X ... 4fr

F# C# F# G#

 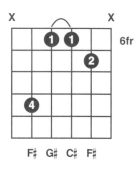

X X ... 6fr

F# G# C# F#

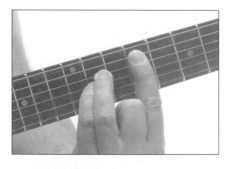 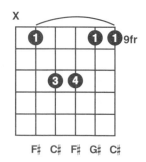

X ... 9fr

F# C# F# G# C#

 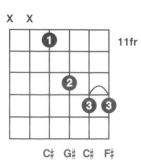

X X ... 11fr

C# G# C# F#

F#add9
F-sharp added ninth

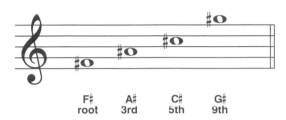

F#	A#	C#	G#
root	3rd	5th	9th

F#6
F-sharp sixth

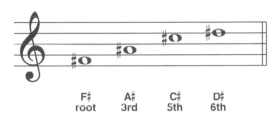

F#	A#	C#	D#
root	3rd	5th	6th

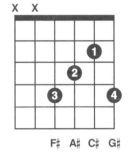

F# A# C# G#

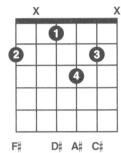

F# D# A# C#

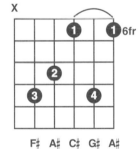

G# C# F# A# — 6fr

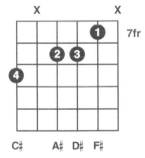

F# C# D# A# — 4fr

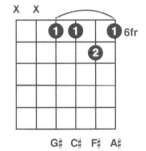

F# A# C# G# A# — 6fr

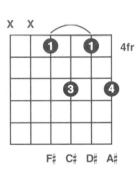

C# A# D# F# — 7fr

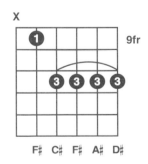

G# C# F# A# — 11fr

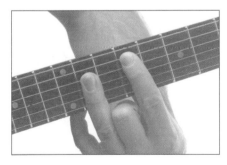

F# C# F# A# D# — 9fr

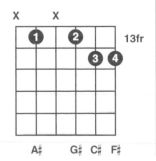

A# G# C# F# — 13fr

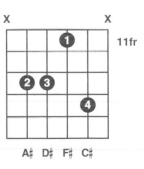

A# D# F# C# — 11fr

F#

F♯6/9 (F♯6 add 9)
F-sharp sixth, added ninth

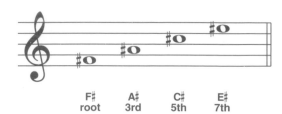

F♯   A♯   C♯   D♯   G♯
root   3rd   5th   6th   9th

F♯   A♯   D♯   G♯   C♯   F♯

C♯   F♯   A♯   D♯   G♯

D♯   G♯   C♯   F♯   A♯   6fr

F♯   A♯   D♯   G♯   C♯   8fr

F♯   G♯   C♯   F♯   A♯   D♯   11fr

F♯maj7 (F♯M7)
F-sharp major seventh

F♯   A♯   C♯   E♯
root   3rd   5th   7th

F♯   A♯   C♯   E♯

F♯   C♯   E♯   A♯   4fr

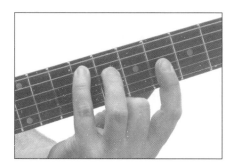

F♯   A♯   C♯   E♯   6fr

F♯   C♯   E♯   A♯   C♯   9fr

F♯   E♯   A♯   C♯   14fr

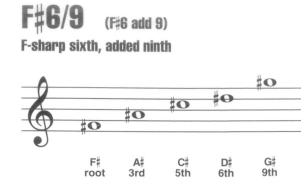
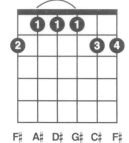
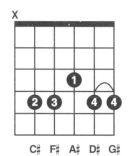
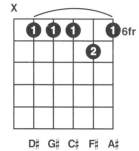
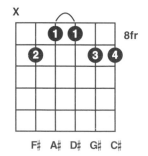
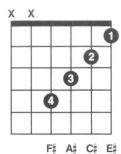
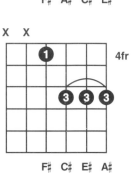
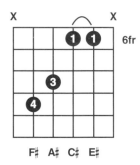
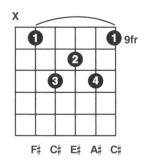
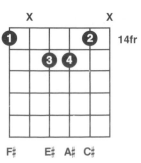

F#maj9 (F#M9)
F-sharp major ninth

F#	A#	C#	E#	G#
root	3rd	5th	7th	9th

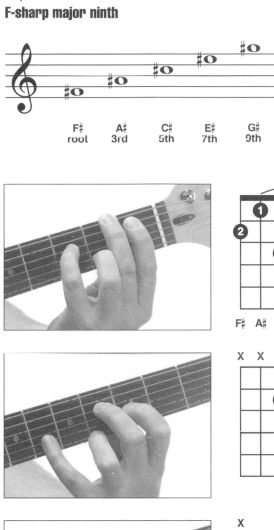
F# A# E# G# C# F#

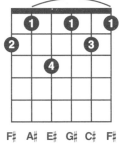
X X
3fr
F# A# E# G#

X
6fr
F# G# C# E# A#

X X
8fr
F# A# E# G#

X
11fr
G# C# F# A# E#

F#maj7#11 (F#M7#11)
F-sharp major seventh, sharp eleventh

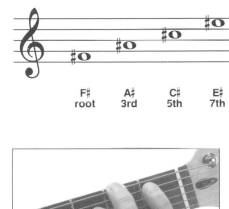

F#	A#	C#	E#	B#
root	3rd	5th	7th	#11th

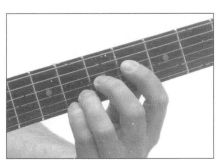
F# A# E# A# B# E#

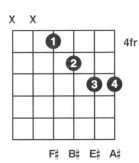
X X
4fr
F# B# E# A#

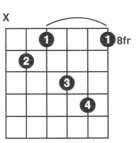
X
8fr
F# A# E# A# B#

X
9fr
F# B# E# A# C#

X X
13fr
F# E# A# B#

F#

F#maj13 (F#M13)
F-sharp major thirteenth

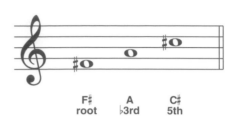

F#	A#	C#	E#	G#	D#
root	3rd	5th	7th	9th	13th

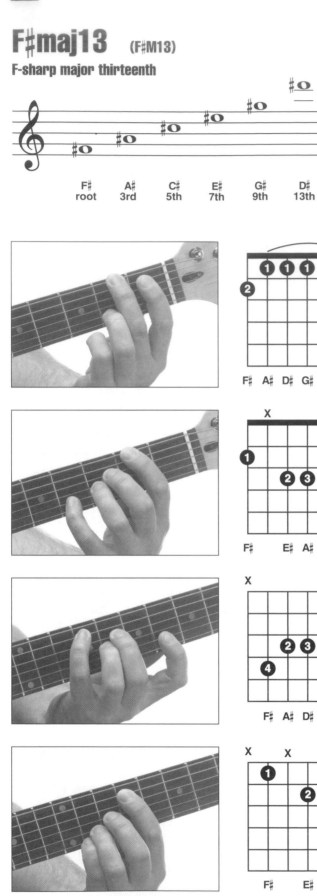

F# A# D# G# C# E#

F# E# A# D#

F# A# D# E# A#   6fr

F# E# A# D#   9fr

D# F# A# E#   11fr

F#m (F#-, F#min)
F-sharp minor

F#	A	C#
root	♭3rd	5th

F# C# F# A C# F#

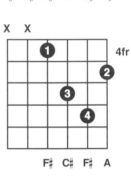

F# C# F# A   4fr

F# C# F# A C#   9fr

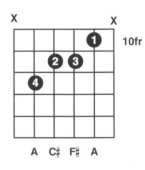

A C# F# A   10fr

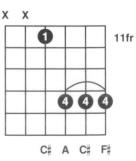

C# A C# F#   11fr

F#m(add9)
F-sharp minor, added ninth

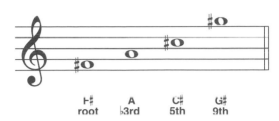

F#	A	C#	G#
root	b3rd	5th	9th

F#m6 (F#-6, F#min6)
F-sharp minor sixth

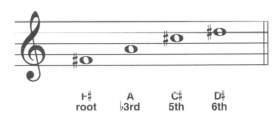

F#	A	C#	D#
root	b3rd	5th	6th

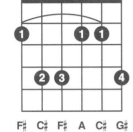
F# C# F# A C# G#

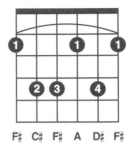
F# C# F# A D# F#

5fr
A G# C# F#

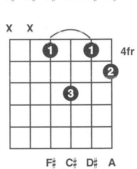
4fr
F# C# D# A

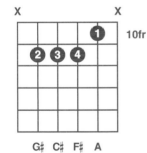
10fr
G# C# F# A

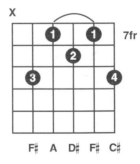
7fr
F# A D# F# C#

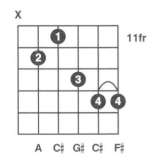
11fr
A C# G# C# F#

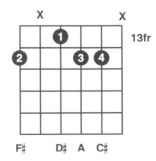
13fr
F# D# A C#

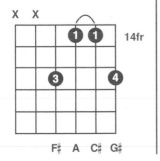
14fr
F# A C# G#

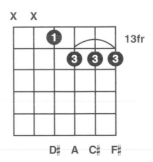
13fr
D# A C# F#

F#

F#m♭6 (F#-(♭6), F#min♭6)
F-sharp minor, flat sixth

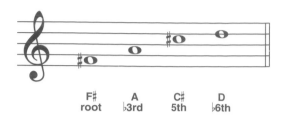

F#	A	C#	D
root	♭3rd	5th	♭6th

F#m6/9
F-sharp minor sixth, added ninth

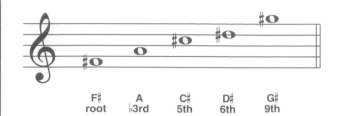

F#	A	C#	D#	G#
root	♭3rd	5th	6th	9th

F# C# F# A D F#

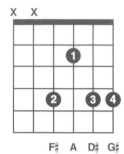

F# A D# G#

5fr
D C# F# A

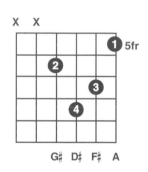

5fr
G# D# F# A

7fr
F# A D F# C#

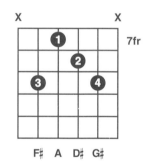

7fr
F# A D# G#

9fr
F# C# F# A D

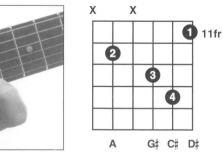

11fr
A G# C# D#

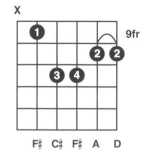
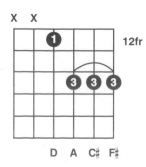

12fr
D A C# F#

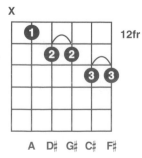

12fr
A D# G# C# F#

F#m7 (F#−7, F#mln7)
F-sharp minor seventh

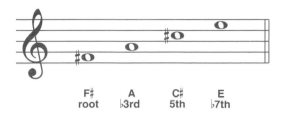

F#	A	C#	E
root	b3rd	5th	b7th

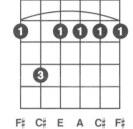

F# C# E A C# F#

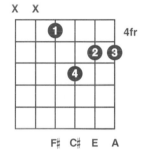

4fr

F# C# E A

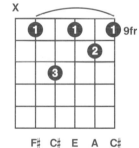

9fr

F# C# E A C#

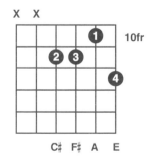

10fr

C# F# A E

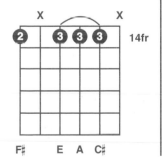

14fr

F# E A C#

F#m7b5 (F#−7b5, F#min7-5)
F-sharp minor seventh, flat fifth

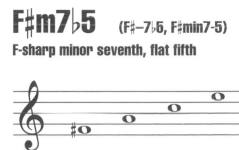

F#	A	C	E
root	b3rd	b5th	b7th

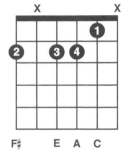

F# E A C

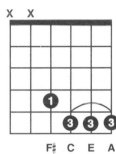

F# C E A

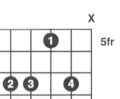

5fr

E A C F#

9fr

F# C E A

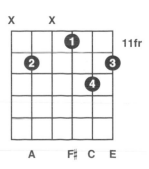

11fr

A F# C E

F#

F#m(maj7) (F#m(+7))
F-sharp minor, major seventh

F#	A	C#	E#
root	b3rd	5th	7th

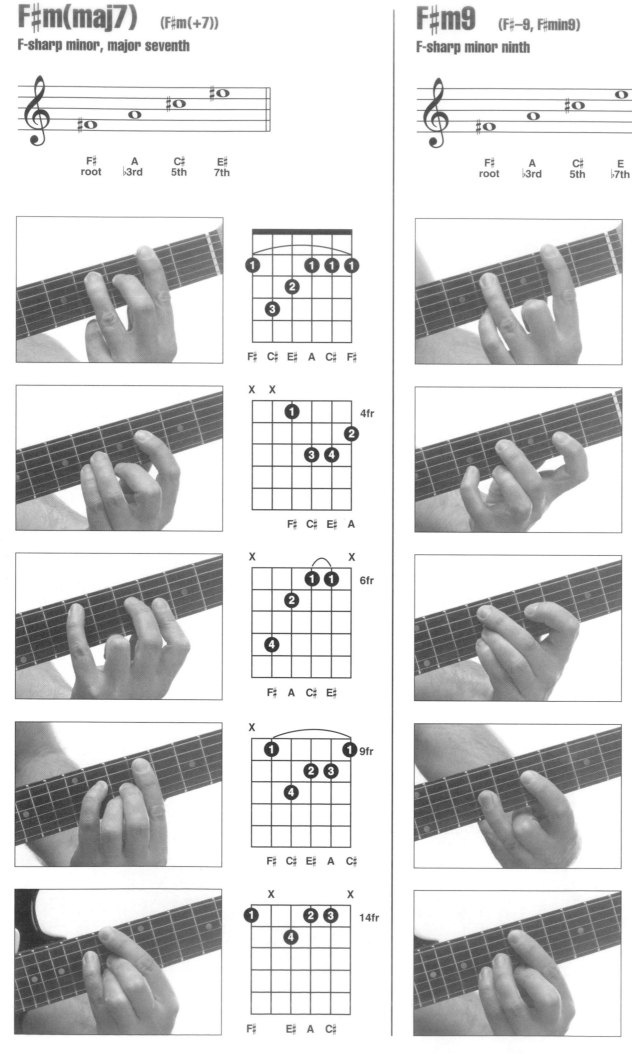

F# C# E# A C# F#

X X
4fr
F# C# E# A

X X
6fr
F# A C# E#

X
9fr
F# C# E# A C#

X X
14fr
F# E# A C#

F#m9 (F#-9, F#min9)
F-sharp minor ninth

F#	A	C#	E	G#
root	b3rd	5th	b7th	9th

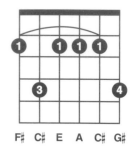

F# C# E A C# G#

X X
F# A E G#

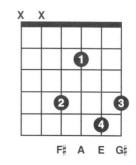

X X
7fr
F# A E G#

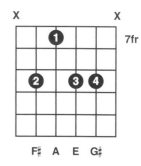

X X
7fr
A E G# C#

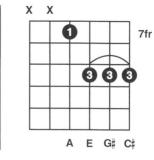

X X
12fr
A G# C# E

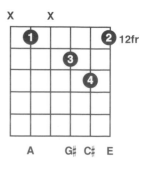

F#m9♭5 (F#m9-5, F#min9♭5)
F-sharp minor ninth, flat fifth

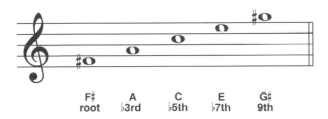

F#	A	C	E	G#
root	♭3rd	♭5th	♭7th	9th

F#m9(maj7) (F#m9+7, F#-9+7)
F-sharp minor ninth, major seventh

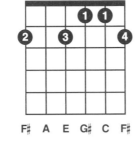

F#	A	C#	E#	G#
root	♭3rd	5th	7th	9th

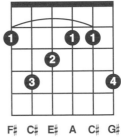

F# A E G# C F#

F# C# E# A C# G#

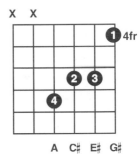

5fr

A G# C E

4fr

A C# E# G#

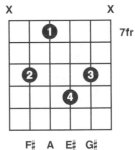

7fr

A E G# C

7fr

F# A E# G#

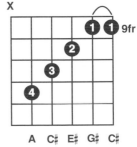

9fr

G# C E A

9fr

A C# E# G# C#

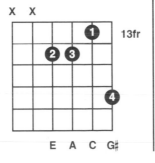

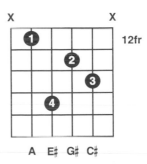

13fr

E A C G#

12fr

A E# G# C#

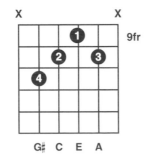
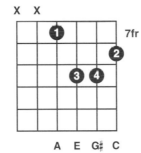

F#

F♯m11 (F♯-11, F♯min11)
F-sharp minor eleventh

F♯	A	C♯	E	G♯	B
root	♭3rd	5th	♭7th	9th	11th

F♯m13 (F♯-13, F♯min13)
F-sharp minor thirteenth

F♯	A	C♯	E	G♯	D♯
root	♭3rd	5th	♭7th	9th	13th

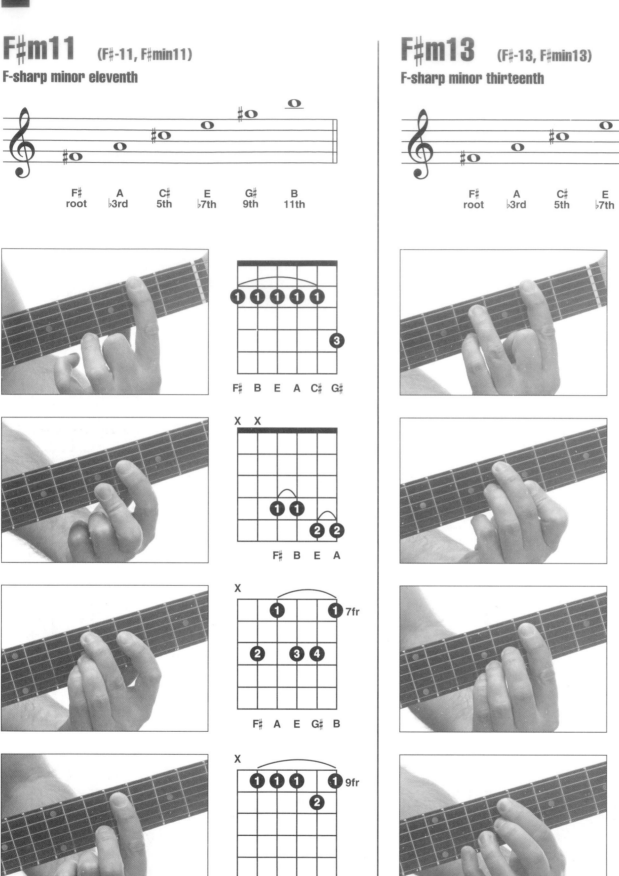

F♯ B E A C♯ G♯

F♯ C♯ E A D♯ F♯

X X

F♯ B E A

X X

D♯ C♯ E A

5fr

X

F♯ A E G♯ B

7fr

X

E A D♯ G♯ C♯

7fr

X

F♯ B E A C♯

9fr

X X

F♯ E A D♯

9fr

X X

F♯ E A B

12fr

X

E D♯ A C♯ F♯

12fr

F#7 (F#dom7)
F-sharp dominant seventh

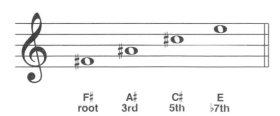

F#   A#   C#   E
root 3rd 5th ♭7th

F#7sus4 (F#7sus)
F-sharp dominant seventh, suspended fourth

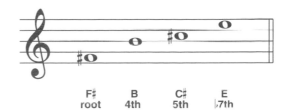

F#   B   C#   E
root 4th 5th ♭7th

X X   O

F# A# C# E

X X   O

F# B C# E

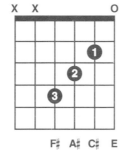

F# C# E A# C# F#

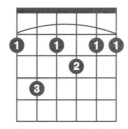

F# C# E B C# F#

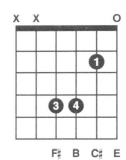

X X   4fr

F# C# E A#

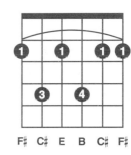

X X   4fr

F# C# E B

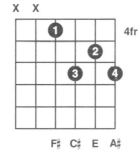

X   9fr

F# C# E A# C#

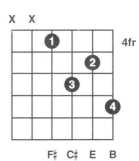

X   9fr

F# C# E B C#

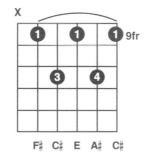

X X   11fr

C# F# A# E

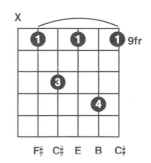

X X   11fr

C# F# B E

F#

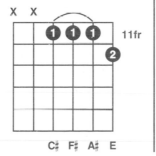

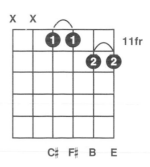

F#7♭5 (F#7-5, F#dom7♭5)
F-sharp dominant seventh, flat fifth

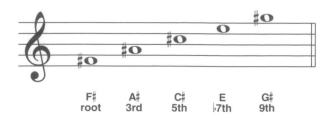

F#	A#	C	E
root	3rd	♭5th	♭7th

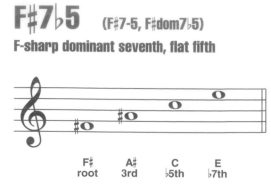

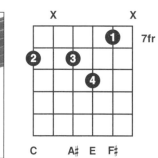

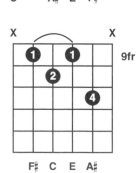

F#9
F-sharp ninth

F#	A#	C#	E	G#
root	3rd	5th	♭7th	9th

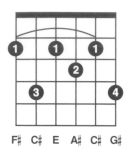

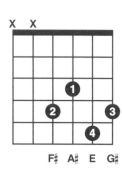

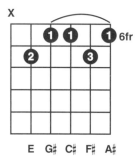

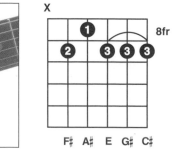

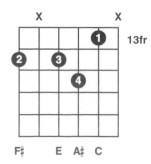

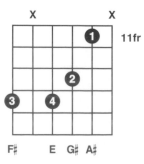

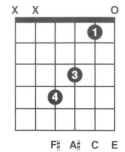

F#9sus4 (F#9sus)

F-sharp ninth, suspended fourth

F#	B	C#	E	G#
root	4th	5th	♭7th	9th

F# C# E B C# G#

X X

F# B E G#

X 6fr

E G# C# F# B

X 9fr

F# B E G# C#

X X 12fr

F# E G# B

F#9♭5 (F#9-5, F#dom9♭5)

F-sharp ninth, flat fifth

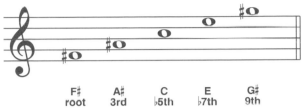

F#	A#	C	E	G#
root	3rd	♭5th	♭7th	9th

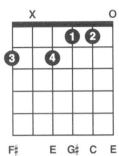

X O

F# E G# C E

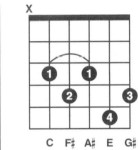

X

C F# A# E G#

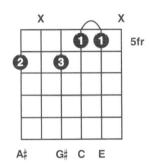

X X 5fr

A# G# C E

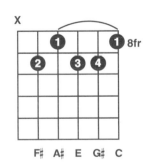

X 8fr

F# A# E G# C

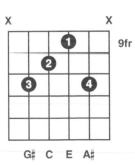

X X 9fr

G# C E A#

F#

F♯7♭9 (F♯7−9, F♯dom7♭9)
F-sharp dominant seventh, flat ninth

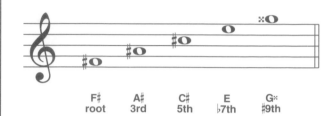

F♯	A♯	C♯	E	G
root	3rd	5th	♭7th	♭9th

F♯7♯9 (F♯7+9, F♯dom7♯9)
F-sharp dominant seventh, sharp ninth

F♯	A♯	C♯	E	G✕
root	3rd	5th	♭7th	♯9th

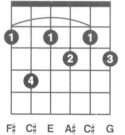

F♯ C♯ E A♯ C♯ G

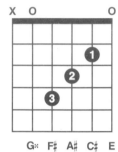

G✕ F♯ A♯ C♯ E

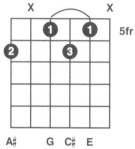

A♯ G C♯ E

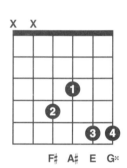

F♯ A♯ E G✕

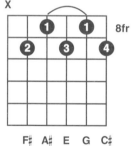

F♯ A♯ E G C♯

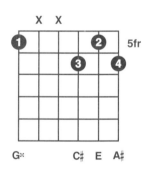

G✕ C♯ E A♯

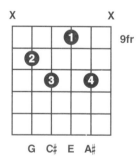

G C♯ E A♯

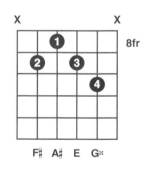

F♯ A♯ E G✕

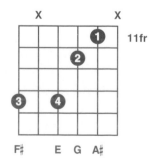

F♯ E G A♯

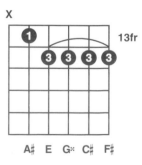

A♯ E G✕ C♯ F♯

F#7♭5(#9) (F#7−5(+9), F#dom7♭5(#9))
F-sharp dominant seventh, flat fifth, sharp ninth

F#	A#	C	E	G✕
root	3rd	♭5th	♭7th	#9th

F#11
F-sharp eleventh

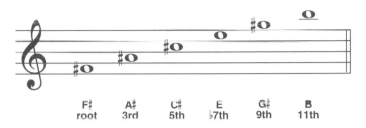

F#	A#	C#	E	G#	B
root	3rd	5th	♭7th	9th	11th

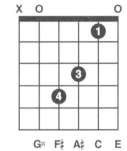

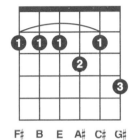

X O   O
G✕ F# A# C E

F# B E A# C# G#

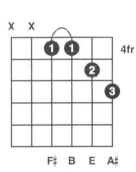

X
C F# A# E G✕

X X 4fr
F# B E A#

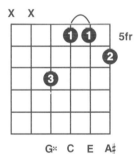

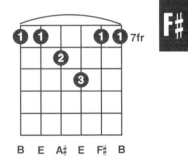

X X 5fr
G✕ C E A#

7fr
B E A# E F# B

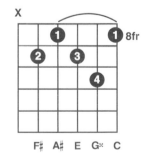
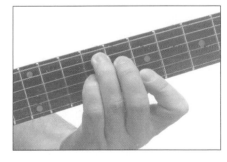
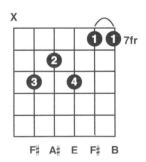

X 8fr
F# A# E G✕ C

X 7fr
F# A# E F# B

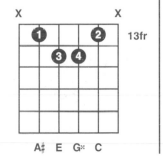

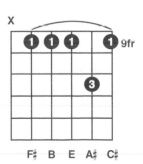

X   X 13fr
A# E G✕ C

X 9fr
F# B E A# C#

F#

F#7#11 (F#7+11, F#dom7#11)
F-sharp dominant seventh, sharp eleventh

F#	A#	C#	E	B#
root	3rd	5th	b7th	#11th

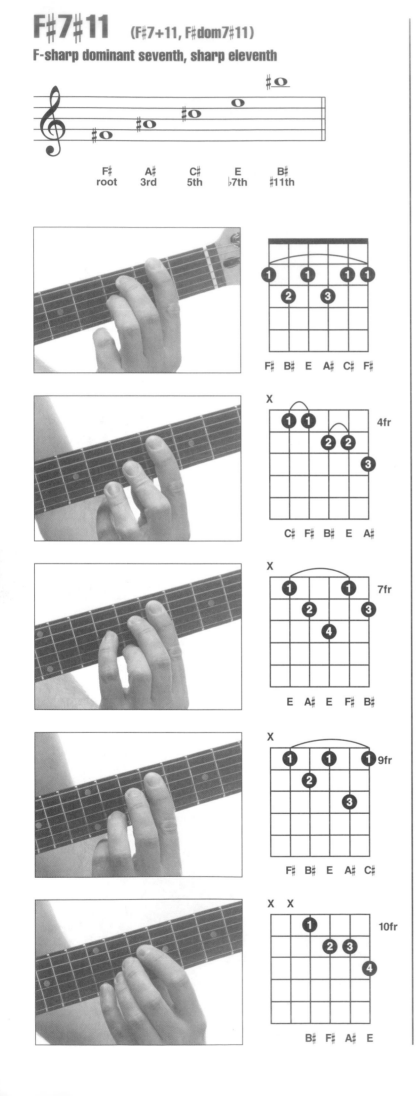

F#13 (F#dom13)
F-sharp thirteenth

F#	A#	C#	E	G#	D#
root	3rd	5th	b7th	9th	13th

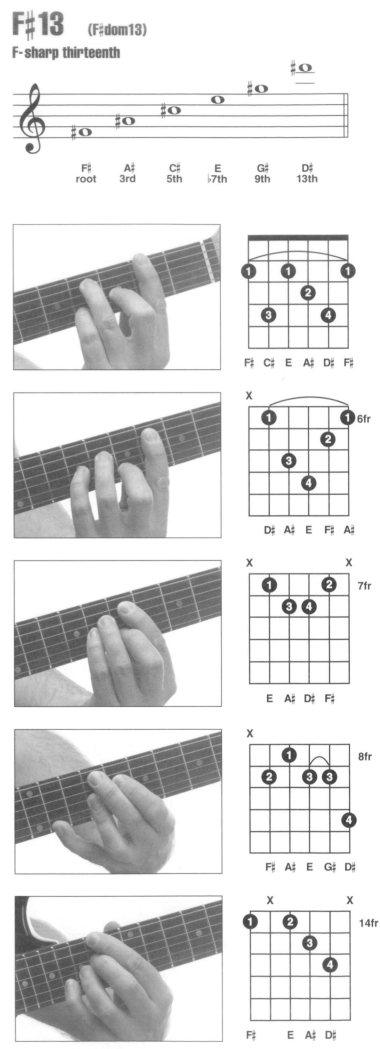

F#13sus4 (F#13sus)
F-sharp thirteenth, suspended fourth

F#	B	C#	E	G#	D#
root	4th	5th	♭7th	9th	13th

F#+ (F#aug, F#(#5))
F-sharp augmented

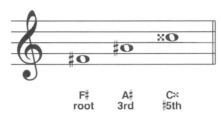

F#	A#	C𝄪
root	3rd	#5th

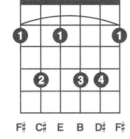

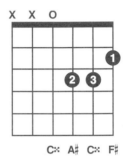

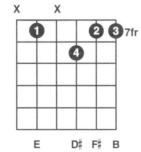

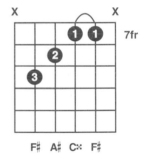

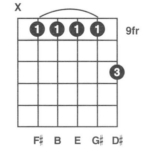

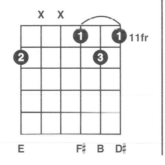

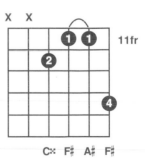

F#

F#+7 (F#7#5)
F-sharp dominant seventh, sharp fifth

F#	A#	C✕	E
root	3rd	#5th	♭7th

F#+9 (F#9#5, F#9+5)
F-sharp ninth, sharp fifth

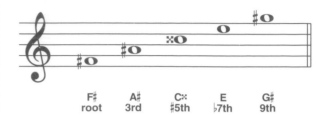

F#	A#	C✕	E	G#
root	3rd	#5th	♭7th	9th

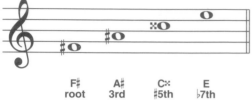

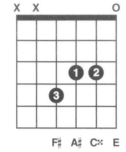

F# A# C✕ E

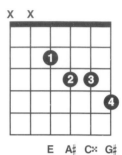

E A# C✕ G#

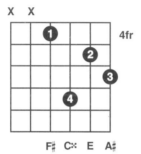

F# C✕ E A#

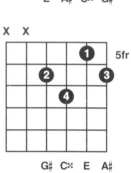

G# C✕ E A#

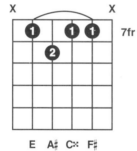

E A# C✕ F#

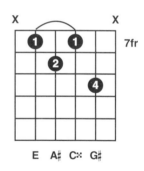

E A# C✕ G#

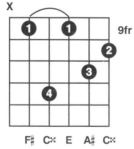

F# C✕ E A# C✕

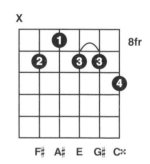

F# A# E G# C✕

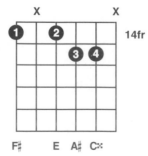

F# E A# C✕

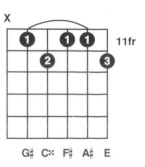

G# C✕ F# A# E

F♯+7♭9 (F♯7+5(♭9))

F-sharp dominant seventh, sharp fifth, flat ninth

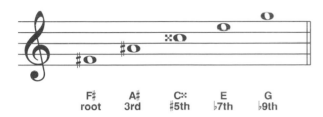

F♯	A♯	C𝄪	E	G
root	3rd	♯5th	♭7th	♭9th

F♯+7♯9 (F♯7+5(♯9))

F-sharp dominant seventh, sharp fifth, sharp ninth

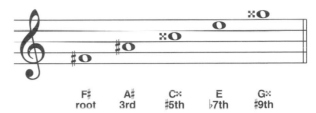

F♯	A♯	C𝄪	E	G𝄪
root	3rd	♯5th	♭7th	♯9th

E A♯ C𝄪 G

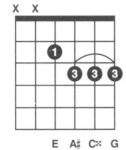

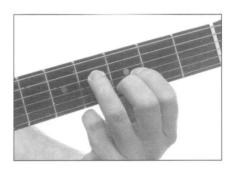

G𝄪 F♯ A♯ C𝄪 E

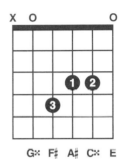

5fr

G C𝄪 E A♯

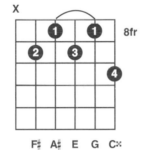

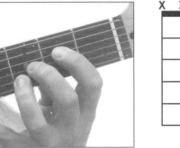

E A♯ C𝄪 G𝄪

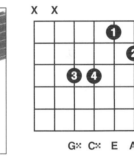

8fr

F♯ A♯ E G C𝄪

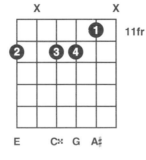

5fr

G𝄪 C𝄪 E A♯

11fr

E C𝄪 G A♯

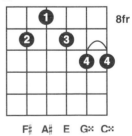

8fr

F♯ A♯ E G𝄪 C𝄪

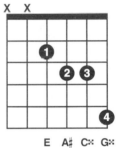

F♯

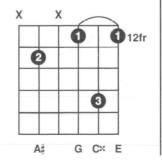

12fr

A♯ G C𝄪 E

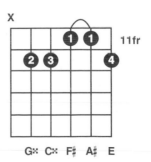

11fr

G𝄪 C𝄪 F♯ A♯ E

F#° (F#dim)
F-sharp diminished

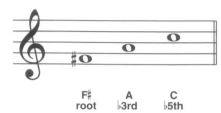

F#	A	C
root	b3rd	b5th

F#°7 (F#dim7)
F-sharp diminished seventh

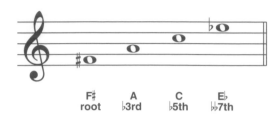

F#	A	C	Eb
root	b3rd	b5th	bb7th

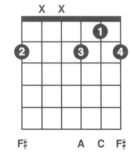
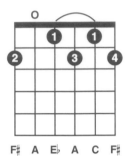

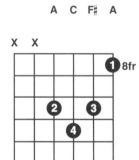

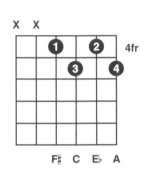

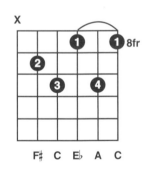

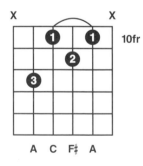
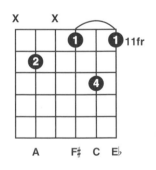

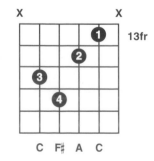
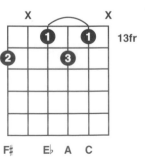

G (Gmaj)
G major

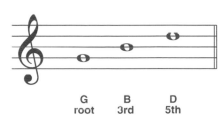

G   B   D
root   3rd   5th

G5 (G5 no 3rd)
G fifth (power chord)

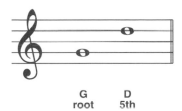

G   D
root   5th

O O O

G B D G B G

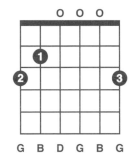

X X O O

D G D G

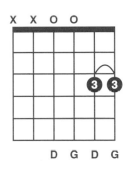

G D G B D G

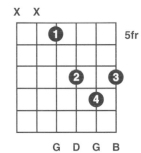

X X X

G D G

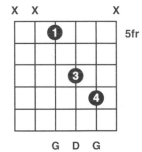

X X 5fr

G D G B

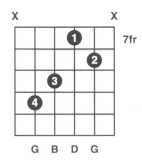

X X X 5fr

G D G

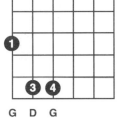

X X 7fr

G B D G

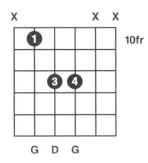

X X X 10fr

G D G

X X 10fr

G D G B

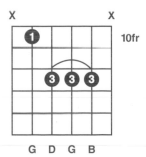

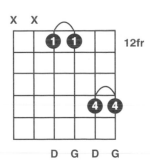

X X 12fr

D G D G

G

Gsus4 (Gsus)
G suspended fourth

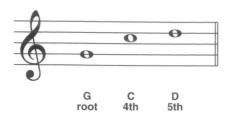

G	C	D
root	4th	5th

G C D G C G

G D G C D G

G D G C 5fr

G C D G 7fr

G D G C 10fr

Gsus2 (G5add2)
G suspended second

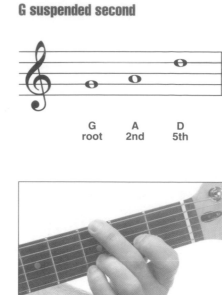

G	A	D
root	2nd	5th

G A D A D G

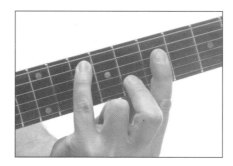
G D G A 5fr

G A D G 7fr

G D G A D 10fr

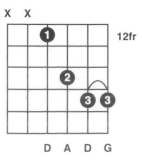
D A D G 12fr

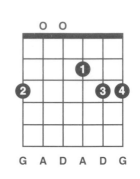
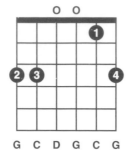
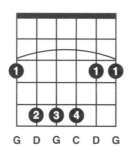
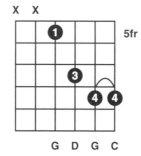
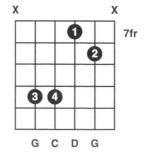
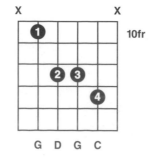
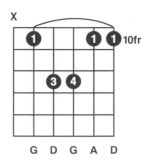
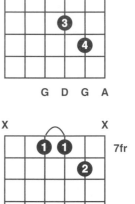

Gadd9

G added ninth

G	B	D	A
root	3rd	5th	9th

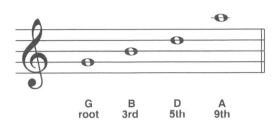

O O O

G A D A B G

X X

G B D A

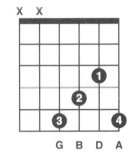

X X

7fr

A D G B

X

7fr

G B D A B

X X

12fr

A D G B

G6

G sixth

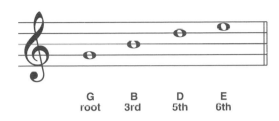

G	B	D	E
root	3rd	5th	6th

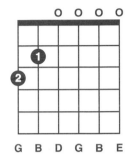

O O O O

G B D G B E

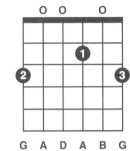

X X

5fr

G D E B

X X

8fr

D B E G

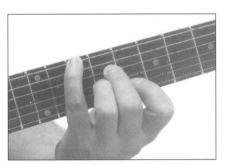
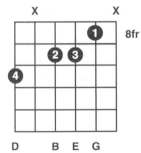

X

10fr

G D G B E

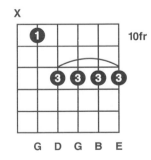

X X

14fr

G E B D

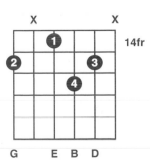

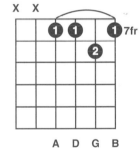
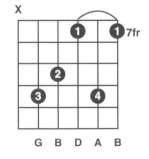
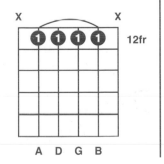

G

G6/9 (G6add9)
G sixth, added ninth

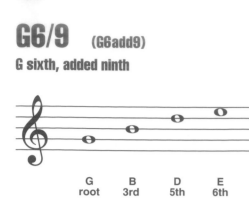

G	B	D	E	A
root	3rd	5th	6th	9th

 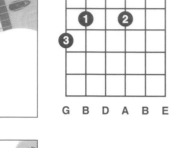

G B D A B E

G B E A D G

X

D G B E A

X

E A D G B — 7fr

X

G B E A D — 9fr

Gmaj7 (GM7)
G major seventh

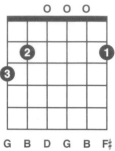

G	B	D	F#
root	3rd	5th	7th

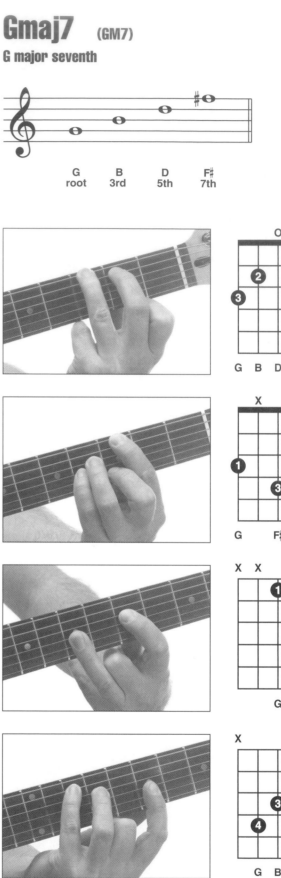

O O O

G B D G B F#

X X

G F# B D

X X

G D F# B — 5fr

X X

G B D F# — 7fr

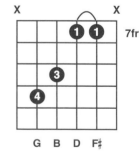

X

G D F# B D — 10fr

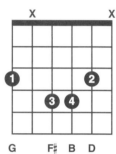
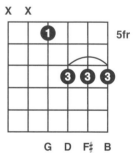
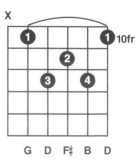

Gmaj9 (GM9)
G major ninth

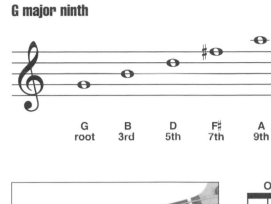

G	B	D	F#	A
root	3rd	5th	7th	9th

Gmaj7#11 (GM7#11)
G major seventh, sharp eleventh

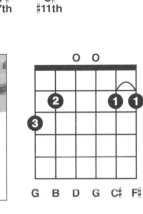

G	B	D	F#	C#
root	3rd	5th	7th	#11th

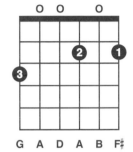
G A D A B F#

G B F# A

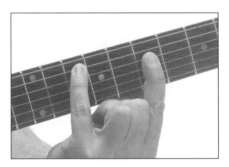
G A D F# B

G B F# A

A D G B F#

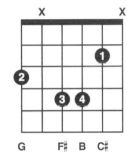
G B D G C# F#

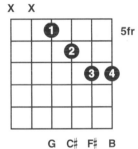
G F# B C#

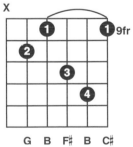
G C# F# B

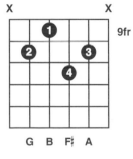
G B F# B C#

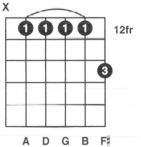

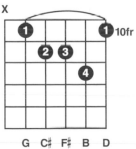
G C# F# B D

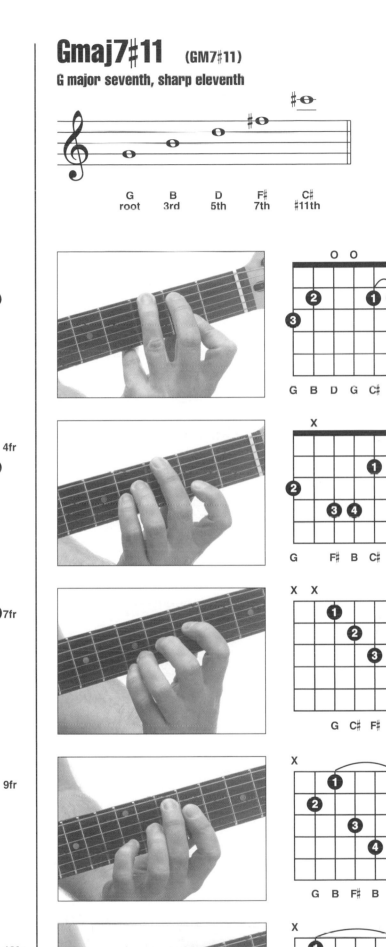

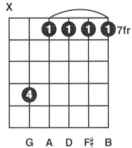

G

Gmaj13 (GM13)
G major thirteenth

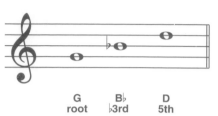

G	B	D	F#	A	E
root	3rd	5th	7th	9th	13th

Gm (G-, Gmin)
G minor

G	B♭	D
root	♭3rd	5th

G B E A D F#

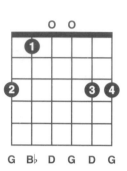

G B♭ D G D G

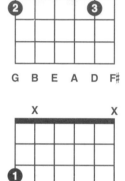

G F# B E

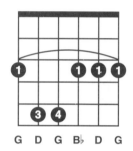

G D G B♭ D G

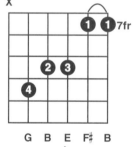

7fr

G B E F# B

5fr

G D G B♭

10fr

G F# B E

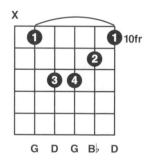

10fr

G D G B♭ D

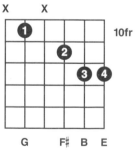

12fr

E A D G B F#

12fr

D B♭ D G

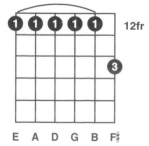

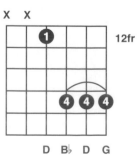

160

Gm(add9)
G minor, added ninth

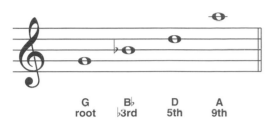

G	B♭	D	A
root	♭3rd	5th	9th

Gm6 (G-6, Gmin6)
G minor sixth

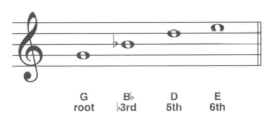

G	B♭	D	E
root	♭3rd	5th	6th

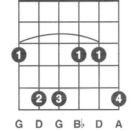
G D G B♭ D A

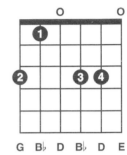
G B♭ D B♭ D E

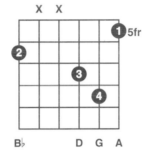
B♭ D G A (5fr)

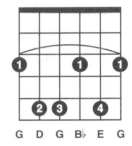
G D G B♭ E G

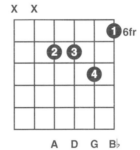
A D G B♭ (6fr)

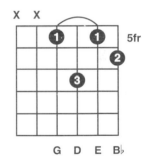
G D E B♭ (5fr)

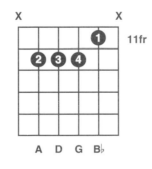
A D G B♭ (11fr)

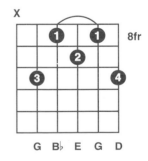
G B♭ E G D (8fr)

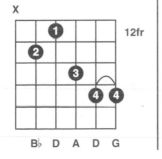
B♭ D A D G (12fr)

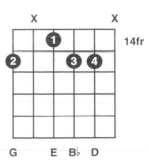
G E B♭ D (14fr)

G

Gm♭6 (G-(♭6), Gmin♭6)
G minor, flat sixth

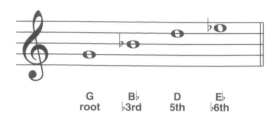

G	B♭	D	E♭
root	♭3rd	5th	♭6th

 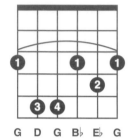

G D G B♭ E♭ G

X X — 6fr
E♭ D G B♭

X — 8fr
G B♭ E♭ G D

X — 10fr
G D G B♭ E♭

 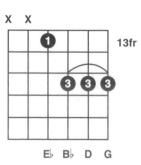

X X — 13fr
E♭ B♭ D G

Gm6/9
G minor sixth, added ninth

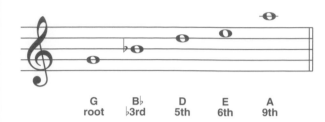

G	B♭	D	E	A
root	♭3rd	5th	6th	9th

 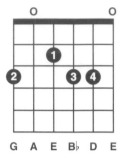

G A E B♭ D E

 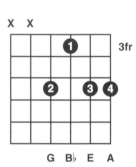

X X — 3fr
G B♭ E A

 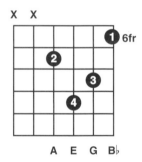

X X — 6fr
A E G B♭

  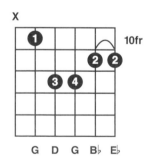

X X — 8fr
G B♭ E A

 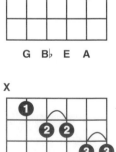 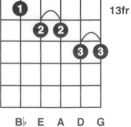

X — 13fr
B♭ E A D G

Gm7 (G-7, Gmin7)
G minor seventh

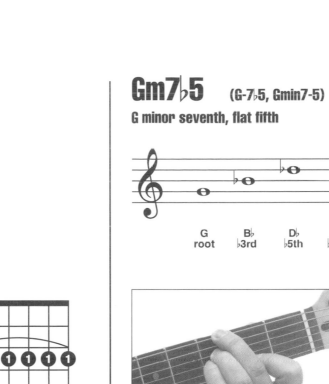

G	B♭	D	F
root	♭3rd	5th	♭7th

Gm7♭5 (G-7♭5, Gmin7-5)
G minor seventh, flat fifth

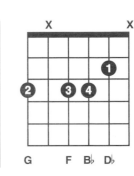

G	B♭	D♭	F
root	♭3rd	♭5th	♭7th

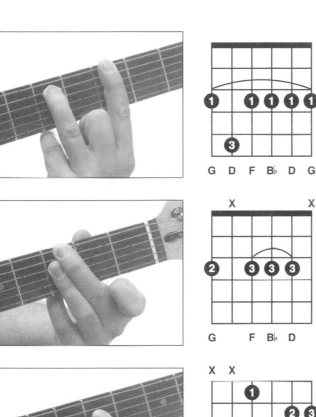

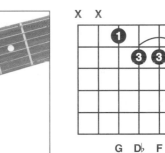

G D F B♭ D G

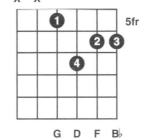

G F B♭ D

G D♭ F B♭   5fr

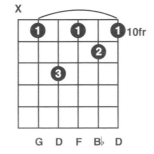

G D F B♭   5fr

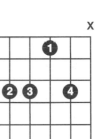

F B♭ D♭ G   6fr

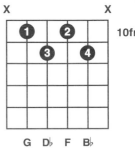

G D F B♭ D   10fr

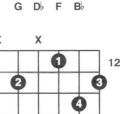

G D♭ F B♭   10fr

F B♭ D G   15fr

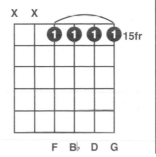

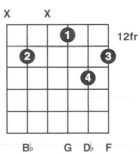

B♭ G D♭ F   12fr

G

Gm(maj7) (Gm(+7))

G minor, major seventh

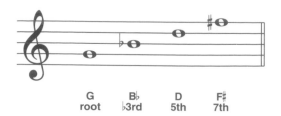

G	B♭	D	F♯
root	♭3rd	5th	7th

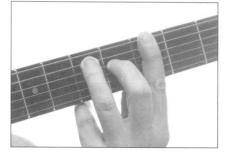 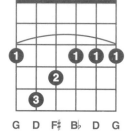

G D F♯ B♭ D G

 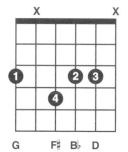

X   X

G   F♯ B♭ D

 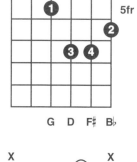

X X   5fr

G D F♯ B♭

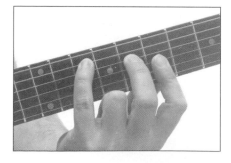 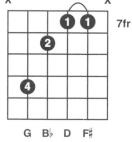

X   X   7fr

G B♭ D F♯

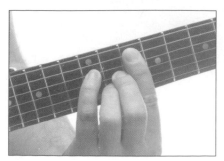 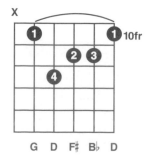

X   10fr

G D F♯ B♭ D

Gm9 (G-9, Gmin9)

G minor ninth

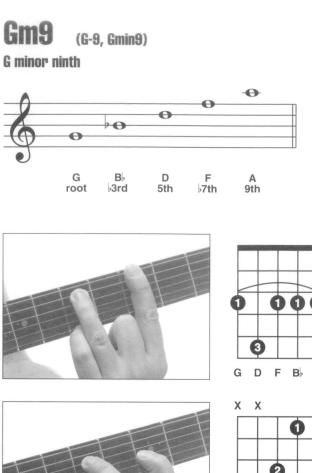

G	B♭	D	F	A
root	♭3rd	5th	♭7th	9th

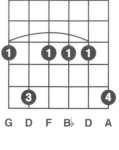

G D F B♭ D A

 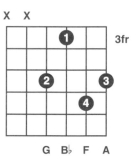

X X   3fr

G B♭ F A

 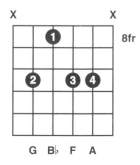

X   X   8fr

G B♭ F A

 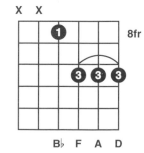

X X   8fr

B♭ F A D

 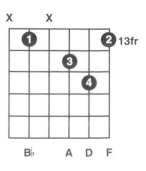

X X   13fr

B♭   A D F

Gm9♭5 (Gm9-5, Gmin9♭5)
G minor ninth, flat fifth

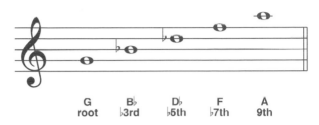

G root	B♭ ♭3rd	D♭ ♭5th	F ♭7th	A 9th

Gm9(maj7) (Gm9+7, G-9+7)
G minor ninth, major seventh

G root	B♭ ♭3rd	D 5th	F♯ 7th	A 9th

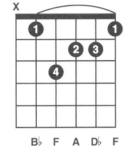

B♭ F A D♭ F

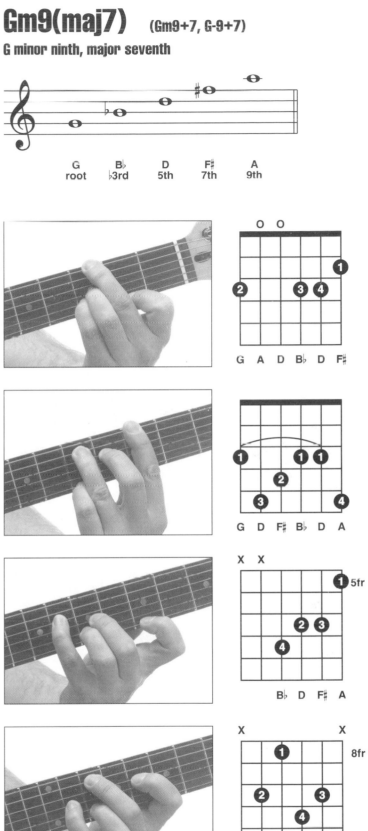

G A D B♭ D F♯

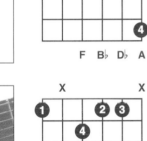

F B♭ D♭ A

G D F♯ B♭ D A

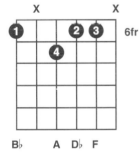

B♭ A D♭ F   6fr

B♭ D F♯ A   5fr

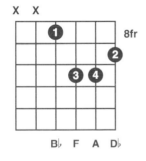

B♭ F A D♭   8fr

G B♭ F♯ A   8fr

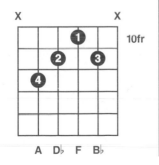

A D♭ F B♭   10fr

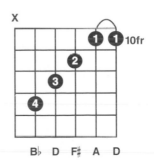
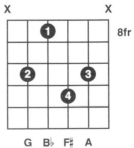

B♭ D F♯ A D   10fr

G

Gm11 (G-11, Gmin11)
G minor eleventh

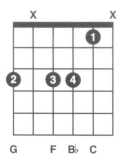

G	B♭	D	F	A	C
root	♭3rd	5th	♭7th	9th	11th

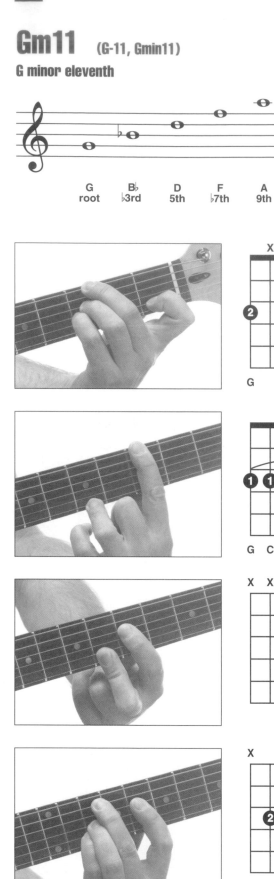
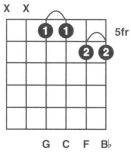
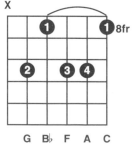

Gm13 (G-13, Gmin13)
G minor thirteenth

G	B♭	D	F	A	E
root	♭3rd	5th	♭7th	9th	13th

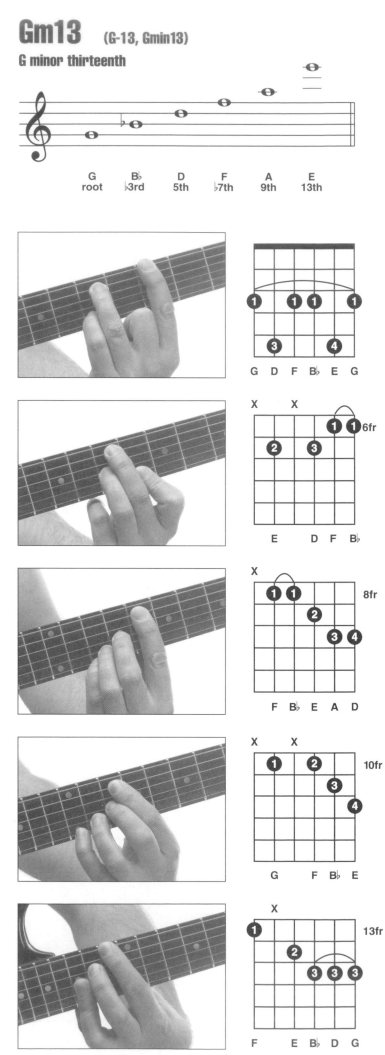
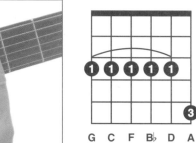

G7 (Gdom7)
G dominant seventh

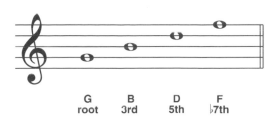

G	B	D	F
root	3rd	5th	♭7th

O O O

G B D G B F

G D F B D G

X X   5fr

G D F B

X   10fr

G D F B D

X X   12fr

D G B F

G7sus4 (G7sus)
G dominant seventh, suspended fourth

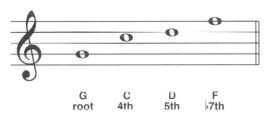

G	C	D	F
root	4th	5th	♭7th

O O

G C D G C F

G D F C D G

X X   5fr

G D F C

X   10fr

G D F C D

X X   12fr

D G C F

G

G7♭5 (G7-5, Gdom7♭5)
G dominant seventh, flat fifth

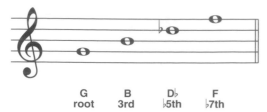

G	B	D♭	F
root	3rd	♭5th	♭7th

G9
G ninth

G	B	D	F	A
root	3rd	5th	♭7th	9th

X   O   O

D♭ F G B F

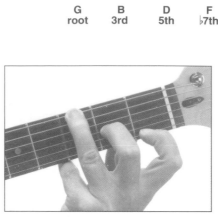

O   O   O

G A D A B F

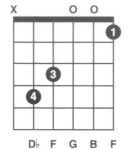

X   X

G   F B D♭

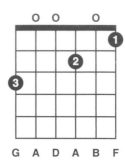

G D F B D A

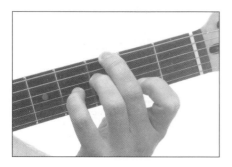

X X   5fr

G D♭ F B

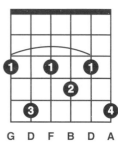

X X   4fr

G B F A

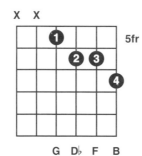

X X   7fr

D♭   F G B

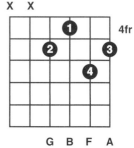

X   9fr

G B F A D

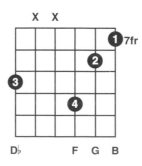

X   X   10fr

G D♭ F B

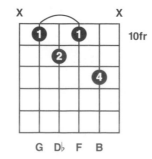

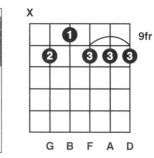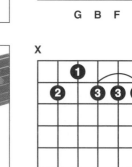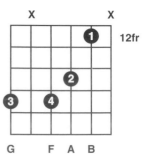

X   X   12fr

G   F A B

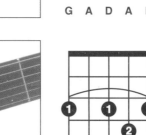

G9sus4 (G9sus)
G ninth, suspended fourth

G	C	D	F	A
root	4th	5th	♭7th	9th

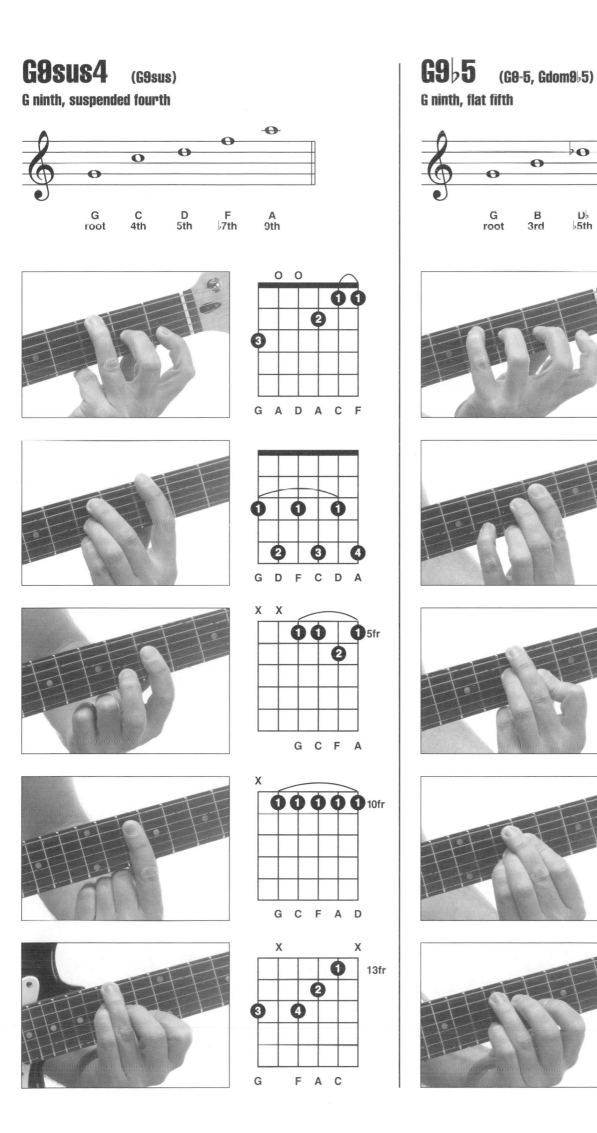

O O
G A D A C F

G D F C D A

X X
G C F A   5fr

X
G C F A D   10fr

X X
G F A C   13fr

G9♭5 (G9-5, Gdom9♭5)
G ninth, flat fifth

G	B	D♭	F	A
root	3rd	♭5th	♭7th	9th

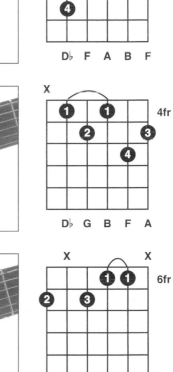

X O
D♭ F A B F

X
D♭ G B F A   4fr

X X
B A D♭ F   6fr

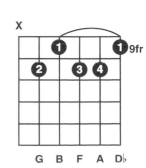

X
G B F A D♭   9fr

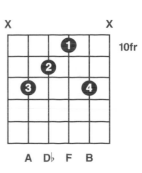

X X
A D♭ F B   10fr

G

G7♭9 (G7-9, Gdom7♭9)
G dominant seventh, flat ninth

G   B   D   F   A♭
root   3rd   5th   ♭7th   ♭9th

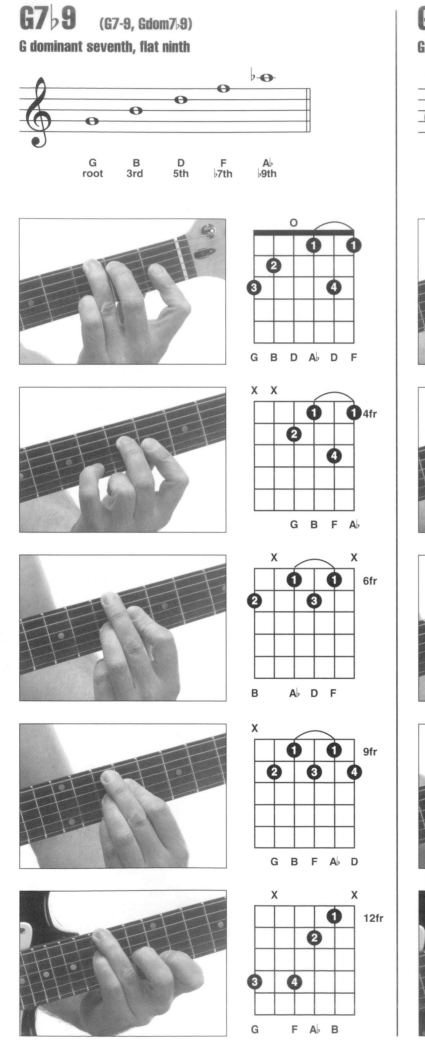

G B D A♭ D F

G B F A♭

B A♭ D F

G B F A♭ D

G F A♭ B

G7♯9 (G7+9, Gdom7♯9)
G dominant seventh, sharp ninth

G   B   D   F   A♯
root   3rd   5th   ♭7th   ♯9th

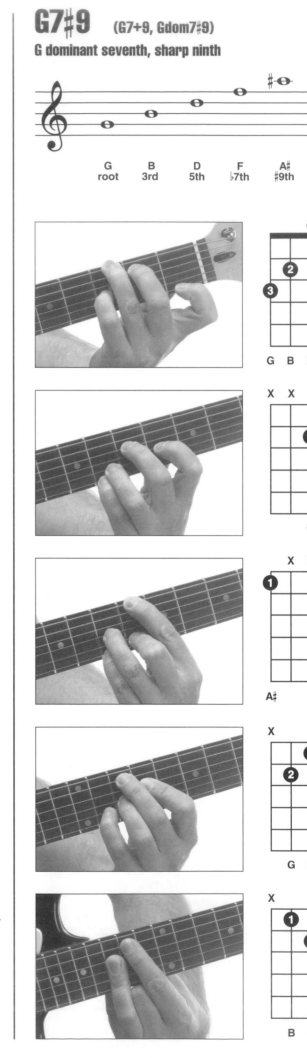
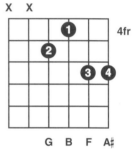
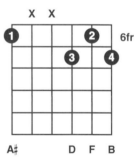
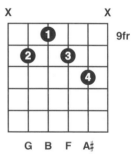
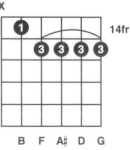

G B D A♯ B F

G B F A♯

A♯ D F B

G B F A♯

B F A♯ D G

G7♭5(♯9) (G7-5(+9), Gdom7♭5(♯9))
G dominant seventh, flat fifth, sharp ninth

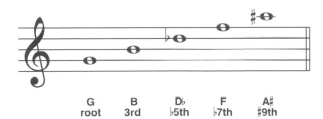

G	B	D♭	F	A♯
root	3rd	♭5th	♭7th	♯9th

G11
G eleventh

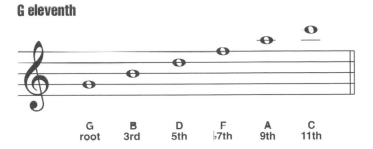

G	B	D	F	A	C
root	3rd	5th	♭7th	9th	11th

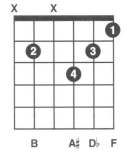

B   A♯ D♭ F

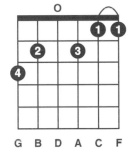

G B D A C F

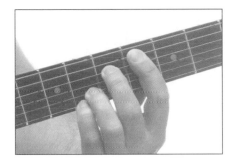

D♭ G B F A♯   4fr

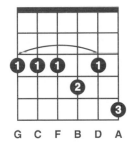

G C F B D A

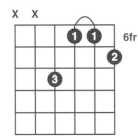

A♯ D♭ F B   6fr

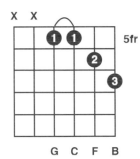

G C F B   5fr

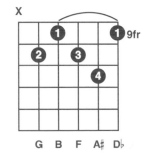

G B F A♯ D♭   9fr

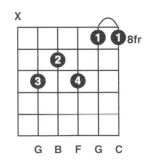

G B F G C   8fr

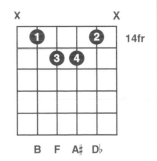

B F A♯ D♭   14fr

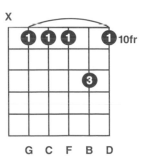

G C F B D   10fr

G

G7♯11 (G7+11, Gdom7♯11)
G dominant seventh, sharp eleventh

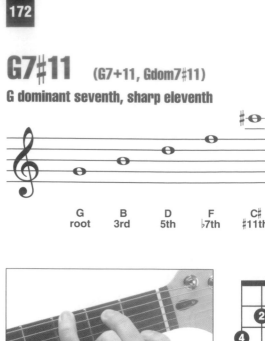

G	B	D	F	C♯
root	3rd	5th	♭7th	♯11th

G B D G C♯ F

D G C♯ F B — 5fr

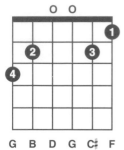

F B F G C♯ — 8fr

G C♯ F B D — 10fr

C♯ G B F — 11fr

G13 (Gdom13)
G thirteenth

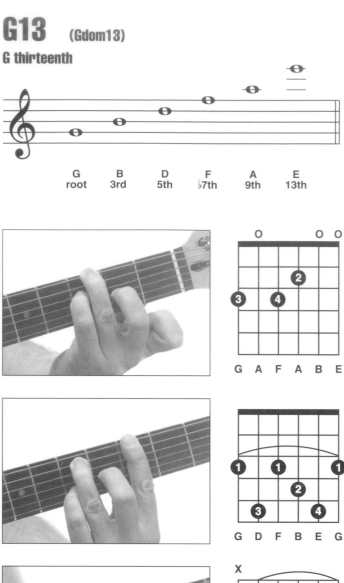

G	B	D	F	A	E
root	3rd	5th	♭7th	9th	13th

G A F A B E

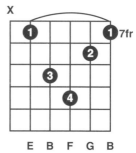

G D F B E G

E B F G B — 7fr

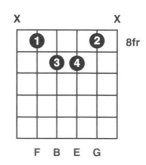

F B E G — 8fr

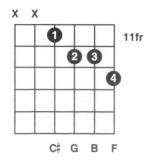
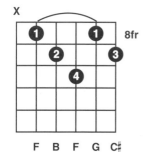
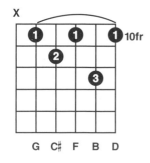
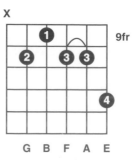

G B F A E — 9fr

G13sus4 (G13sus)
G thirteenth, suspended fourth

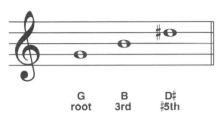

G	C	D	F	A	E
root	4th	5th	♭7th	9th	13th

G+ (Gaug, G(♯5))
G augmented

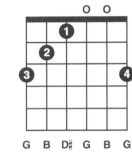

G	B	D♯
root	3rd	♯5th

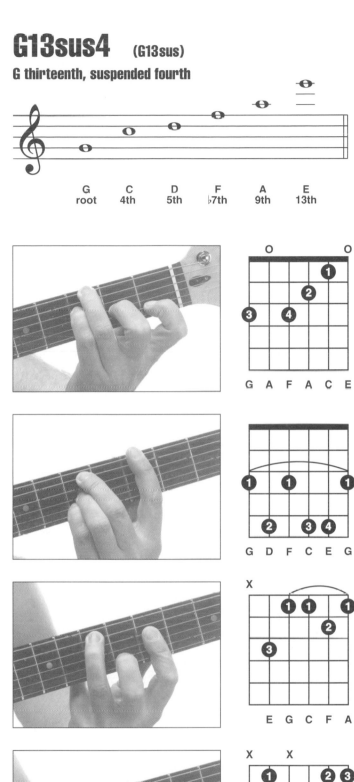

G A F A C E

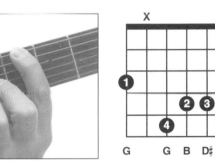

G B D♯ G B G

G D F C E G

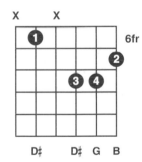

G G B D♯

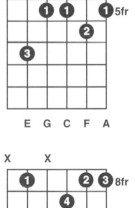

E G C F A

D♯ D♯ G B — 6fr

F E G C — 8fr

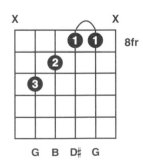

G B D♯ G — 8fr

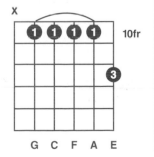

G C F A E — 10fr

D♯ G B G — 12fr

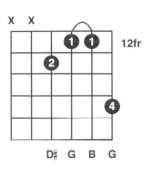

G

G+7 (G7#5)

G dominant seventh, sharp fifth

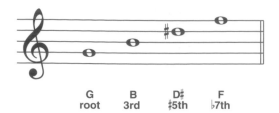

G	B	D#	F
root	3rd	#5th	b7th

G+9 (G9#5, G9+5)

G ninth, sharp fifth

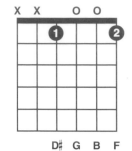

G	B	D#	F	A
root	3rd	#5th	b7th	9th

X X O O

D# G B F

X X

G F B D#

X X 5fr

G D# F B

X X 8fr

F B D# G

X 10fr

G D# F B D#

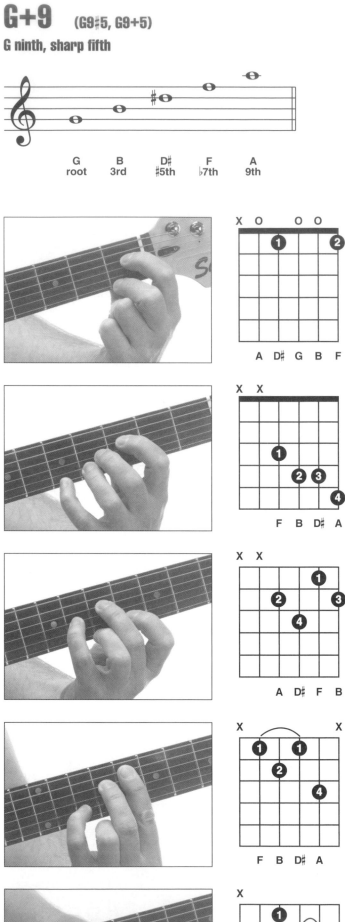

X O O O

A D# G B F

X X

F B D# A

X X 6fr

A D# F B

X X 8fr

F B D# A

X 9fr

G B F A D#

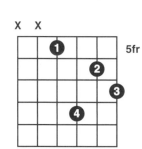
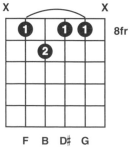
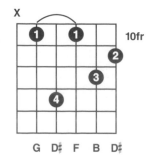
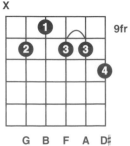

G+7♭9 (G7+5(♭9))
G dominant seventh, sharp fifth, flat ninth

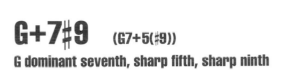

G	B	D#	F	A♭
root	3rd	#5th	♭7th	♭9th

G+7♯9 (G7+5(♯9))
G dominant seventh, sharp fifth, sharp ninth

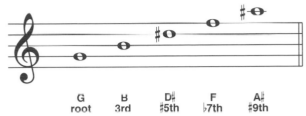

G	B	D#	F	A#
root	3rd	#5th	♭7th	#9th

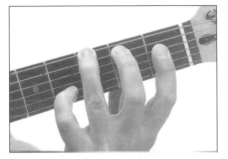
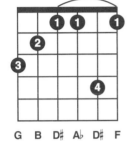
G B D# A♭ D# F

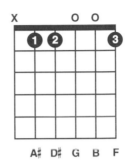
A# D# G B F

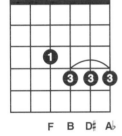
F B D# A♭

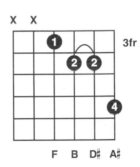
F B D# A#

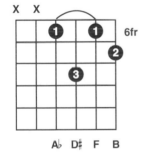
A♭ D# F B

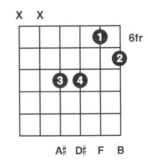
A# D# F B

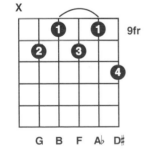
G B F A♭ D#

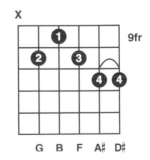
G B F A# D#

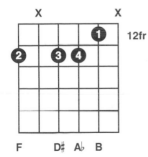
F D# A♭ B

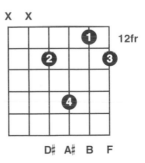
D# A# B F

G° (Gdim)
G diminished

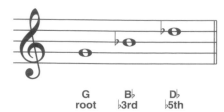

G root | B♭ ♭3rd | D♭ ♭5th

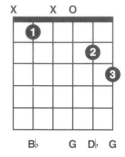

X X O
B♭ G D♭ G

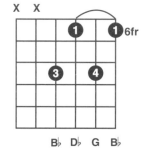

X X — 6fr
B♭ D♭ G B♭

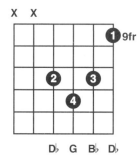

X X — 9fr
D♭ G B♭ D♭

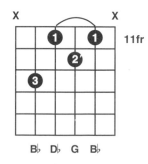

X X — 11fr
B♭ D♭ G B♭

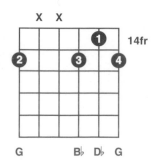

X X — 14fr
G B♭ D♭ G

G°7 (Gdim7)
G diminished seventh

G root | B♭ ♭3rd | D♭ ♭5th | F♭ ♭♭7th

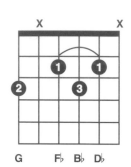

X X
G F♭ B♭ D♭

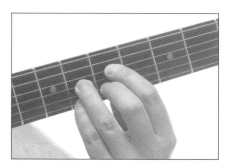
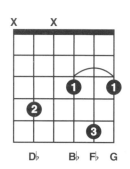

X X
D♭ B♭ F♭ G

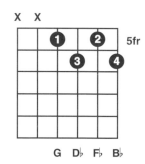

X X — 5fr
G D♭ F♭ B♭

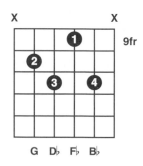

X X — 9fr
G D♭ F♭ B♭

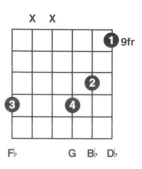

X X — 9fr
F♭ G B♭ D♭

A♭ (A♭maj)
A-flat major

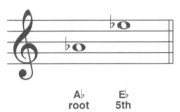

A♭   C   E♭
root   3rd   5th

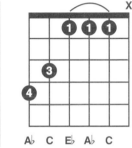

A♭ C E♭ A♭ C

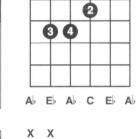

A♭ E♭ A♭ C E♭ A♭   4fr

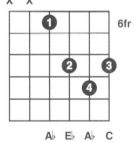

A♭ E♭ A♭ C   6fr

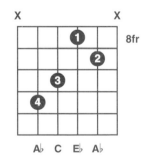

A♭ C E♭ A♭   8fr

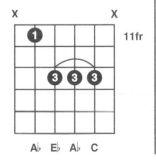

A♭ E♭ A♭ C   11fr

A♭5 (A♭ no 3rd)
A-flat fifth (power chord)

A♭   E♭
root   5th

E♭ A♭ E♭ A♭

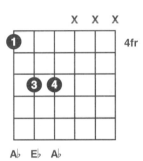

A♭ E♭ A♭   4fr

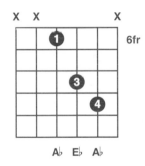

A♭ E♭ A♭   6fr

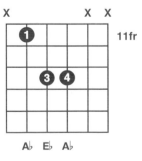

A♭ E♭ A♭   11fr

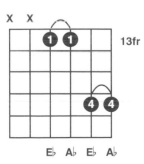

E♭ A♭ E♭ A♭   13fr

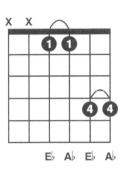

A♭sus4 (A♭sus)
A-flat suspended fourth

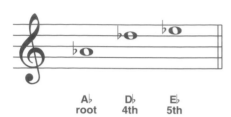

A♭ root   D♭ 4th   E♭ 5th

E♭ A♭ D♭ A♭

A♭ E♭ A♭ D♭ E♭ A♭   4fr

A♭ E♭ A♭ D♭   6fr

A♭ D♭ E♭ A♭   8fr

A♭ E♭ A♭ D♭   11fr

A♭sus2 (A♭5add2)
A-flat suspended second

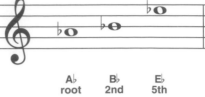

A♭ root   B♭ 2nd   E♭ 5th

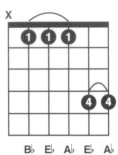

B♭ E♭ A♭ E♭ A♭

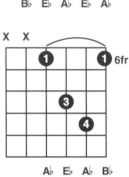

A♭ E♭ A♭ B♭   6fr

A♭ B♭ E♭ A♭   8fr

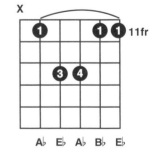

A♭ E♭ A♭ B♭ E♭   11fr

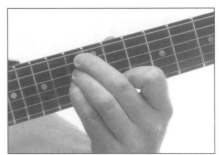
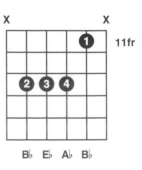

B♭ E♭ A♭ B♭   11fr

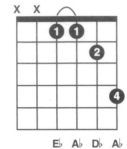
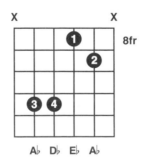
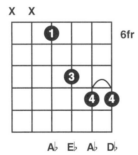
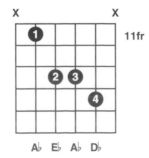

A♭add9
A-flat added ninth

A♭	C	E♭	B♭
root	3rd	5th	9th

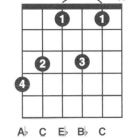

A♭ C E♭ B♭ C

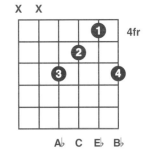

A♭ C E♭ B♭ — 4fr

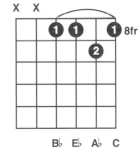

B♭ E♭ A♭ C — 8fr

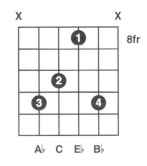

A♭ C E♭ B♭ — 8fr

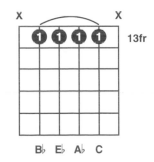

B♭ E♭ A♭ C — 13fr

A♭6
A-flat sixth

A♭	C	E♭	F
root	3rd	5th	6th

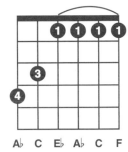

A♭ C E♭ A♭ C F

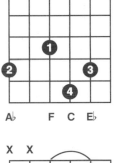

A♭ F C E♭ — 4fr

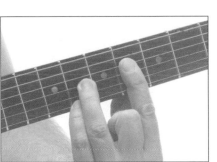
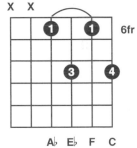

A♭ E♭ F C — 6fr

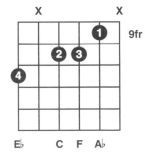

E♭ C F A♭ — 9fr

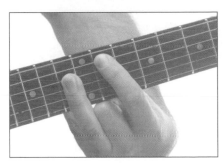
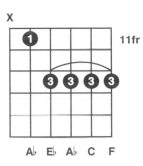

A♭ E♭ A♭ C F — 11fr

A♭

A♭6/9 (A♭6add9)
A-flat sixth, added ninth

A♭	C	E♭	F	B♭
root	3rd	5th	6th	9th

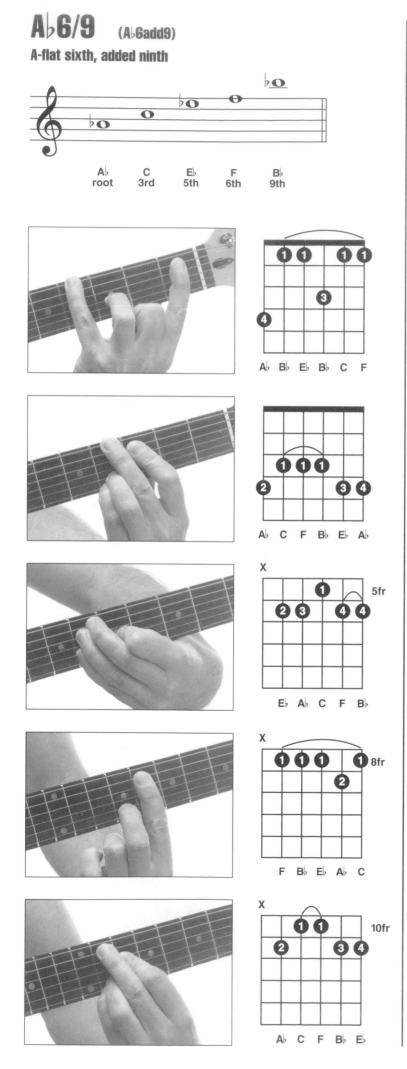

A♭ B♭ E♭ B♭ C F

A♭ C F B♭ E♭ A♭

E♭ A♭ C F B♭ — 5fr

F B♭ E♭ A♭ C — 8fr

A♭ C F B♭ E♭ — 10fr

A♭maj7 (A♭M7)
A-flat major seventh

A♭	C	E♭	G
root	3rd	5th	7th

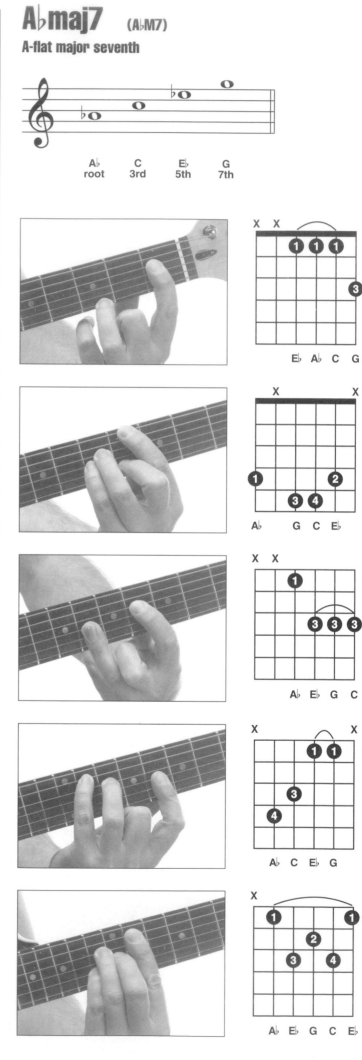

E♭ A♭ C G

A♭ G C E♭

A♭ E♭ G C — 6fr

A♭ C E♭ G — 8fr

A♭ E♭ G C E♭ — 11fr

A♭maj9 (A♭M9)
A-flat major ninth

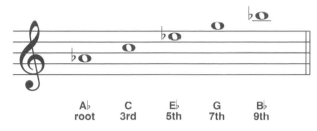

A♭	C	E♭	G	B♭
root	3rd	5th	7th	9th

A♭ B♭ E♭ B♭ C G

A♭ C G B♭ — 5fr

A♭ B♭ E♭ G C — 8fr

A♭ C G B♭ — 10fr

B♭ E♭ A♭ C G — 13fr

A♭maj7#11 (A♭M7#11)
A-flat major seventh, sharp eleventh

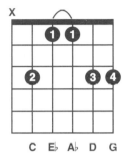

A♭	C	E♭	G	D
root	3rd	5th	7th	#11th

C E♭ A♭ D G

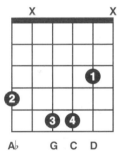

A♭ G C D

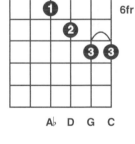

A♭ D G C — 6fr

A♭ C G C D — 10fr

A♭ D G C E♭ — 11fr

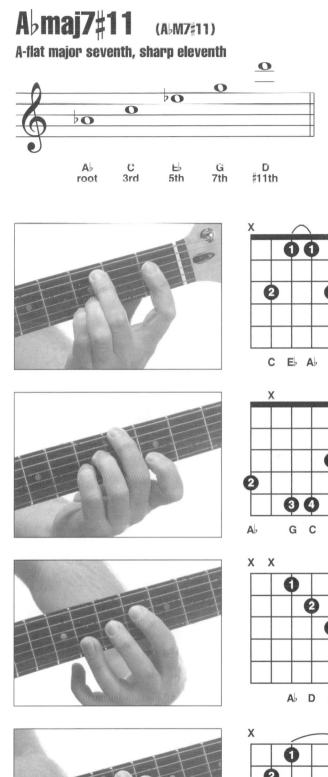
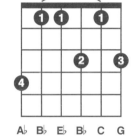
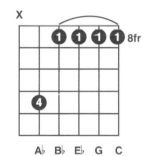
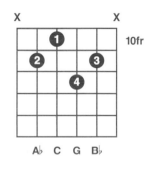
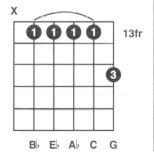
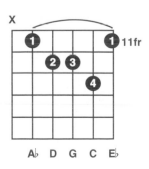
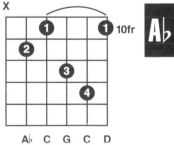

A♭

A♭maj13 (A♭M13)
A-flat major thirteenth

A♭	C	E♭	G	B♭	F
root	3rd	5th	7th	9th	13th

A♭m (A♭min, A♭-)
A-flat minor

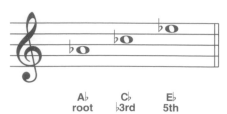

A♭	C♭	E♭
root	♭3rd	5th

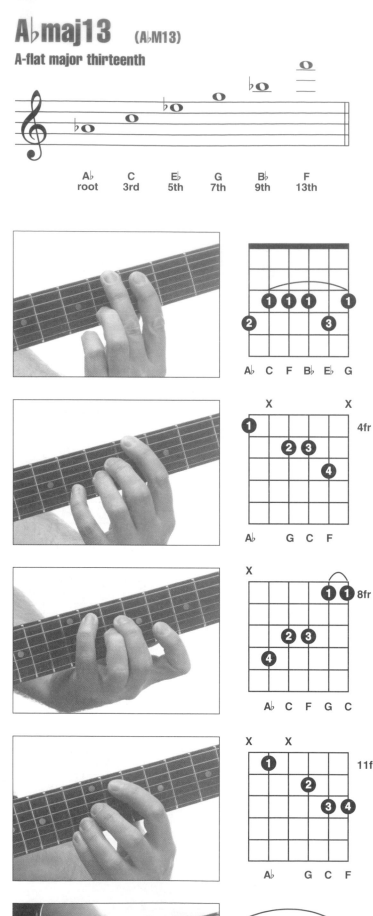

A♭ C F B♭ E♭ G

X   X   4fr

A♭   G C F

X   8fr

A♭ C F G C

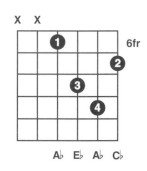

X   X   11fr

A♭   G C F

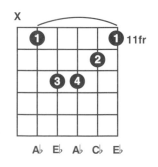

13fr

F B♭ E A♭ C G

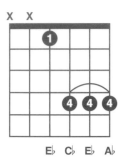

X X

E♭ C♭ E♭ A♭

4fr

A♭ E♭ A♭ C♭ E♭ A♭

X X   6fr

A♭ E♭ A♭ C♭

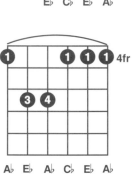

X   11fr

A♭ E♭ A♭ C♭ E♭

X   X   12fr

C♭ E♭ A♭ C♭

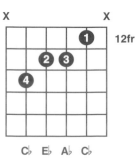

A♭m(add9)
A-flat minor, added ninth

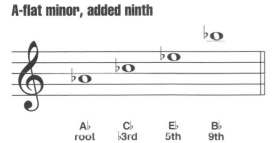

A♭	C♭	E♭	B♭
root	♭3rd	5th	9th

A♭m6 (A♭min6, A♭-6)
A-flat minor sixth

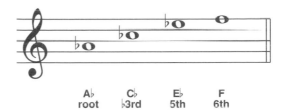

A♭	C♭	E♭	F
root	♭3rd	5th	6th

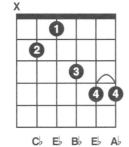

C♭ E♭ B♭ E♭ A♭

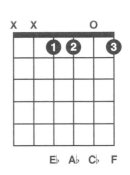

E♭ A♭ C♭ F

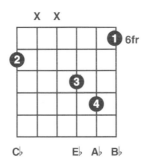

4fr
A♭ E♭ A♭ C♭ E♭ B♭

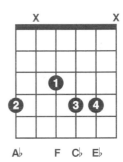

A♭ F C♭ E♭

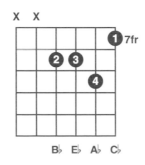

6fr
C♭ E♭ A♭ B♭

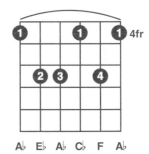

4fr
A♭ E♭ A♭ C♭ F A♭

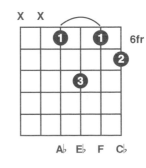

7fr
B♭ E♭ A♭ C♭

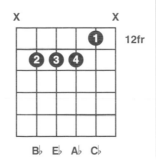

6fr
A♭ E♭ F C♭

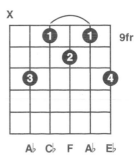

12fr
B♭ E♭ A♭ C♭

9fr
A♭ C♭ F A♭ E♭

A♭

A♭m♭6 (A♭-(♭6), A♭min♭6)
A-flat minor, flat sixth

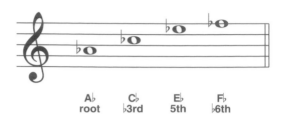

A♭	C♭	E♭	F♭
root	♭3rd	5th	♭6th

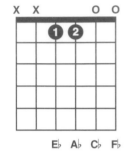

E♭ A♭ C♭ F♭

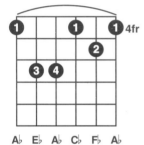

A♭ E♭ A♭ C♭ F♭ A♭

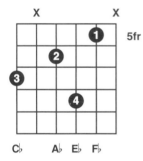

C♭ A♭ E♭ F♭

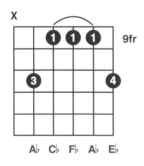

A♭ C♭ F♭ A♭ E♭

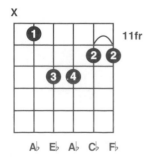

A♭ E♭ A♭ C♭ F♭

A♭m6/9
A-flat minor sixth, added ninth

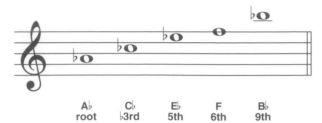

A♭	C♭	E♭	F	B♭
root	♭3rd	5th	6th	9th

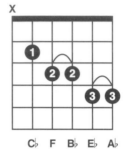

C♭ F B♭ E♭ A♭

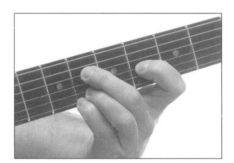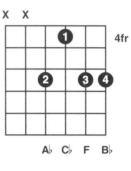

A♭ C♭ F B♭

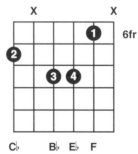

C♭ B♭ E♭ F

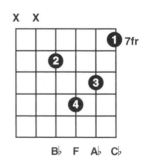

B♭ F A♭ C♭

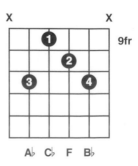

A♭ C♭ F B♭

A♭m7 (A♭-7, A♭min7)
A-flat minor seventh

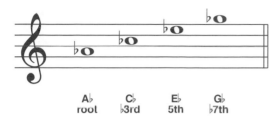

A♭   C♭   E♭   G♭
root   ♭3rd   5th   ♭7th

X   X

A♭   G♭ C♭ E♭

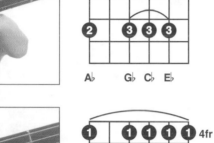

4fr

A♭ E♭ G♭ C♭ E♭ A♭

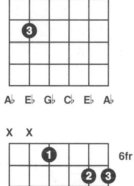
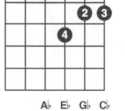

X X

6fr

A♭ E♭ G♭ C♭

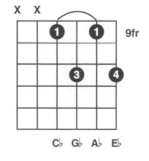

X X

9fr

C♭ G♭ A♭ E♭

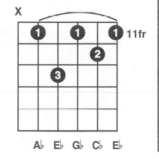

X

11fr

A♭ E♭ G♭ C♭ E♭

A♭m7♭5 (A♭-7♭5, A♭min7-5)
A-flat minor seventh, flat fifth

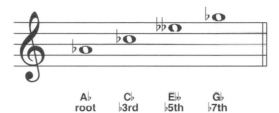

A♭   C♭   E♭♭   G♭
root   ♭3rd   ♭5th   ♭7th

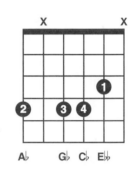

X   X

A♭   G♭ C♭ E♭♭

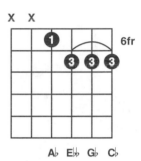

X X

6fr

A♭ E♭♭ G♭ C♭

X   X

7fr

G♭ C♭ E♭♭ A♭

X   X

11fr

A♭ E♭♭ G♭ C♭

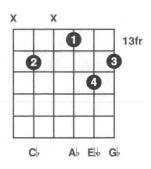

X   X

13fr

C♭   A♭ E♭♭ G♭

A♭

A♭m(maj7) (A♭-(+7))
A-flat minor, major seventh

A♭	C♭	E♭	G
root	♭3rd	5th	7th

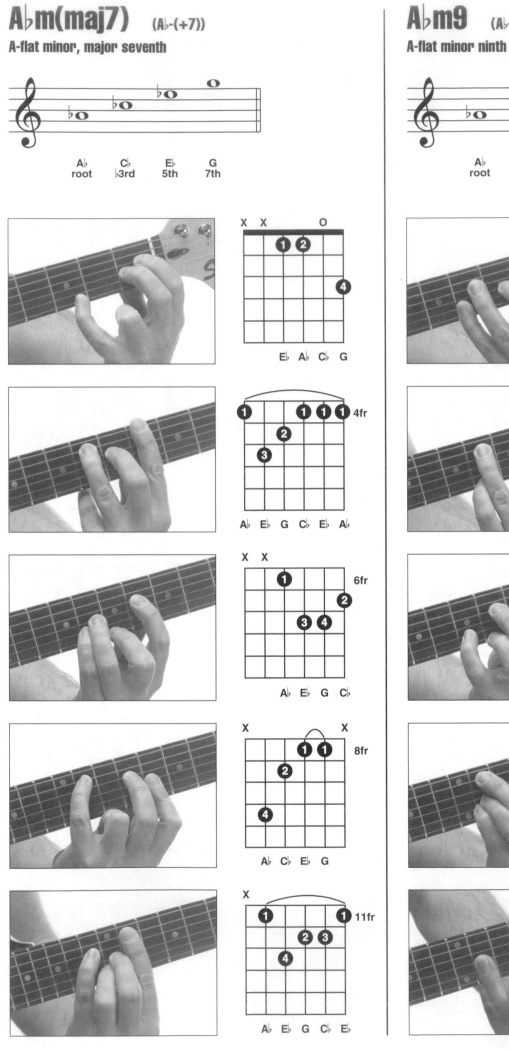

A♭m9 (A♭-9, A♭min9)
A-flat minor ninth

A♭	C♭	E♭	G♭	B♭
root	♭3rd	5th	♭7th	9th

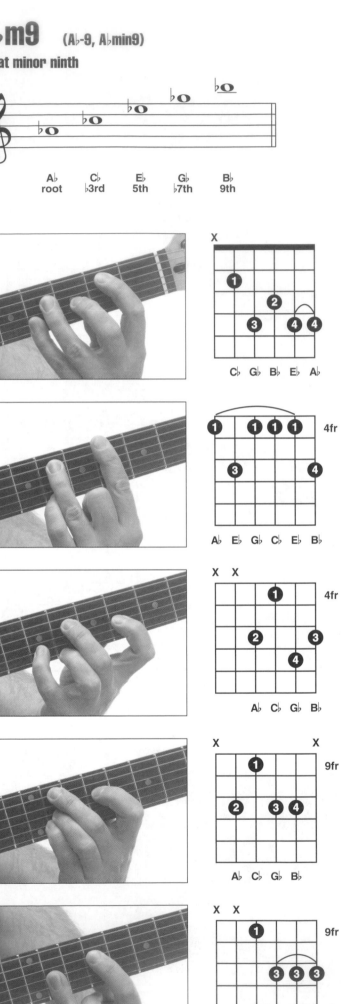

A♭m9♭5 (A♭m9-5, A♭min9♭5)
A-flat minor ninth, flat fifth

A♭	C♭	E♭♭	G♭	B♭
root	♭3rd	♭5th	♭7th	9th

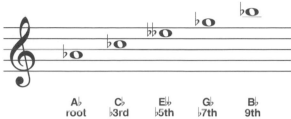

C♭ G♭ B♭ E♭♭ G♭

3fr
G♭ C♭ E♭♭ B♭

7fr
C♭ B♭ E♭♭ G♭

9fr
C♭ G♭ B♭ E♭♭

11fr
B♭ E♭♭ G♭ C♭

A♭m9(maj7) (A♭m9+7, A♭-9+7)
A-flat minor ninth, major seventh

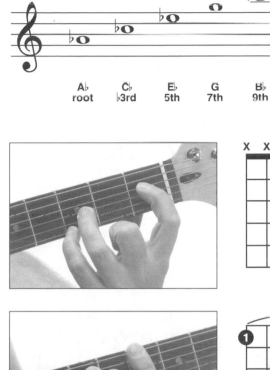

A♭	C♭	E♭	G	B♭
root	♭3rd	5th	7th	9th

E♭ B♭ C♭ G

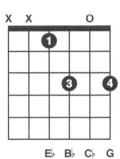

4fr
A♭ E♭ G C♭ E♭ B♭

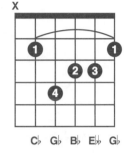

6fr
C♭ E♭ G B♭

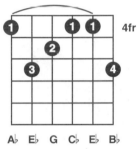

9fr
A♭ C♭ G B♭

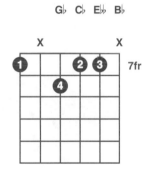

11fr
C♭ E♭ G B♭ E♭

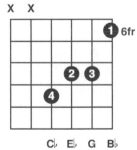

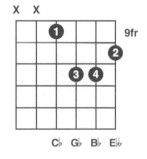

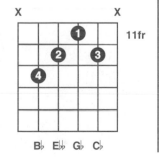
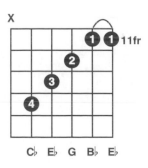
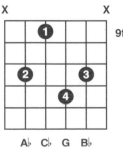

A♭

A♭m11 (A♭-11, A♭min11)
A-flat minor eleventh

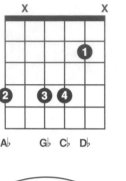

A♭	C♭	E♭	G♭	B♭	D♭
root	♭3rd	5th	♭7th	9th	11th

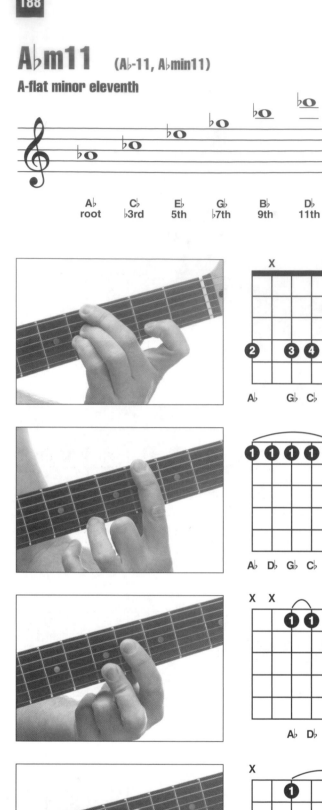

X   X

| 2 | | 3 | 4 | 1 |

A♭ G♭ C♭ D♭

1 1 1 1 1   4fr
        3

A♭ D♭ G♭ C♭ E♭ B♭

X X
1 1
  2 2   6fr

A♭ D♭ G♭ C♭

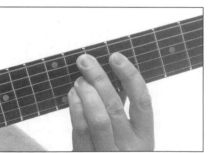

X
1   1   9fr
2   3 4

A♭ C♭ G♭ B♭ D♭

1 1 1 1 1   11fr
      2

A♭ D♭ G♭ C♭ E♭

A♭m13 (A♭-13, A♭min13)
A-flat minor thirteenth

A♭	C♭	E♭	G♭	B♭	F
root	♭3rd	5th	♭7th	9th	13th

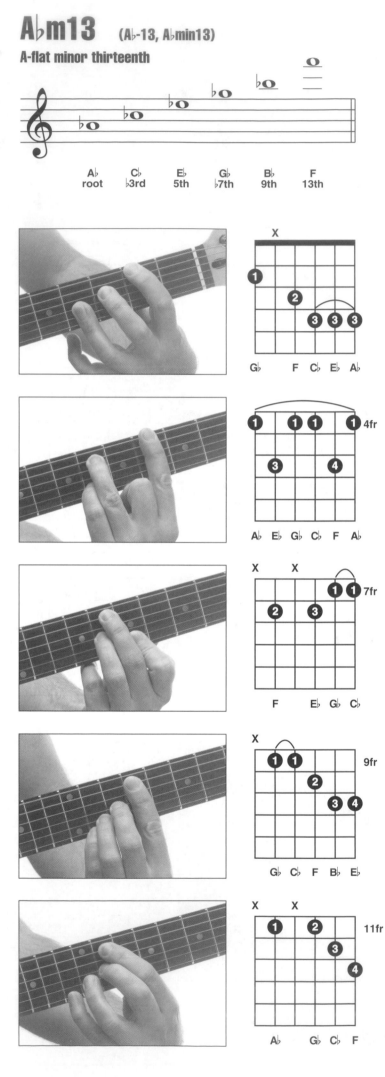

X
1
  2
    3 3 3

G♭ F C♭ E♭ A♭

1 1 1 1   4fr
3   4

A♭ E♭ G♭ C♭ F A♭

X X
      1 1   7fr
2   3

F   E♭ G♭ C♭

X
1 1   9fr
  2
    3 4

G♭ C♭ F B♭ E♭

X X
1   2   11fr
    3
      4

A♭ G♭ C♭ F

A♭7 (A♭dom7)
A-flat dominant seventh

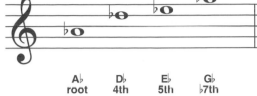

A♭	C	E♭	G♭
root	3rd	5th	♭7th

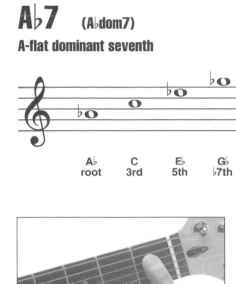 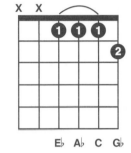

E♭ A♭ C G♭

 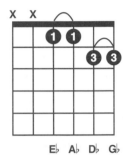

A♭ E♭ G♭ C E♭ A♭

 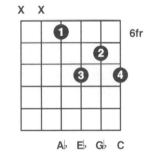

A♭ E♭ G♭ C 6fr

 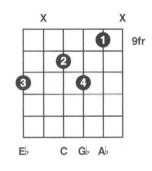

E♭ C G♭ A♭ 9fr

 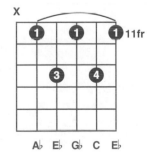

A♭ E♭ G♭ C E♭ 11fr

A♭7sus4 (A♭7sus)
A-flat dominant seventh, suspended fourth

A♭	D♭	E♭	G♭
root	4th	5th	♭7th

E♭ A♭ D♭ G♭

 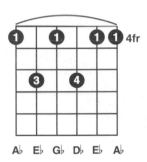

A♭ E♭ G♭ D♭ E♭ A♭ 4fr

 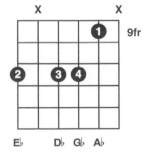

A♭ E♭ G♭ D♭ 6fr

E♭ D♭ G♭ A♭ 9fr

 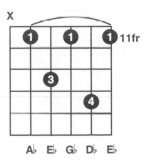

A♭ E♭ G♭ D♭ E♭ 11fr

A♭

A♭7♭5 (A♭7-5, A♭dom7♭5)
A-flat dominant seventh, flat fifth

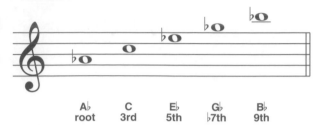

A♭ — root
C — 3rd
E♭♭ — ♭5th
G♭ — ♭7th

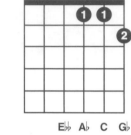

X X O
① ①
②

E♭♭ A♭ C G♭

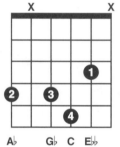

X X
①
② ③
④

A♭ G♭ C E♭♭

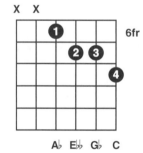

X X
①
② ③
④ 6fr

A♭ E♭♭ G♭ C

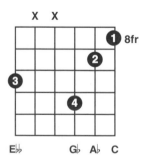

X X
① 8fr
②
③
④

E♭♭ G♭ A♭ C

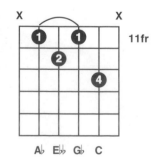

X X
① ①
②
④ 11fr

A♭ E♭♭ G♭ C

A♭9
A-flat ninth

A♭ — root
C — 3rd
E♭ — 5th
G♭ — ♭7th
B♭ — 9th

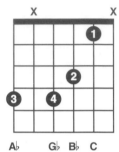

X X
①
②
③ ④

A♭ G♭ B♭ C

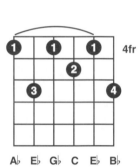

① ① ① 4fr
②
③ ④

A♭ E♭ G♭ C E♭ B♭

X X
① 5fr
② ③
④

A♭ C G♭ B♭

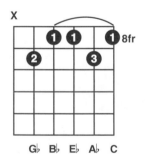

X
① ① ① 8fr
② ③

G♭ B♭ E♭ A♭ C

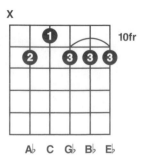

X
① 10fr
② ③ ③ ③

A♭ C G♭ B♭ E♭

A♭9sus4 (A♭9sus)
A-flat ninth, suspended fourth

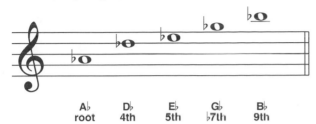

A♭	D♭	E♭	G♭	B♭
root	4th	5th	♭7th	9th

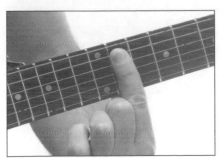
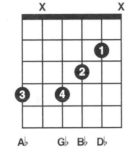
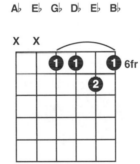
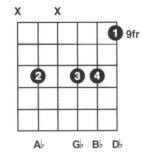

A♭ G♭ B♭ D♭

A♭ E♭ G♭ D♭ E♭ B♭ — 4fr

A♭ D♭ G♭ B♭ — 6fr

A♭ G♭ B♭ D♭ — 9fr

A♭ D♭ G♭ B♭ E♭ — 11fr

A♭9♭5 (A♭9-5, A♭dom9♭5)
A-flat ninth, flat fifth

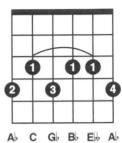

A♭	C	E♭♭	G♭	B♭
root	3rd	♭5th	♭7th	9th

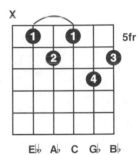

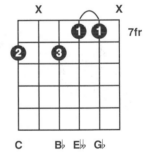

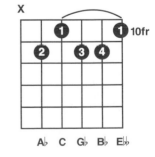

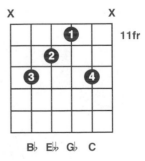

A♭ C G♭ B♭ E♭♭ A♭

E♭♭ A♭ C G♭ B♭ — 5fr

C B♭ E♭♭ G♭ — 7fr

A♭ C G♭ B♭ E♭♭ — 10fr

B♭ E♭♭ G♭ C — 11fr

A♭

A♭7♭9 (A♭7-9, A♭dom7♭9)
A-flat dominant seventh, flat ninth

A♭	C	E♭	G♭	B♭♭
root	3rd	5th	♭7th	♭9th

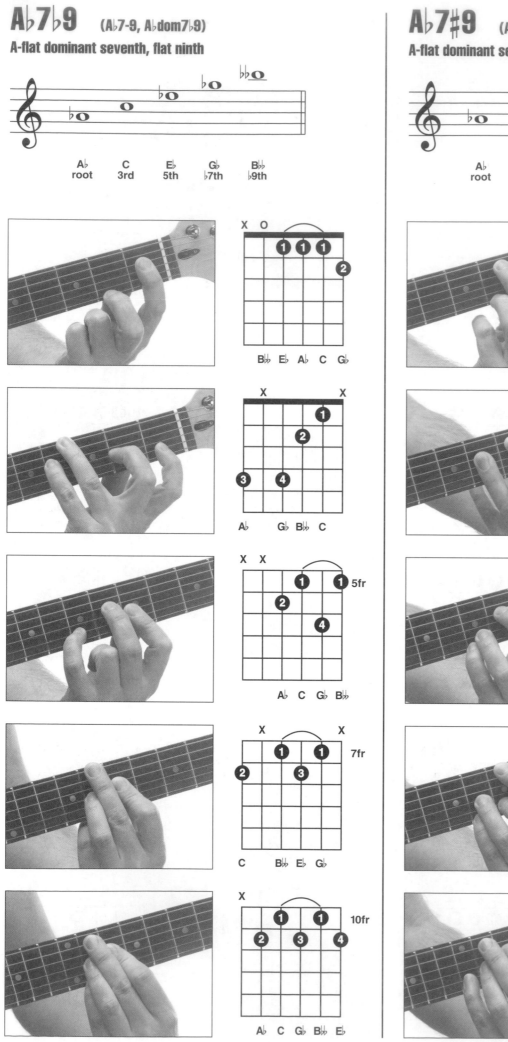

X O
B♭♭ E♭ A♭ C G♭

X X
A♭ G♭ B♭♭ C

X X
5fr
A♭ C G♭ B♭♭

X X
7fr
C B♭♭ E♭ G♭

X
10fr
A♭ C G♭ B♭♭ E♭

A♭7♯9 (A♭7+9, A♭dom7♯9)
A-flat dominant seventh, sharp ninth

A♭	C	E♭	G♭	B
root	3rd	5th	♭7th	♯9th

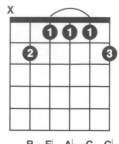

X
B E♭ A♭ C G♭

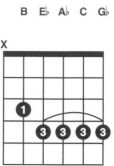

X
C G♭ B E♭ A♭

X X
5fr
A♭ C G♭ B

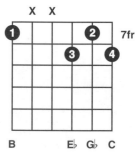

X X
7fr
B E♭ G♭ C

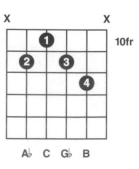

X X
10fr
A♭ C G♭ B

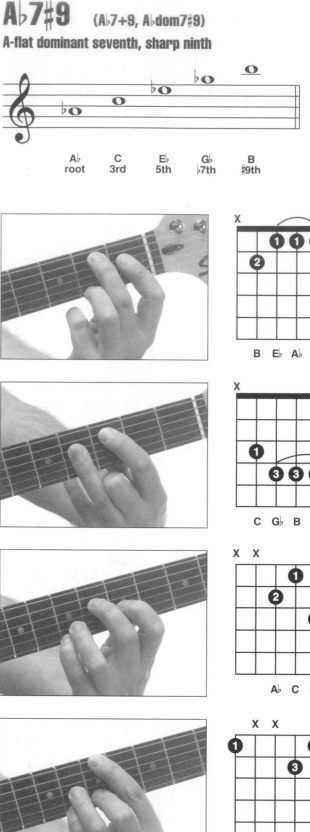

A♭7♭5(♯9) (A♭7-5(+9), A♭dom7♭5(♯9))
A-flat dominant seventh, flat fifth, sharp ninth

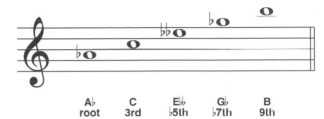

A♭	C	E♭♭	G♭	B
root	3rd	♭5th	♭7th	9th

A♭11
A-flat eleventh

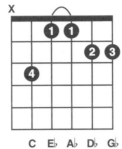
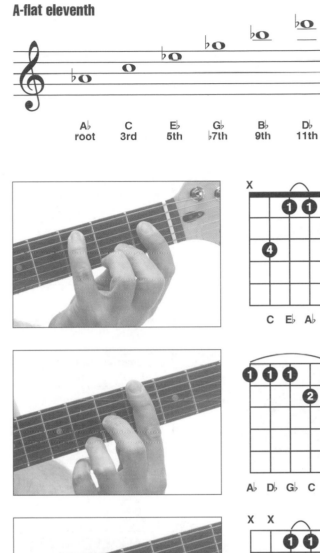

A♭	C	E♭	G♭	B♭	D♭
root	3rd	5th	♭7th	9th	11th

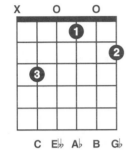

C E♭♭ A♭ B G♭

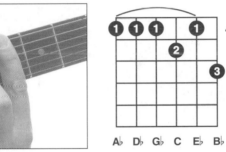

A♭ E♭♭ G♭ C G♭ B

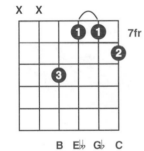
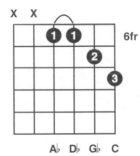

B E♭♭ G♭ C

A♭ D♭ G♭ C

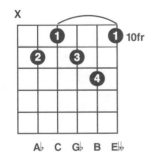

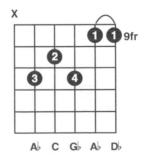

A♭ C G♭ B E♭♭

A♭ C G♭ A♭ D♭

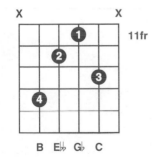

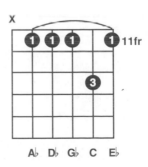

B E♭♭ G♭ C

A♭ D♭ G♭ C E♭

Ab

A♭7♯11 (A♭7+11, A♭dom7♯11)
A-flat dominant seventh, sharp eleventh

A♭	C	E♭	G♭	D
root	3rd	5th	♭7th	♯11th

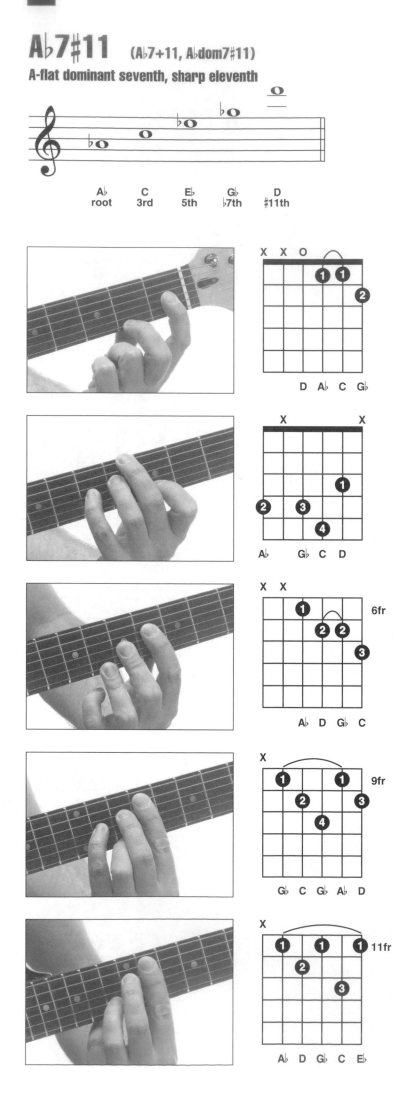

A♭13 (A♭dom13)
A-flat thirteenth

A♭	C	E♭	G♭	B♭	F
root	3rd	5th	♭7th	9th	13th

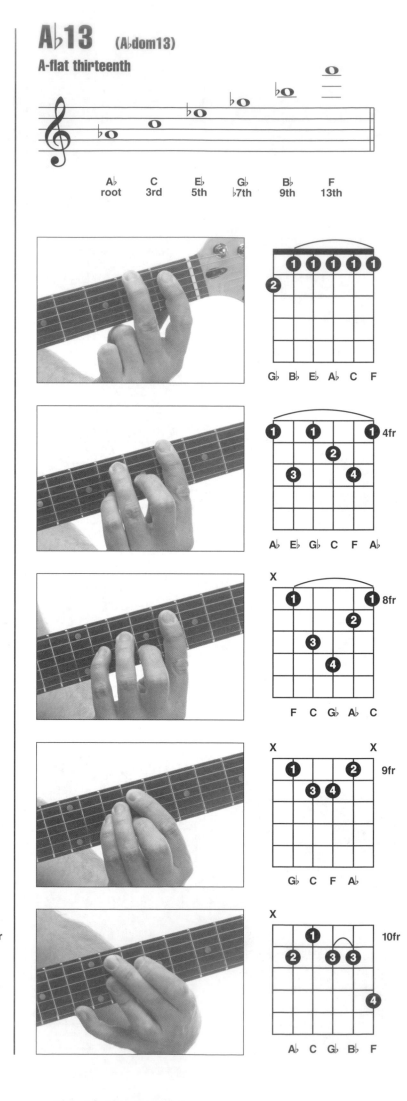

A♭13sus4 (A♭13sus)

A-flat thirteenth, suspended fourth

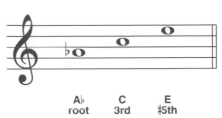

A♭	D♭	E♭	G♭	B♭	F
root	4th	5th	♭7th	9th	13th

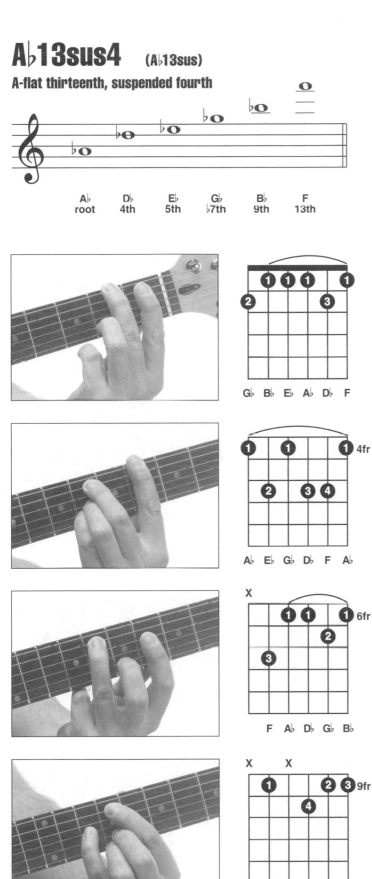

G♭ B♭ E♭ A♭ D♭ F

A♭ E♭ G♭ D♭ F A♭

F A♭ D♭ G♭ B♭

G♭ F A♭ D♭

A♭ D♭ G♭ B♭ F

A♭+ (A♭aug, A♭(♯5))

A-flat augmented

A♭	C	E
root	3rd	♯5th

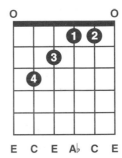

E C E A♭ C E

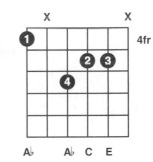

A♭ A♭ C E

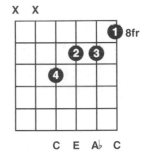

C E A♭ C

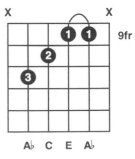

A♭ C E A♭

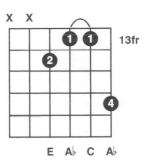

E A♭ C A♭

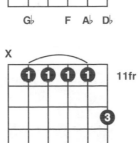

A♭

A♭+7 (A♭7♯5)
A-flat dominant seventh, sharp fifth

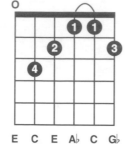

A♭	C	E	G♭
root	3rd	♯5th	♭7th

E C E A♭ C G♭

A♭ G♭ C E

6fr

A♭ E G♭ C

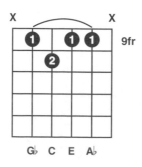

9fr

G♭ C E A♭

11fr

A♭ E G♭ C E

A♭+9 (A♭9♯5, A♭9+5)
A-flat ninth, sharp fifth

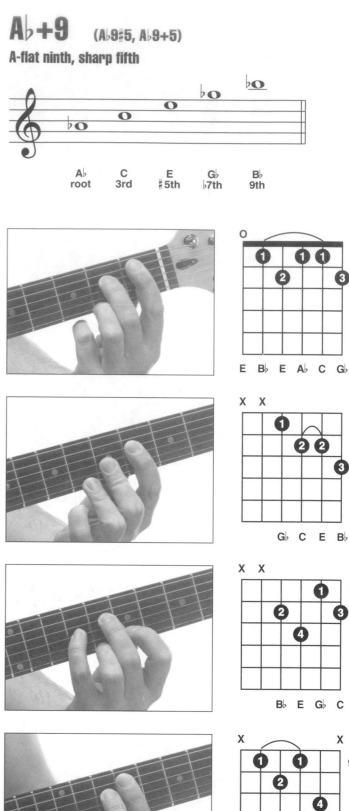

A♭	C	E	G♭	B♭
root	3rd	♯5th	♭7th	9th

E B♭ E A♭ C G♭

4fr

G♭ C E B♭

7fr

B♭ E G♭ C

9fr

G♭ C E B♭

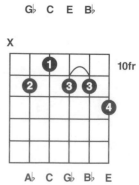

10fr

A♭ C G♭ B♭ E

A♭+7♭9 (A♭7+5(♭9))

A-flat dominant seventh, sharp fifth, flat ninth

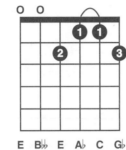

A♭	C	E	G♭	B♭♭
root	3rd	#5th	♭7th	♭9th

O O

E B♭♭ E A♭ C G♭

A♭ C E B♭♭ E G♭

X X 7fr

B♭♭ E G♭ C

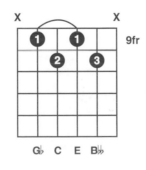

X X 9fr

G♭ C E B♭♭

X 10fr

A♭ C G♭ B♭♭ E

A♭+7♯9 (A♭7+5(♯9))

A-flat dominant seventh, sharp fifth, sharp ninth

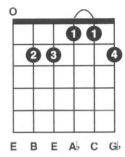

A♭	C	E	G♭	B
root	3rd	#5th	♭7th	#9th

O

E B E A♭ C G♭

X X 4fr

G♭ C E B

X X 7fr

C E G♭ B

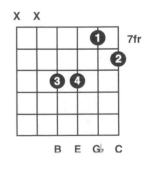

X X 7fr

B E G♭ C

X 10fr

A♭ C G♭ B E

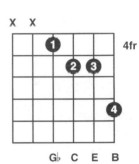
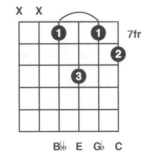
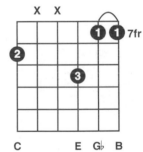

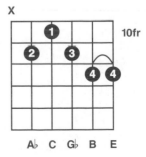
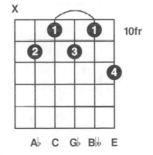
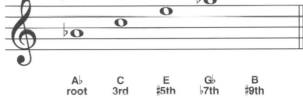

A♭

198

A♭° (A♭dim)
A-flat diminished

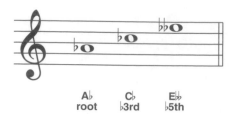

A♭ C♭ E♭♭
root ♭3rd ♭5th

A♭°7 (A♭dim7)
A-flat diminished seventh

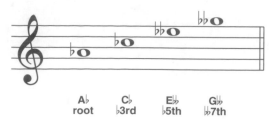

A♭ C♭ E♭♭ G♭♭
root ♭3rd ♭5th ♭♭7th

 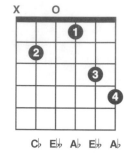

C♭ E♭♭ A♭ E♭♭ A♭

 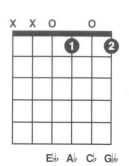

E♭♭ A♭ C♭ G♭♭

 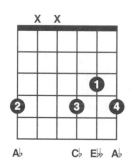

A♭ C♭ E♭♭ A♭

 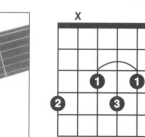

A♭ G♭♭ C♭ E♭♭

 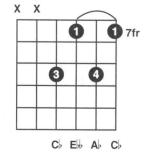

C♭ E♭♭ A♭ C♭ 7fr

 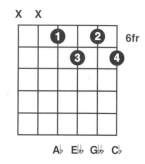

A♭ E♭♭ G♭♭ C♭ 6fr

 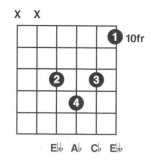

E♭♭ A♭ C♭ E♭♭ 10fr

 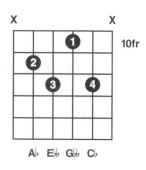

A♭ E♭♭ G♭♭ C♭ 10fr

 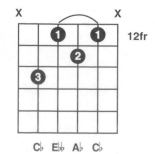

C♭ E♭♭ A♭ C♭ 12fr

 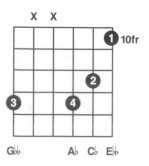

G♭♭ A♭ C♭ E♭♭ 10fr

A (Amaj)
A major

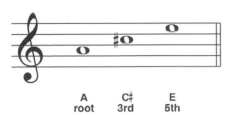

A   C#   E
root   3rd   5th

A5 (A no 3rd)
A fifth (power chord)

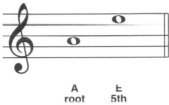

A   E
root   5th

X O   O

A E A C# E

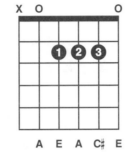

X O   X X

A E A

5fr

A E A C# E A

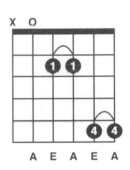

X O

A E A E A

X X   7fr

A E A C#

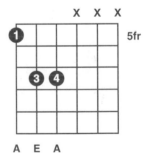

X X X

5fr

A E A

X   X

9fr

A C# E A

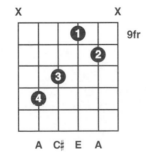

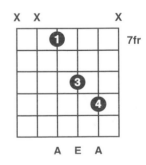

X X   X

7fr

A E A

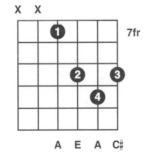

X   X

12fr

A E A C#

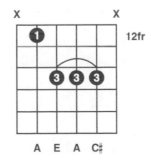

X   X X

12fr

A E A

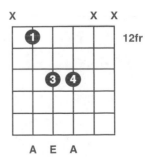

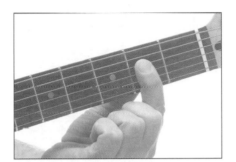

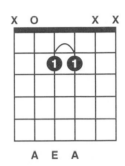

A

Asus4 (Asus)
A suspended fourth

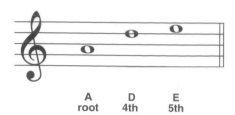

A root   D 4th   E 5th

A E A D E

A E A D E A

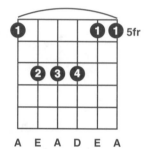
A E A D

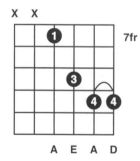
A D E A

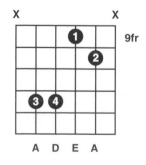

E A D A D E

Asus2 (A5add2)
A suspended second

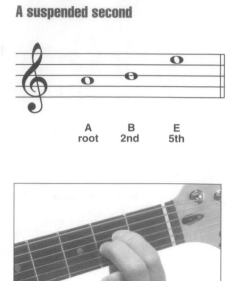

A root   B 2nd   E 5th

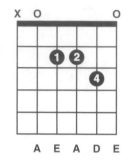
A E A B E

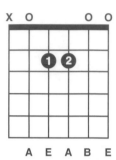
A B E A

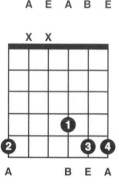
A E A B

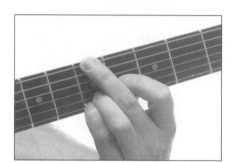
A B E A

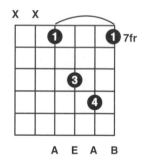
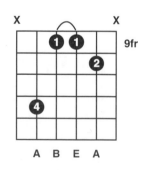
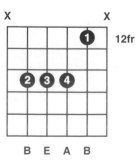
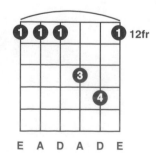

B E A B

Aadd9
A added ninth

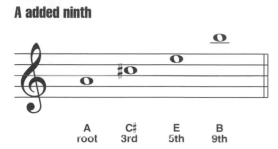

A	C#	E	B
root	3rd	5th	9th

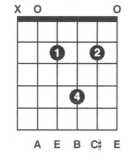

A E B C# E

A C# E B — 5fr

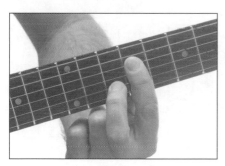
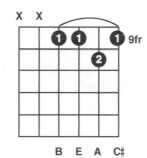

B E A C# — 9fr

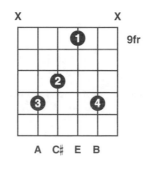

A C# E B — 9fr

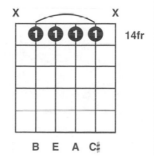

B E A C# — 14fr

A6
A sixth

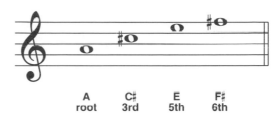

A	C#	E	F#
root	3rd	5th	6th

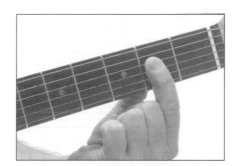
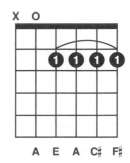

A E A C# F#

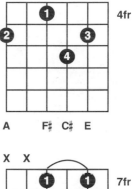

A F# C# E — 4fr

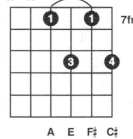

A E F# C# — 7fr

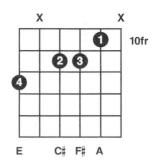

E C# F# A — 10fr

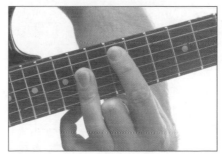
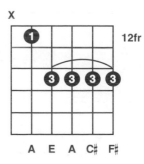

A E A C# F# — 12fr

A

A6/9 (A6add9)
A sixth, added ninth

A	C#	E	F#	B
root	3rd	5th	6th	9th

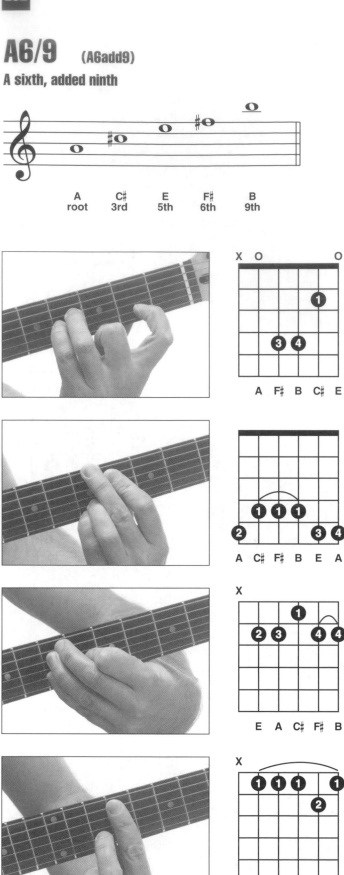

X O   O

A F# B C# E

A C# F# B E A

X   6fr

E A C# F# B

X   9fr

F# B E A C#

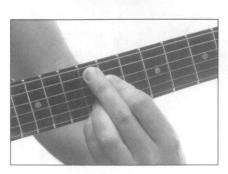

X   11fr

A C# F# B E

Amaj7 (AM7)
A major seventh

A	C#	E	G#
root	3rd	5th	7th

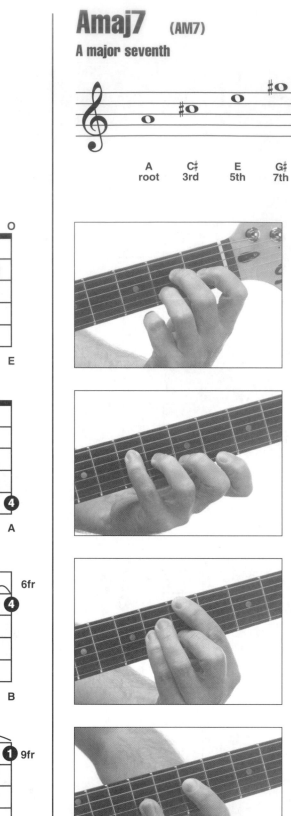

X O   O

A E G# C# E

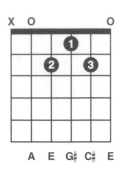

X X   4fr

A C# E G#

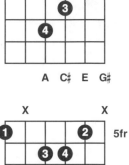

X   X   5fr

A G# C# E

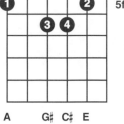

X X   7fr

A E G# C#

X   X   9fr

A C# E G#

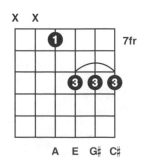

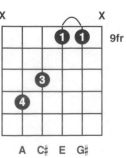

Amaj9 (AM9)
A major ninth

A	C#	E	G#	B
root	3rd	5th	7th	9th

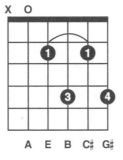

A E B C# G#

A C# G# B   6fr

A B E G# C#   9fr

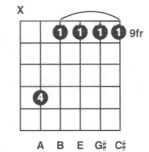

A C# G# B   11fr

B E A C# G#   14fr

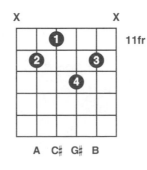

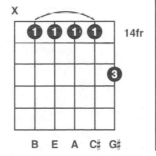

Amaj7#11 (AM7#11)
A major seventh, sharp eleventh

A	C#	E	G#	D#
root	3rd	5th	7th	#11th

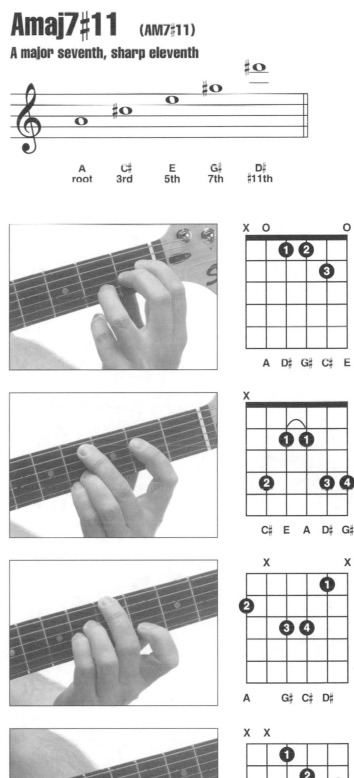

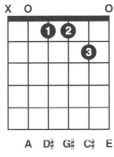

A D# G# C# E

C# E A D# G#

A G# C# D#   4fr

A D# G# C#   7fr

A C# G# C# D#   11fr

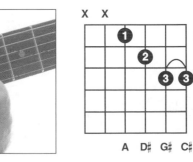

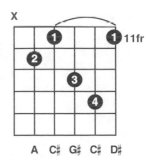

A

Amaj13 (AM13)
A major thirteenth

A	C#	E	G#	B	F#
root	3rd	5th	7th	9th	13th

Am (Amin, A-)
A minor

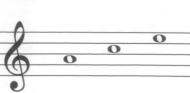

A	C	E
root	♭3rd	5th

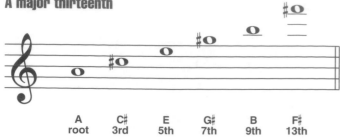
X O
1
2   3 4
A E G# C# F#

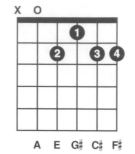
A E A C E

X
1 1 1   1
2   3
A C# F# B E G#

1 1 1 1   5fr
3 4
A E A C E A

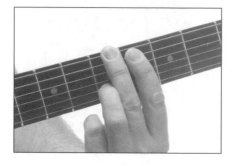
X   X
1   5fr
2 3
4
A   G# C# F#

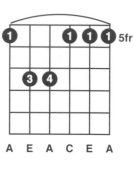
X X
1   7fr
2
3
4
A E A C

X
1 1 9fr
2 3
4
A C# F# G# C#

X   X
1   9fr
2   3
4
A C E A

1 1 1 1 1 1 14fr
3
F# B E A C# G#

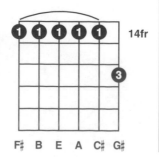
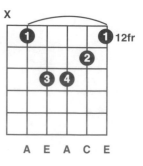
X
1   1 12fr
2
3 4
A E A C E

Am(add9)
A minor, added ninth

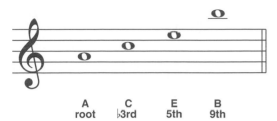

A	C	E	B
root	♭3rd	5th	9th

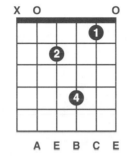

X O   O
A E B C E

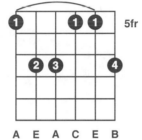

5fr
A E A C E B

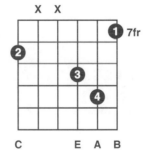

X X   7fr
C   E A B

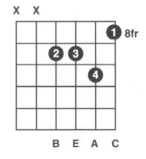

X X   8fr
B E A C

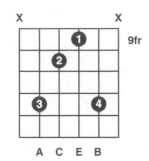

X   X   9fr
A C E B

Am6 (Amin6, A-6)
A minor sixth

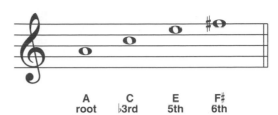

A	C	E	F♯
root	♭3rd	5th	6th

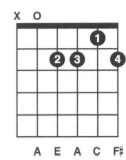

X O
A E A C F♯

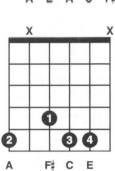

X   X
A   F♯ C E

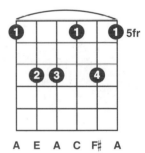

5fr
A E A C F♯ A

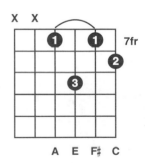

X X   7fr
A E F♯ C

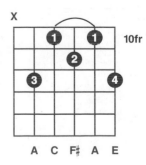

X   10fr
A C F♯ A E

A

Am♭6 (A-(♭6), Amin♭6)
A minor, flat sixth

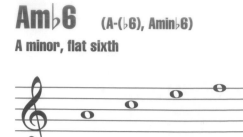

A	C	E	F
root	♭3rd	5th	♭6th

A E A C F

A E A C F A — 5fr

C A E F — 6fr

A C F A E — 10fr

A E A C F — 12fr

Am6/9
A minor sixth, added ninth

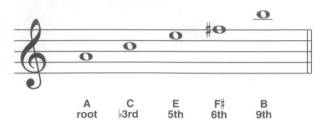

A	C	E	F♯	B
root	♭3rd	5th	6th	9th

C E A B F♯

A C F♯ B — 5fr

C B E F♯ — 7fr

B F♯ A C — 8fr

A C F♯ B — 10fr

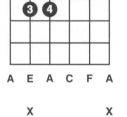
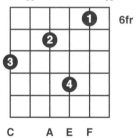
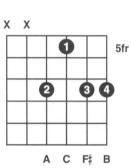
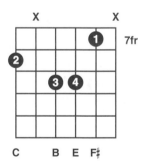
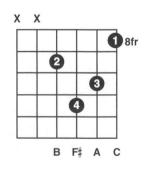
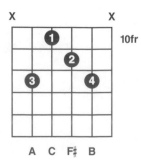
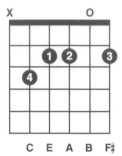
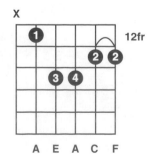

Am7 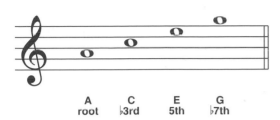(A-7, Amin7)
A minor seventh

A root | C ♭3rd | E 5th | G ♭7th

Am7♭5 (A-7♭5, Amin7♭5)
A minor seventh, flat fifth

A root | C ♭3rd | E♭ ♭5th | G ♭7th

A E A C G

A E♭ A C G

A E G C E A 5fr

A G C E♭

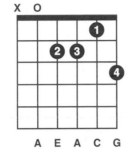
A E G C 7fr

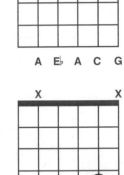
A E♭ G C 7fr

A C G A E 10fr

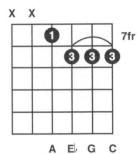
G C E♭ A 8fr

A E G C E 12fr

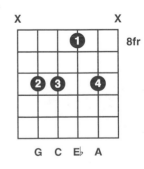
A E♭ G C 12fr

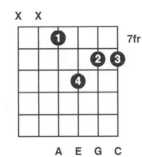
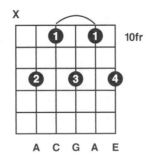
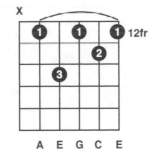

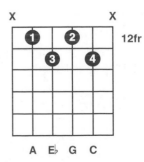

A

Am(maj7) (A-(+7))
A minor, major seventh

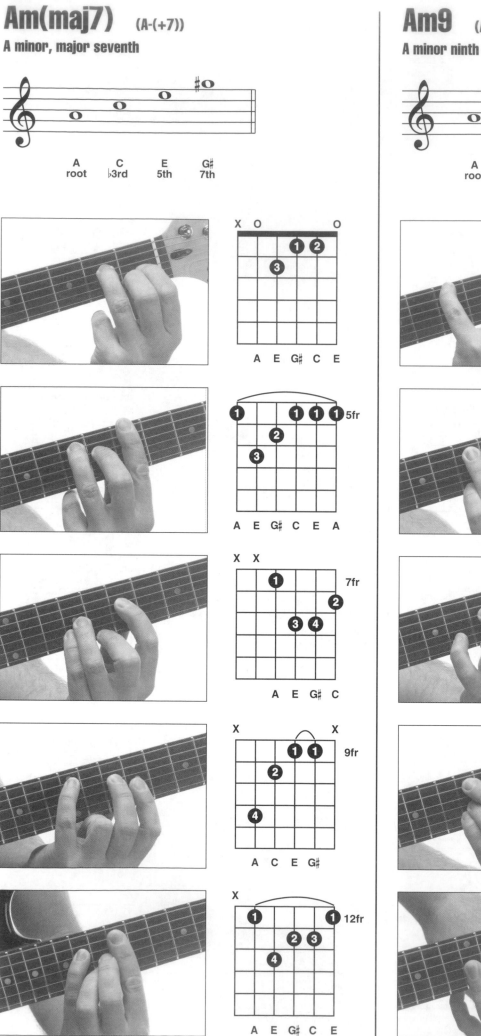

A	C	E	G#
root	♭3rd	5th	7th

X O   O

A E G# C E

A E G# C E A   5fr

X X   7fr

A E G# C

X   X   9fr

A C E G#

X   12fr

A E G# C E

Am9 (A-9, Amin9)
A minor ninth

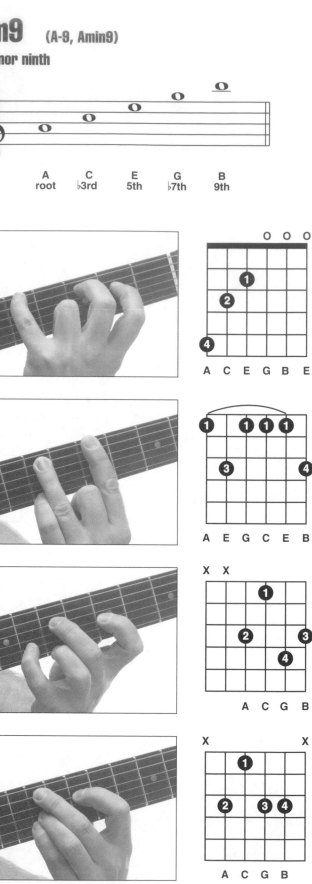

A	C	E	G	B
root	♭3rd	5th	♭7th	9th

O O O

A C E G B E

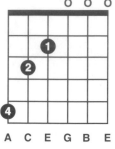

A E G C E B   5fr

X X   5fr

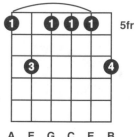

A C G B

X   X   10fr

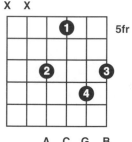

A C G B

X X   10fr

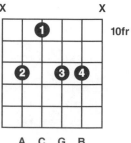

C G B E

Am9♭5 (Am9-5, Amin9♭5)
A minor ninth, flat fifth

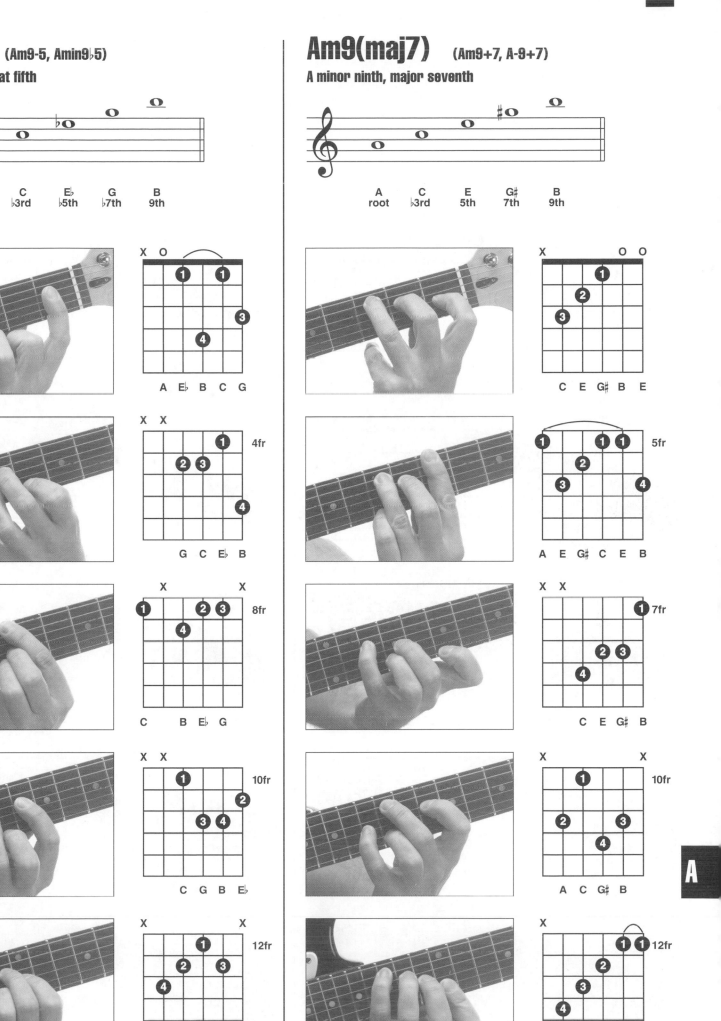

A	C	E♭	G	B
root	♭3rd	♭5th	♭7th	9th

Am9(maj7) (Am9+7, A-9+7)
A minor ninth, major seventh

A	C	E	G#	B
root	♭3rd	5th	7th	9th

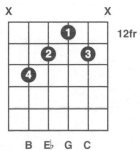

A

Am11 (A-11, Amin11)
A minor eleventh

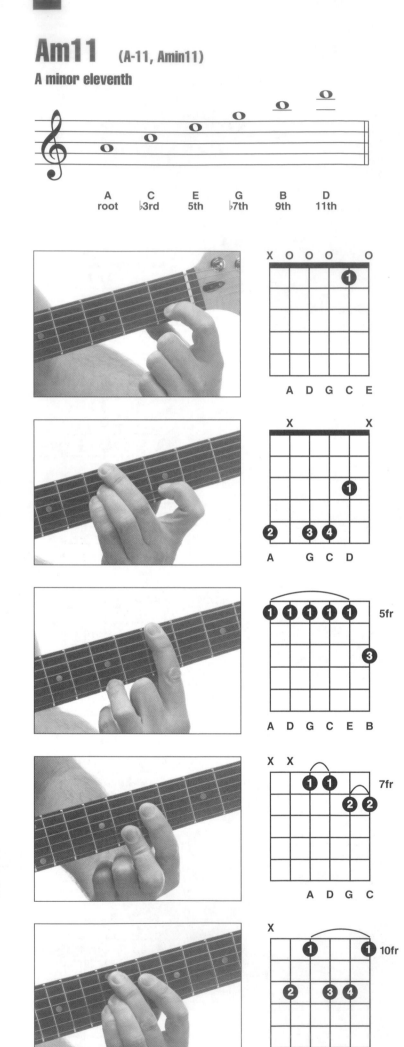

A	C	E	G	B	D
root	♭3rd	5th	♭7th	9th	11th

X O O O

A D G C E

X X

A G C D

A D G C E B — 5fr

X X — 7fr

A D G C

X — 10fr

A C G B D

Am13 (A-13, Amin13)
A minor thirteenth

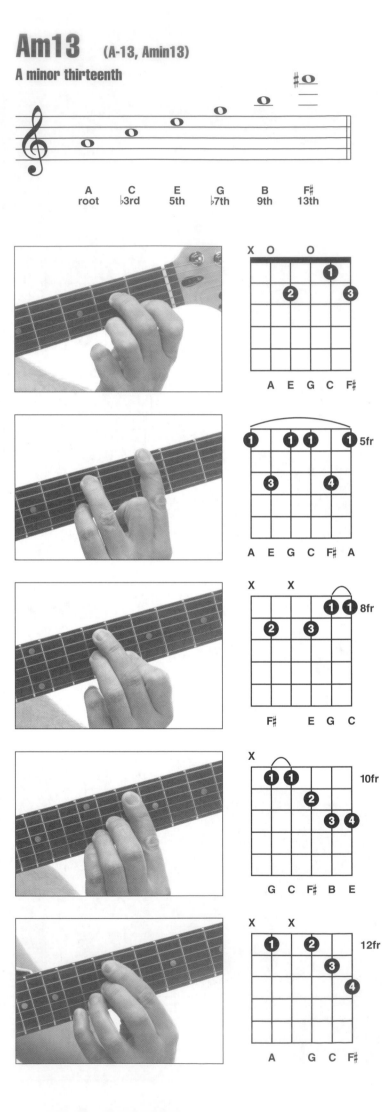

A	C	E	G	B	F♯
root	♭3rd	5th	♭7th	9th	13th

X O O

A E G C F♯

A E G C F♯ A — 5fr

X X — 8fr

F♯ E G C

X — 10fr

G C F♯ B E

X X — 12fr

A G C F♯

A7 (Adom7)
A dominant seventh

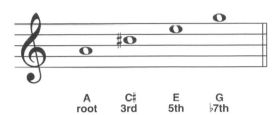

A	C#	E	G
root	3rd	5th	♭7th

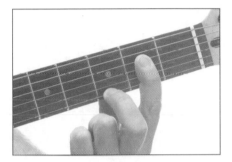
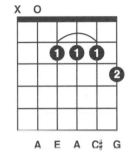

A E A C# G

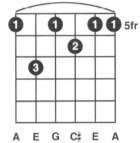

A E G C# E A

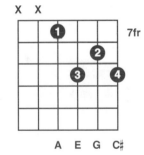

7fr
A E G C#

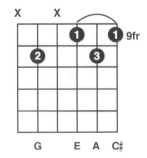

9fr
G E A C#

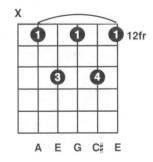

12fr
A E G C# E

A7sus4 (A7sus)
A dominant seventh, suspended fourth

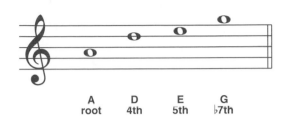

A	D	E	G
root	4th	5th	♭7th

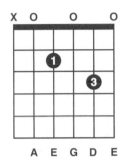

A E G D E

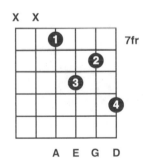

A E G D E A

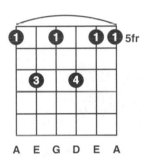

7fr
A E G D

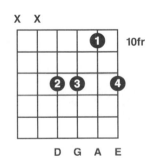

10fr
D G A E

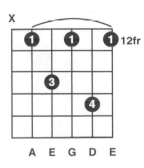

12fr
A E G D E

A

A7♭5 (A7-5, Adom7♭5)
A dominant seventh, flat fifth

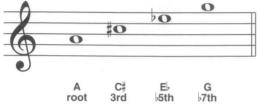

A   C#   E♭   G
root   3rd   ♭5th   ♭7th

A9
A ninth

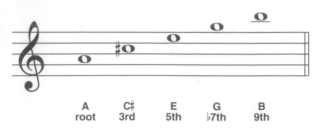

A   C#   E   G   B
root   3rd   5th   ♭7th   9th

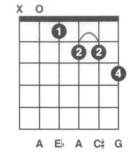
A E♭ A C# G

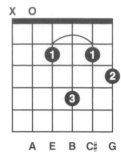
A E B C# G

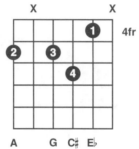
4fr
A G C# E♭

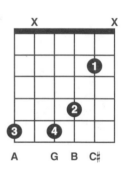
A G B C#

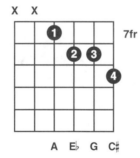
7fr
A E♭ G C#

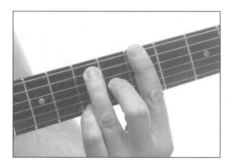
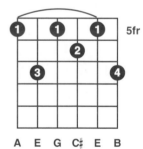
5fr
A E G C# E B

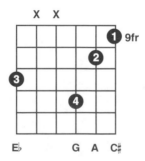
9fr
E♭ G A C#

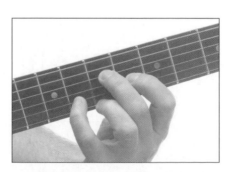
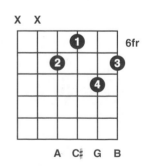
6fr
A C# G B

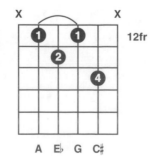
12fr
A E♭ G C#

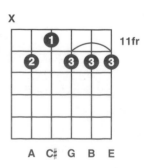
11fr
A C# G B E

A9sus4 (A9sus)
A ninth, suspended fourth

A	D	E	G	B
root	4th	5th	7th	9th

X O
A E B D G

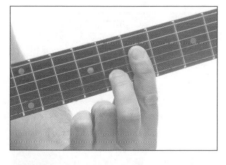

X X
A G B D

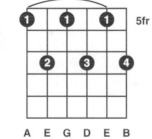

1 1 1 5fr
2 3 4
A E G D E B

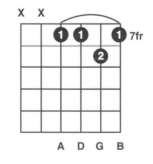

X X
1 1 1 7fr
2
A D G B

X
1 1 1 1 1 12fr
A D G B E

A9♭5 (A9-5, Adom9♭5)
A ninth, flat fifth

A	C#	E♭	G	B
root	3rd	♭5th	♭7th	9th

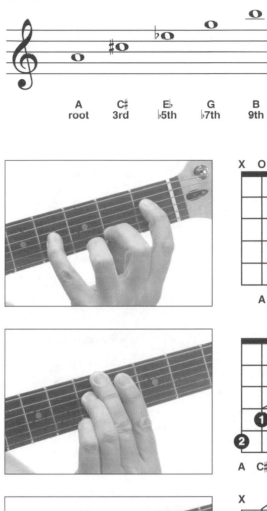

X O
A E♭ B C# G

1 1 1
2 3 4
A C# G B E♭ A

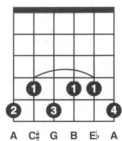

X
1 1 6fr
2 3
4
E♭ A C# G B

X X
1 1 8fr
2 3
C# B E♭ G

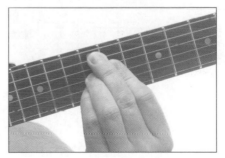

X
1 1 11fr
2 3 4
A C# G B E♭

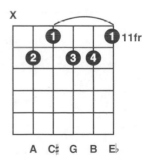

A7♭9 (A7-9, Adom7♭9)
A dominant seventh, flat ninth

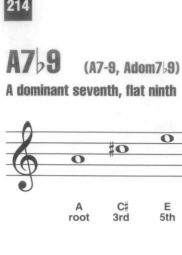

A	C♯	E	G	B♭
root	3rd	5th	♭7th	♭9th

A7♯9 (A7+9, Adom7♯9)
A dominant seventh, sharp ninth

A	C♯	E	G	B♯
root	3rd	5th	♭7th	♯9th

X O

A E B♭ C♯ G

X   X

A   G B♭ C♯

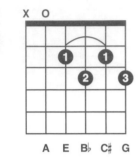

X X

A C♯ G B♭   6fr

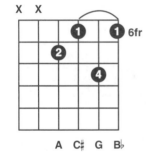

X   X

C♯   B♭ E G   8fr

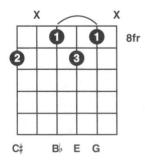

X

A C♯ G B♭ E   11fr

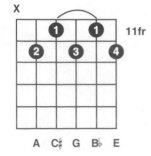

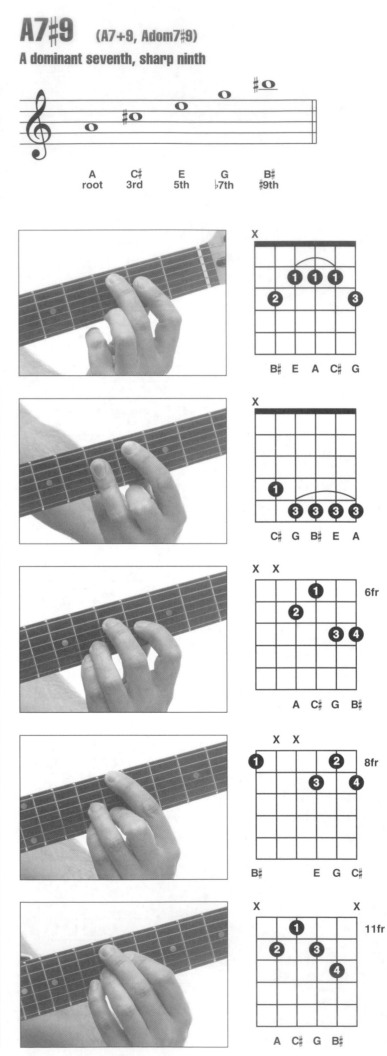

X

B♯ E A C♯ G

X

C♯ G B♯ E A

X X

A C♯ G B♯   6fr

X X

B♯   E G C♯   8fr

X   X

A C♯ G B♯   11fr

A7♭5(♯9) (A7-5(+9), Adom7♭5(♯9))
A dominant seventh, flat fifth, sharp ninth

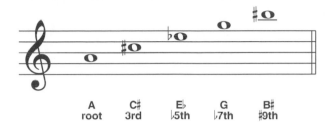

A	C♯	E♭	G	B♯
root	3rd	♭5th	♭7th	♯9th

A11
A eleventh

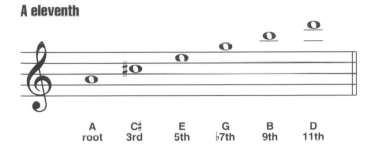

A	C♯	E	G	B	D
root	3rd	5th	♭7th	9th	11th

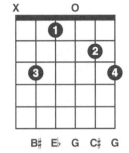

B♯ E♭ G C♯ G

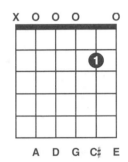

A D G C♯ E

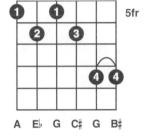

A E♭ G C♯ G B♯

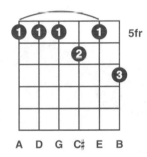

A D G C♯ E B

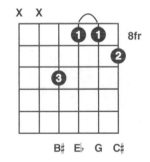

B♯ E♭ G C♯

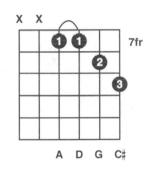

A D G C♯

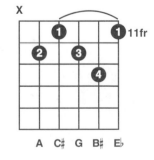

A C♯ G B♯ E♭

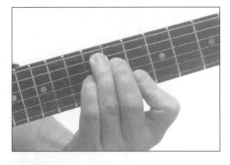
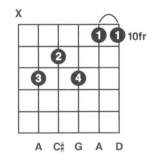

A C♯ G A D

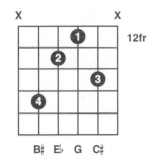

B♯ E♭ G C♯

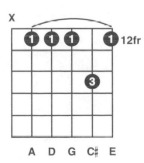

A D G C♯ E

A

A7♯11 (A7+11, Adom7♯11)
A dominant seventh, sharp eleventh

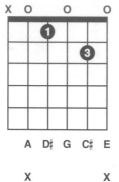

A	C♯	E	G	D♯
root	3rd	5th	♭7th	♯11th

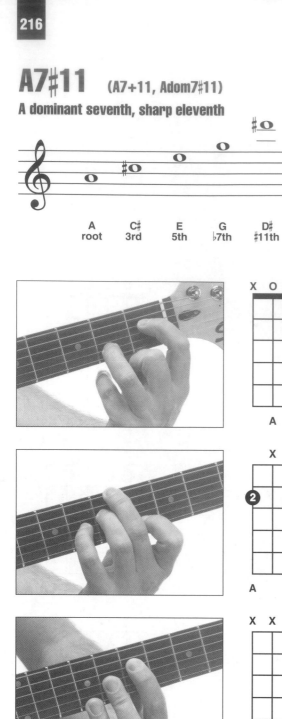

X O O O

A D♯ G C♯ E

X X
4fr

A G C♯ D♯

X X
7fr

A D♯ G C♯

X X
9fr

D♯ G A C♯

X
12fr

A D♯ G C♯ E

A13 (Adom13)
A thirteenth

A	C♯	E	G	B	F♯
root	3rd	5th	♭7th	9th	13th

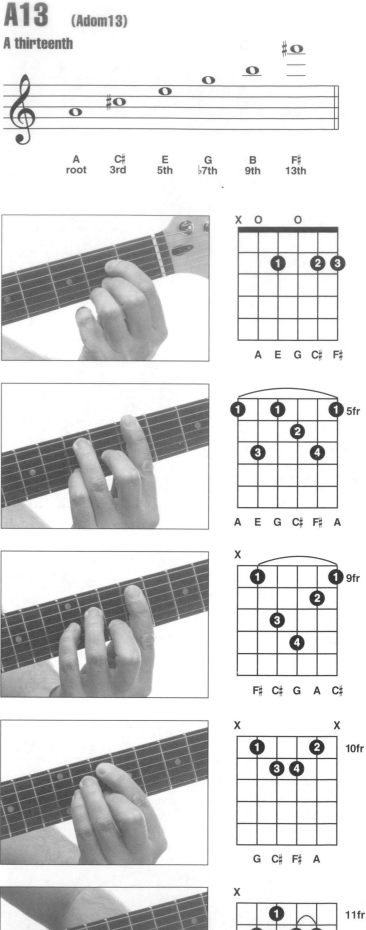

X O O

A E G C♯ F♯

5fr

A E G C♯ F♯ A

X
9fr

F♯ C♯ G A C♯

X X
10fr

G C♯ F♯ A

X
11fr

A C♯ G B F♯

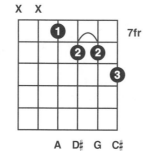

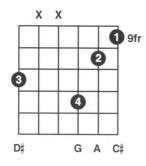

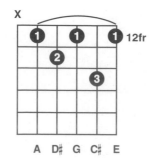
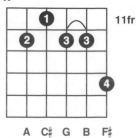

A13sus4 (A13sus)
A thirteenth, suspended fourth

A	D	E	G	B	F#
root	4th	5th	♭7th	9th	13th

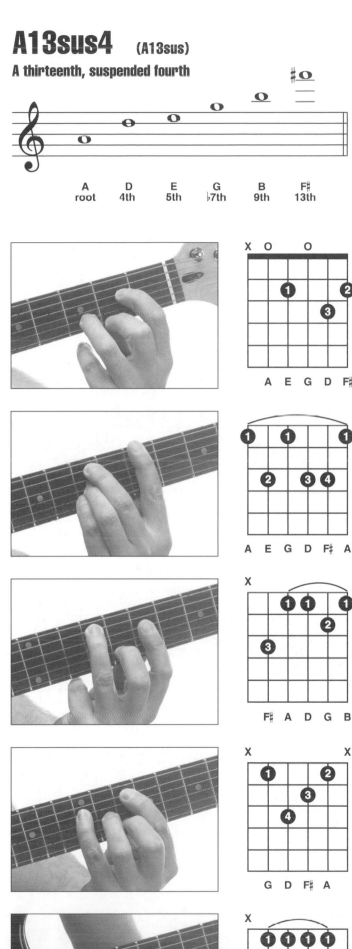

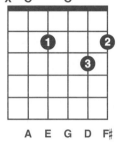

A E G D F#

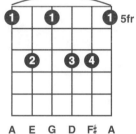

A E G D F# A 5fr

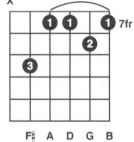

F# A D G B 7fr

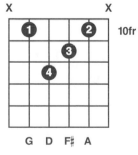

G D F# A 10fr

A D G B F# 12fr

A+ (Aaug, A(♯5))
A augmented

A	C#	E#
root	3rd	♯5th

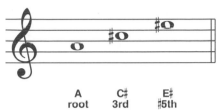

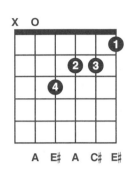

A E# A C# E#

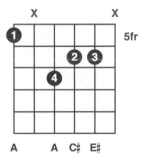

A A C# E# 5fr

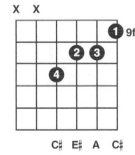
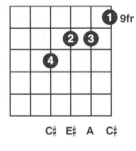

C# E# A C# 9fr

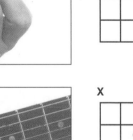

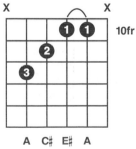

A C# E# A 10fr

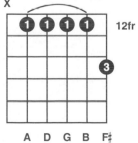

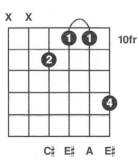

C# E# A E# 10fr

A

A+7 (A7#5)
A dominant seventh, sharp fifth

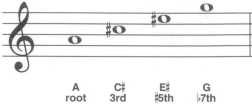

A root | C# 3rd | E# #5th | G ♭7th

X O O

A E# G C# E#

X X

5fr

A G C# E#

X X

7fr

A E# G C#

X X

10fr

G C# E# A

X X

12fr

A E# G C#

A+9 (A9#5, A9+5)
A ninth, sharp fifth

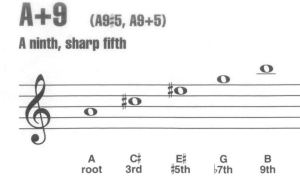

A root | C# 3rd | E# #5th | G ♭7th | B 9th

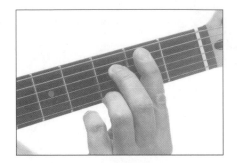

X

B E# A C# G

X X

5fr

G C# E# B

X X

8fr

B E# G C#

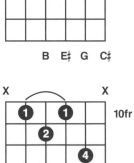

X X

10fr

G C# E# B

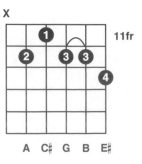

X

11fr

A C# G B E#

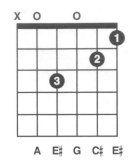
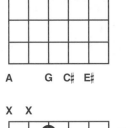
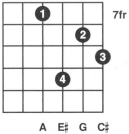
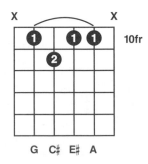
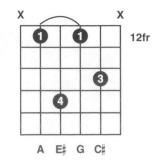
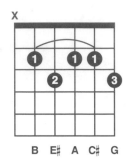
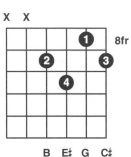
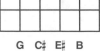

A+7♭9 (A7+5(♭9))
A dominant seventh, sharp fifth, flat ninth

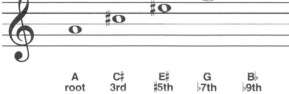

A	C#	E#	G	B♭
root	3rd	#5th	♭7th	♭9th

A+7#9 (A7+5(#9))
A dominant seventh, sharp fifth, sharp ninth

A	C#	E#	G	B#
root	3rd	#5th	♭7th	#9th

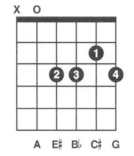

A E# B♭ C# G

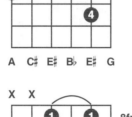

A C# E# B♭ E# G

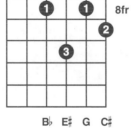

B♭ E# G C#

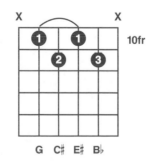

G C# E# B♭

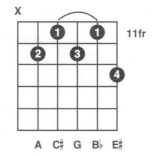

A C# G B♭ E#

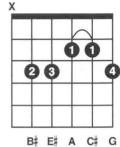
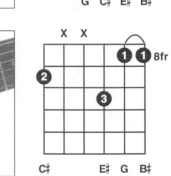
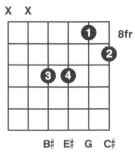

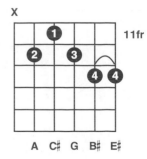

B# E# A C# G

G C# E# B#

C# E# G B#

B# E# G C#

A C# G B# E#

A

A° (Adim)
A diminished

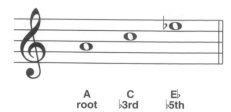

A   C   E♭
root   ♭3rd   ♭5th

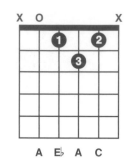

A E♭ A C

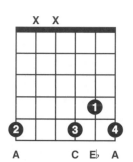

A   C E♭ A

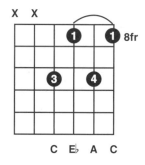

8fr

C E♭ A C

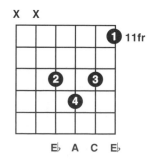

11fr

E♭ A C E♭

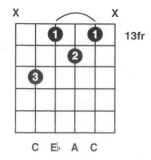

13fr

C E♭ A C

A°7 (Adim7)
A diminished seventh

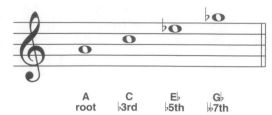

A   C   E♭   G♭
root   ♭3rd   ♭5th   ♭♭7th

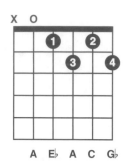

A E♭ A C G♭

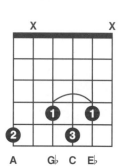

A   G♭ C E♭

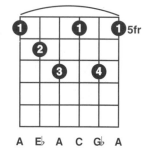

5fr

A E♭ A C G♭ A

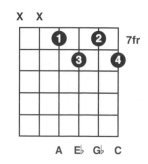

7fr

A E♭ G♭ C

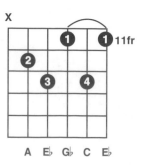

11fr

A E♭ G♭ C E♭

B♭ (B♭maj)
B-flat major

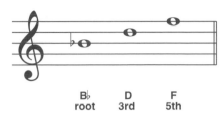

B♭	D	F
root	3rd	5th

 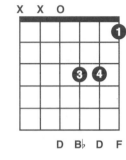

X X O

D B♭ D F

 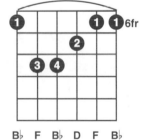

X   X

B♭ F B♭ D

6fr

B♭ F B♭ D F B♭

 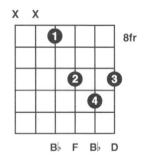

X X   8fr

B♭ F B♭ D

 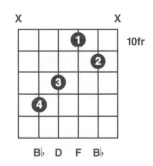

X   X   10fr

B♭ D F B♭

B♭5 (B♭ no 3rd)
B-flat fifth (power chord)

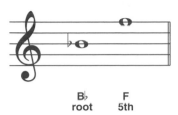

B♭	F
root	5th

 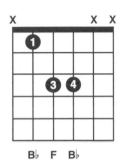

X   X X

B♭ F B♭

 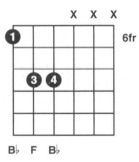

X X   3fr

F B♭ F B♭

 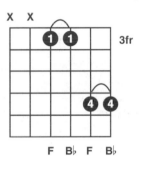

X X X   6fr

B♭ F B♭

 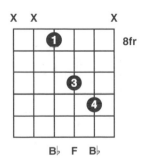

X X   X   8fr

B♭ F B♭

 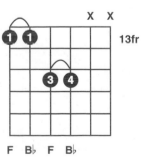

X X   13fr

F B♭ F B♭

 B♭

B♭sus4 (B♭sus)
B-flat suspended fourth

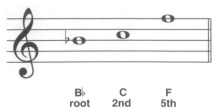

B♭	E♭	F
root	4th	5th

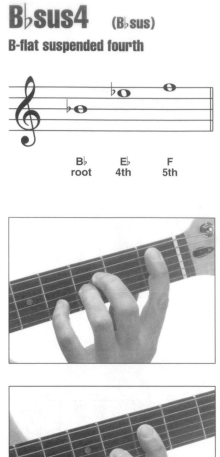

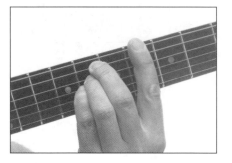

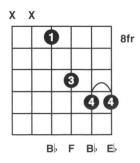

B♭sus2 (B♭5add2)
B-flat suspended second

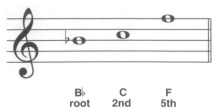

B♭	C	F
root	2nd	5th

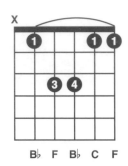

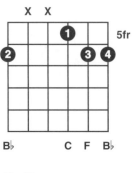

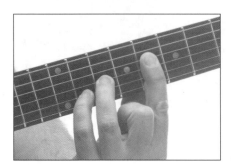

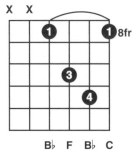

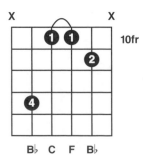

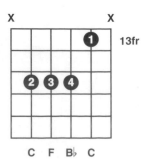

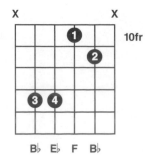

B♭add9

B-flat added ninth

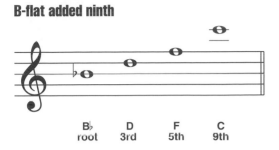

B♭	D	F	C
root	3rd	5th	9th

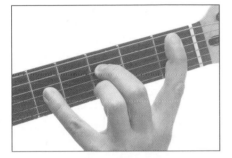

Bb F C D F

C F Bb D

X X 6fr
Bb D F C

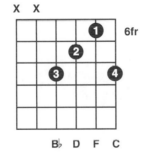

X X 10fr
C F Bb D

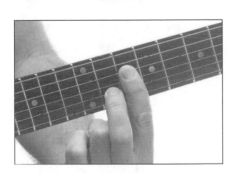

X X 10fr
Bb D F C

B♭6

B-flat sixth

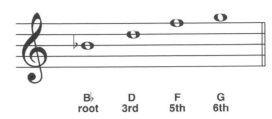

B♭	D	F	G
root	3rd	5th	6th

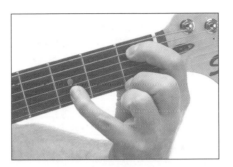

X O O
Bb D G D F

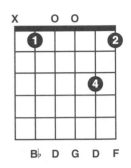

3fr
Bb D F Bb D G

X X 5fr
Bb G D F

X X 8fr
Bb F G D

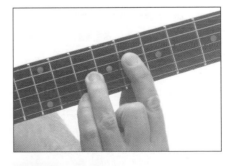

X 13fr
Bb F Bb D G

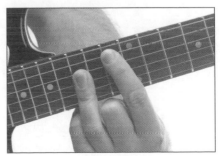

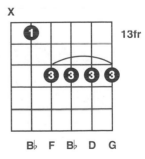
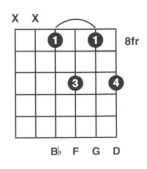
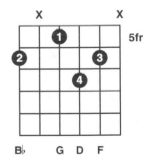
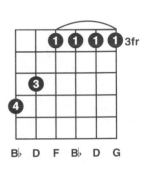
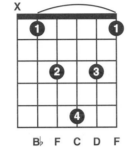
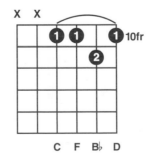
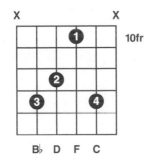

B♭

Bb6/9 (Bb6add9)
B-flat sixth, added ninth

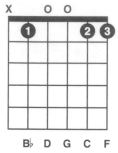

Bb	D	F	G	C
root	3rd	5th	6th	9th

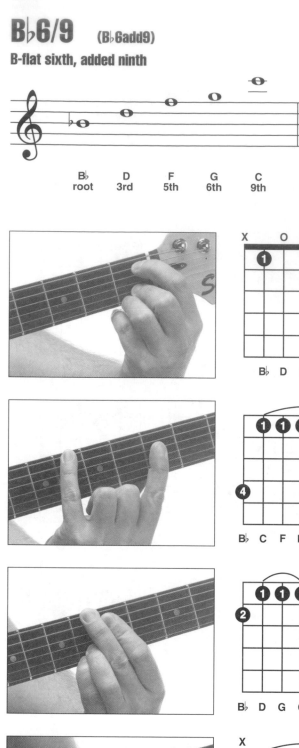

X O O

Bb D G C F

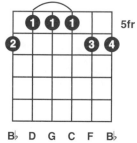

1 1 1 1 1 3fr
4

Bb C F Bb D G

1 1 1 5fr
2 3 4

Bb D G C F Bb

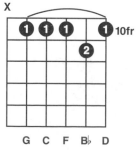

X
1 1 1 1 10fr
2

G C F Bb D

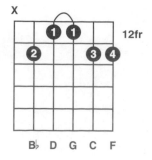

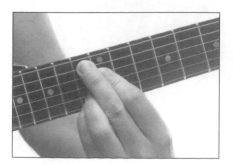

X
1 1 12fr
2 3 4

Bb D G C F

Bbmaj7 (BbM7)
B-flat major seventh

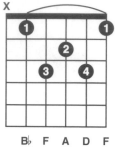

Bb	D	F	A
root	3rd	5th	7th

X
1 1
2
3 4

Bb F A D F

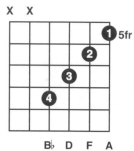

X X
1 5fr
2
3
4

Bb D F A

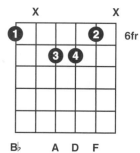

X   X
1   2 6fr
3 4

Bb A D F

X X
1 8fr
3 3 3

Bb F A D

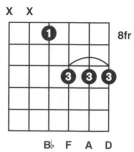

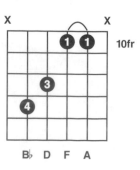

X X
1 1 10fr
3
4

Bb D F A

B♭maj9 (B♭M9)
B-flat major ninth

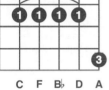

B♭	D	F	A	C
root	3rd	5th	7th	9th

B♭maj7♯11 (B♭M7♯11)
B-flat major seventh, sharp eleventh

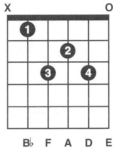

B♭	D	F	A	E
root	3rd	5th	7th	♯11th

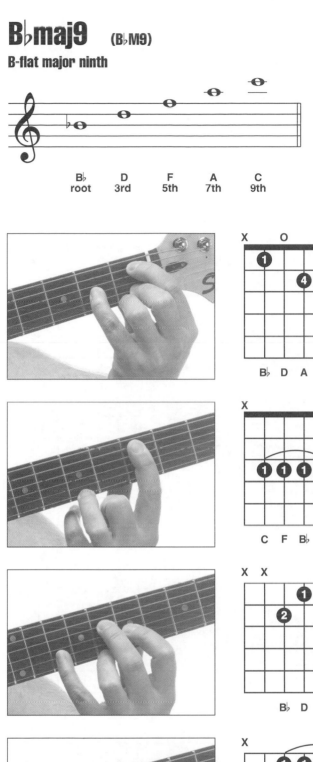
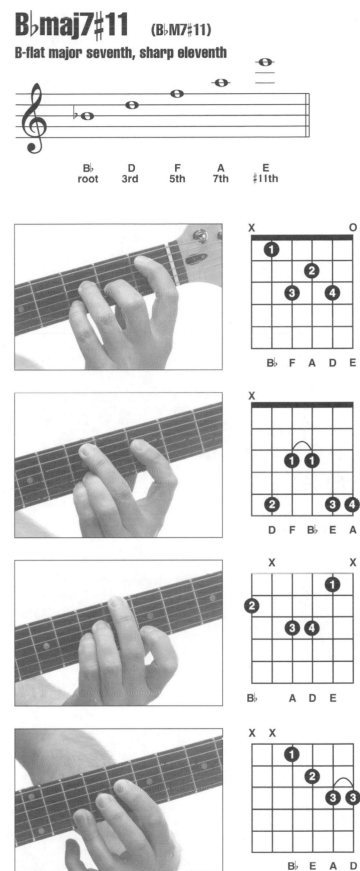

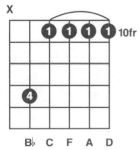

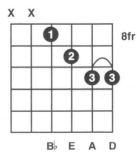

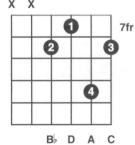
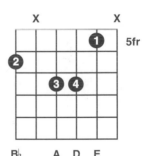

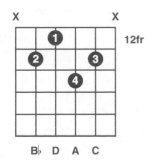

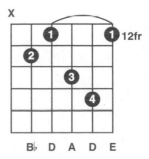

B♭

226

B♭maj13 (B♭M13)
B-flat major thirteenth

B♭	D	F	A	C	G
root	3rd	5th	7th	9th	13th

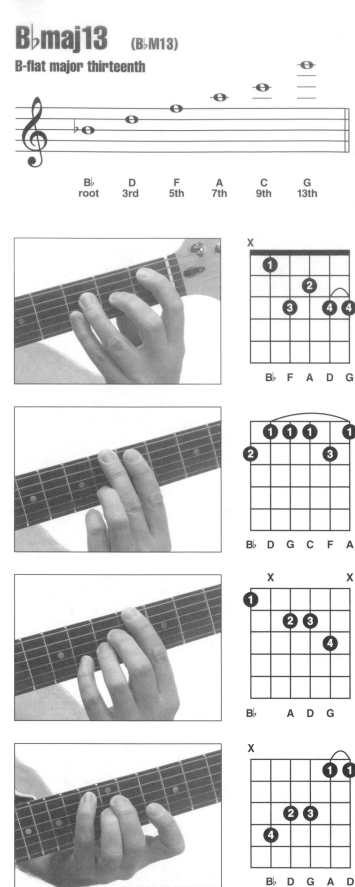
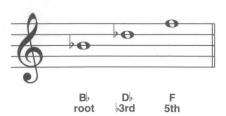

B♭m (B♭min, B♭-)
B-flat minor

B♭	D♭	F
root	♭3rd	5th

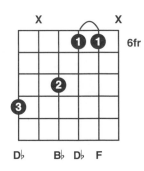
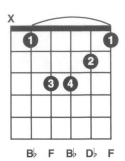
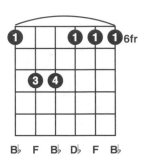
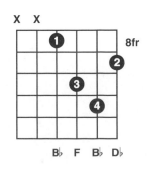
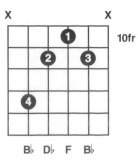

B♭m(add9)

B-flat minor, added ninth

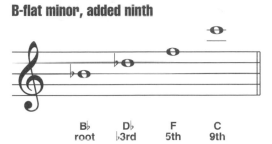

B♭	D♭	F	C
root	♭3rd	5th	9th

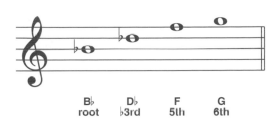

B♭m6 (B♭min6, B♭-6)

B-flat minor sixth

B♭	D♭	F	G
root	♭3rd	5th	6th

X

D♭ F B♭ C F

X O

B♭ F G D♭ G

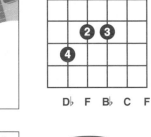

6fr

B♭ F B♭ D♭ F C

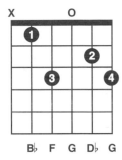

X X

5fr

B♭ G D♭ F

X X

8fr

D♭ F B♭ C

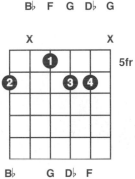

6fr

B♭ F B♭ D♭ G B♭

X X

9fr

C F B♭ D♭

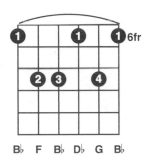

X X

8fr

B♭ F G D♭

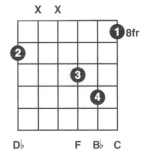

X X

10fr

B♭ D♭ F C

X

11fr

B♭ D♭ G B♭ F

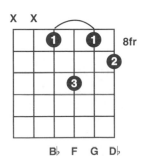

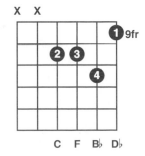

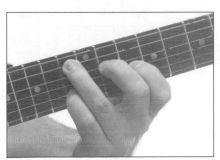

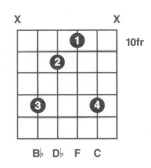

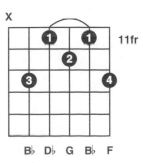

B♭

B♭m♭6 (B♭-(♭6), B♭min♭6)
B-flat minor, flat sixth

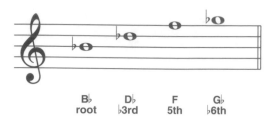

B♭	D♭	F	G♭
root	♭3rd	5th	♭6th

B♭m6/9
B-flat minor sixth, added ninth

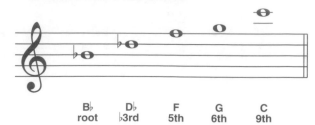

B♭	D♭	F	G	C
root	♭3rd	5th	6th	9th

 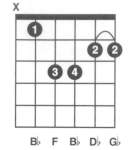

 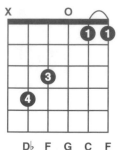

 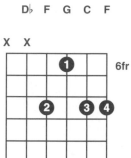

 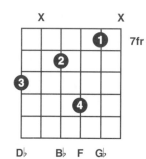

 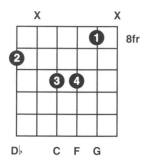

 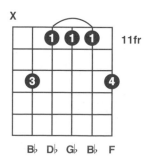

 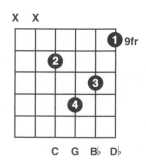

 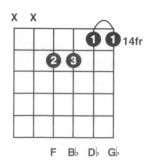

 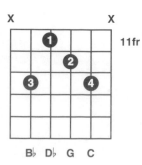

B♭m7 (B♭-7, B♭min7)
B-flat minor seventh

B♭m7♭5 (B♭-7♭5, B♭min7♭5)
B-flat minor seventh, flat fifth

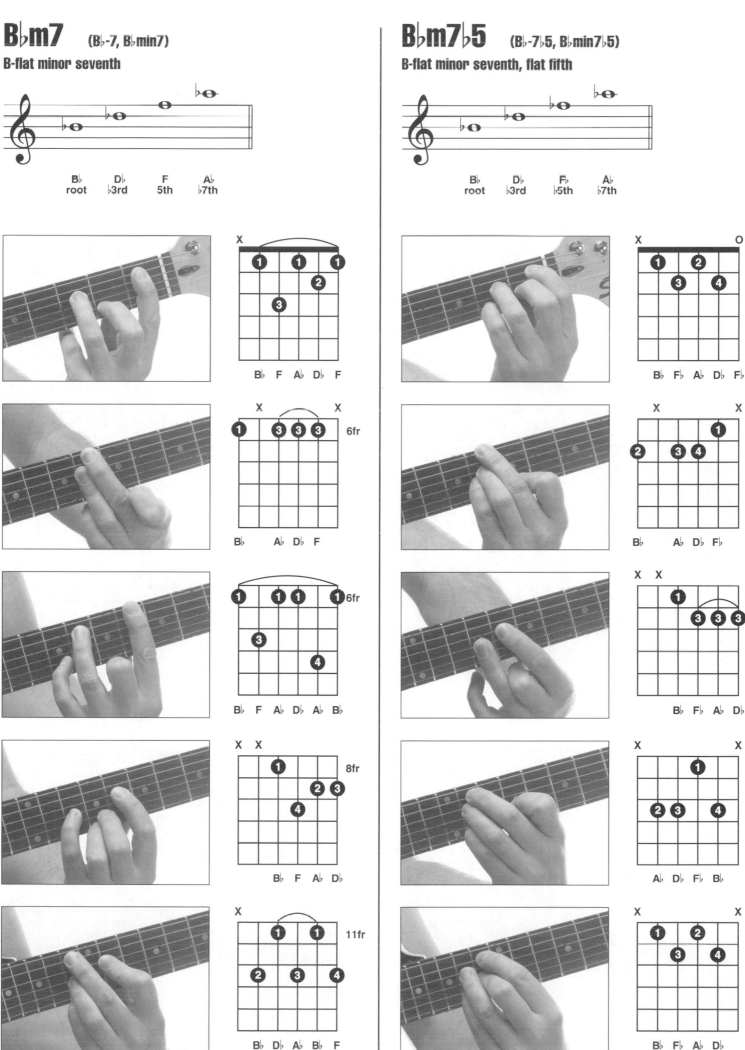

B♭m(maj7) (B♭-(+7))
B-flat minor, major seventh

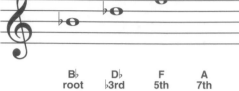

B♭	D♭	F	A
root	♭3rd	5th	7th

B♭ F A D♭ F

6fr

B♭ F A D♭ F B♭

8fr

B♭ F A D♭

10fr

B♭ D♭ F A

13fr

B♭ A D♭ F

B♭m9 (B♭-9, B♭min9)
B-flat minor ninth

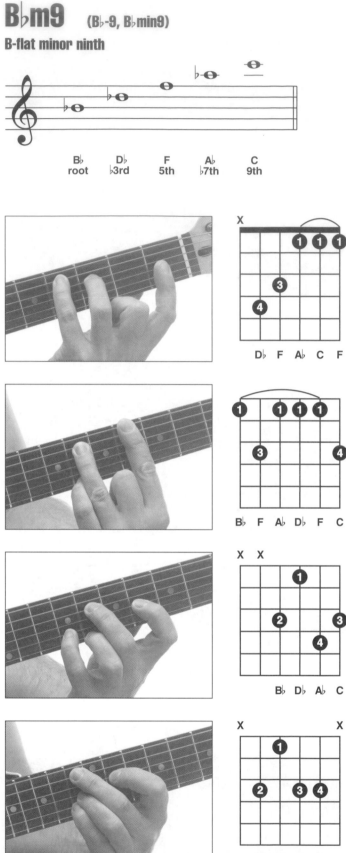

B♭	D♭	F	A♭	C
root	♭3rd	5th	♭7th	9th

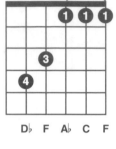

D♭ F A♭ C F

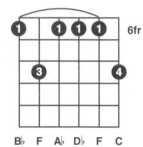

6fr

B♭ F A♭ D♭ F C

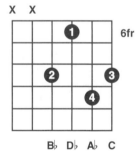

6fr

B♭ D♭ A♭ C

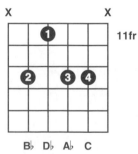

11fr

B♭ D♭ A♭ C

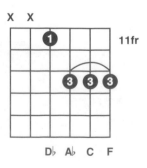

11fr

D♭ A♭ C F

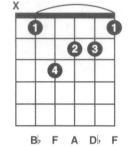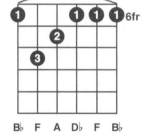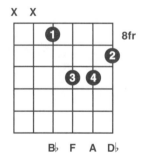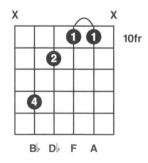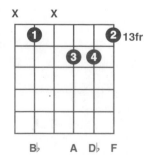

B♭m9♭5 (B♭m9-5, B♭min9♭5)
B-flat minor ninth, flat fifth

B♭	D♭	F♭	A♭	C
root	♭3rd	♭5th	♭7th	9th

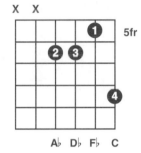

X
C F♭ B♭ D♭ A♭

X X
5fr
A♭ D♭ F♭ C

X X
9fr
D♭ C F♭ A♭

X X
11fr
D♭ A♭ C F♭

X X
13fr
C F♭ A♭ D♭

B♭m9(maj7) (B♭m9+7, B♭-9+7)
B-flat minor ninth, major seventh

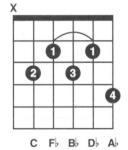

B♭	D♭	F	A	C
root	♭3rd	5th	7th	9th

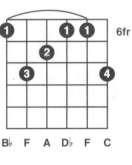

X
D♭ F A C F

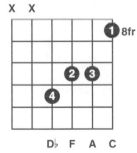

6fr
B♭ F A D♭ F C

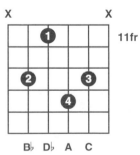

X X
8fr
D♭ F A C

X X
11fr
B♭ D♭ A C

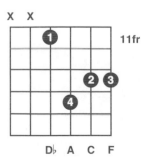

X X
11fr
D♭ A C F

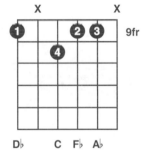
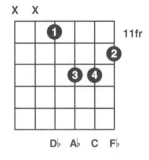
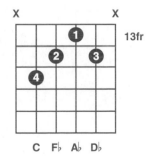

B♭

B♭m11 (B♭-11, B♭min11)
B-flat minor eleventh

B♭	D♭	F	A♭	C	E♭
root	♭3rd	5th	♭7th	9th	11th

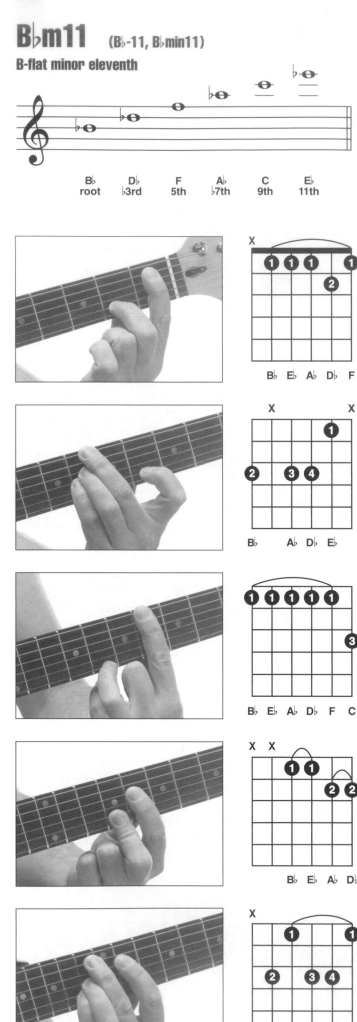

X

① ① ① ① ①
②

B♭ E♭ A♭ D♭ F

X X

① 4fr
② ③ ④

B♭ A♭ D♭ E♭

① ① ① ① ① 6fr
③

B♭ E♭ A♭ D♭ F C

X X

① ① 8fr
② ②

B♭ E♭ A♭ D♭

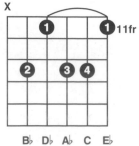

X

① ① 11fr
② ③ ④

B♭ D♭ A♭ C E♭

B♭m13 (B♭-13, B♭min13)
B-flat minor thirteenth

B♭	D♭	F	A♭	C	G
root	♭3rd	5th	♭7th	9th	13th

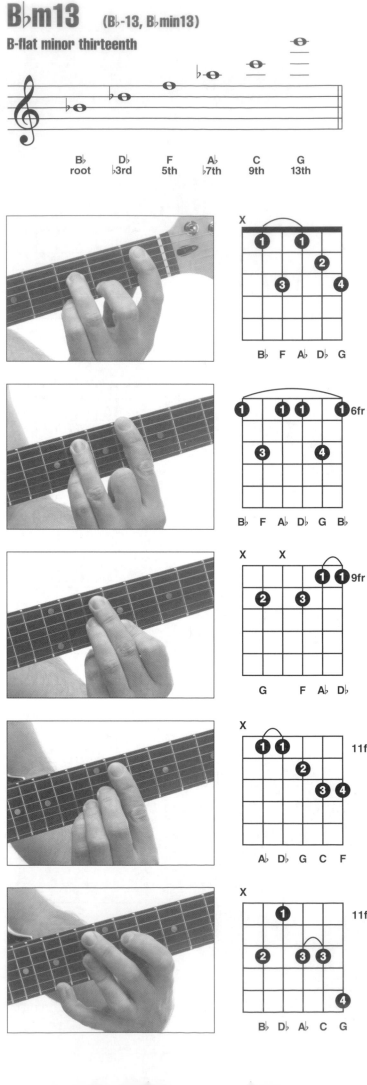

X

① ①
②
③ ④

B♭ F A♭ D♭ G

① ① ① ① 6fr
③ ④

B♭ F A♭ D♭ G B♭

X X

① ① 9fr
② ③

G F A♭ D♭

X

① ① 11fr
②
③ ④

A♭ D♭ G C F

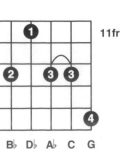

X

① 11fr
② ③ ③
④

B♭ D♭ A♭ C G

B♭7 (B♭dom7)
B-flat dominant seventh

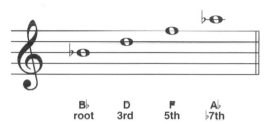

B♭   D   F   A♭
root   3rd   5th   ♭7th

B♭7sus4 (B♭7sus)
B-flat dominant seventh, suspended fourth

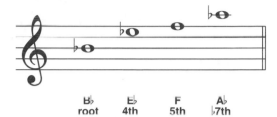

B♭   E♭   F   A♭
root   4th   5th   ♭7th

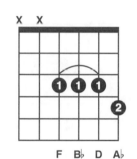
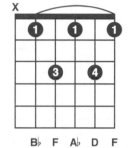
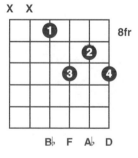
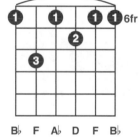
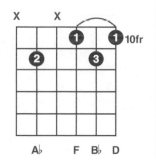

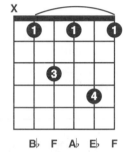
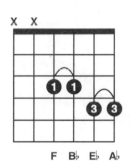
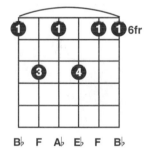
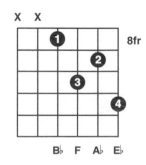
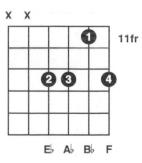

B♭

B♭7♭5 (B♭7-5, B♭dom7♭5)
B-flat dominant seventh, flat fifth

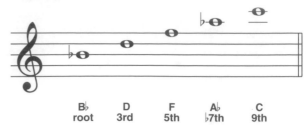

B♭   D   F♭   A♭
root   3rd   ♭5th   ♭7th

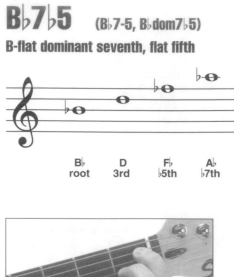 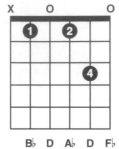

B♭ D A♭ D F♭

 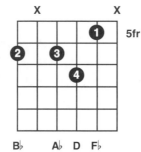

B♭ F♭ A♭ D

B♭ A♭ D F♭   5fr

 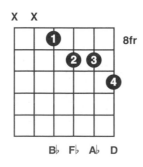

B♭ F♭ A♭ D   8fr

 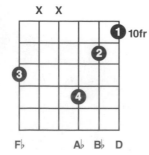

F♭ A♭ B♭ D   10fr

B♭9
B-flat ninth

B♭   D   F   A♭   C
root   3rd   5th   ♭7th   9th

B♭ D A♭ C F

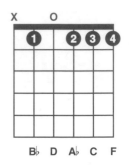

B♭ A♭ C D   3fr

 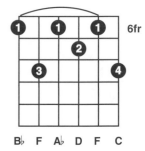

B♭ F A♭ D F C   6fr

 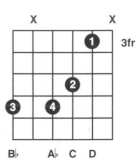

B♭ D A♭ C   7fr

 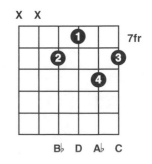

B♭ D A♭ C F   12fr

 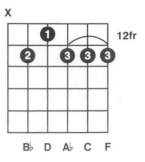

B♭9sus4 (B♭9sus)
B-flat ninth, suspended fourth

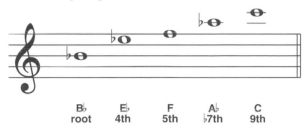

B♭	E♭	F	A♭	C
root	4th	5th	♭7th	9th

 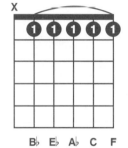

Bb Eb Ab C F

 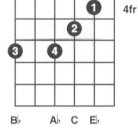

Bb Ab C Eb

 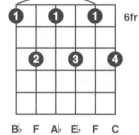

Bb F Ab Eb F C

 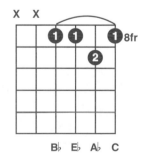

Bb Eb Ab C

 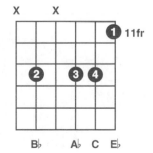

Bb Ab C Eb

B♭9♭5 (B♭9-5, B♭dom9♭5)
B-flat ninth, flat fifth

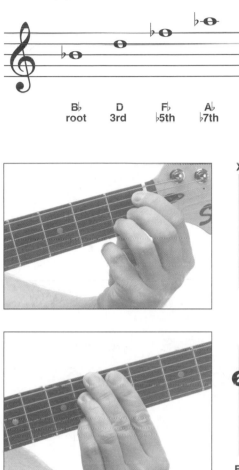

B♭	D	F♭	A♭	C
root	3rd	♭5th	♭7th	9th

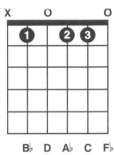

Bb D Ab C Fb

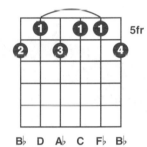

Bb D Ab C Fb Bb

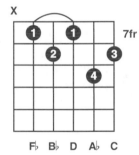 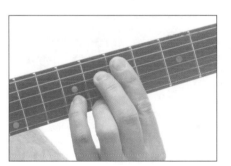

Fb Bb D Ab C

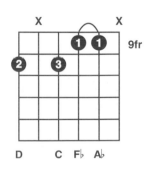 

D C Fb Ab

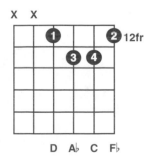 

D Ab C Fb

B♭7♭9 (B♭7-9, B♭dom7♭9)
B-flat dominant seventh, flat ninth

B♭	D	F	A♭	C♭
root	3rd	5th	♭7th	♭9th

B♭7♯9 (B♭7+9, B♭dom7♯9)
B-flat dominant seventh, sharp ninth

B♭	D	F	A♭	C♯
root	3rd	5th	♭7th	♯9th

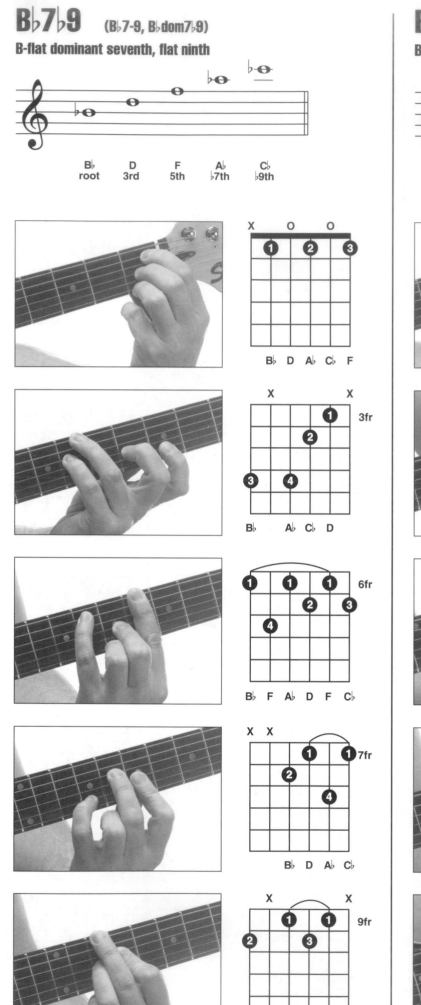

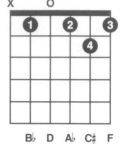

B♭ D A♭ C♯ F

D A♭ C♯ F B♭   5fr

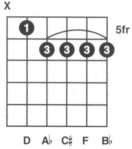

B♭ D A♭ C♯   7fr

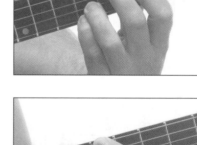

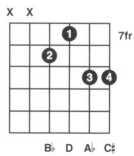

C♯ F A♭ D   9fr

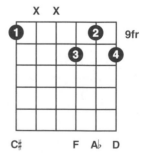

B♭ D A♭ C♯   12fr

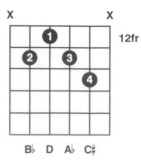

B♭7♭5(♯9) (B♭7-5(+9), B♭dom7♭5(♯9))

B-flat dominant seventh, flat fifth, sharp ninth

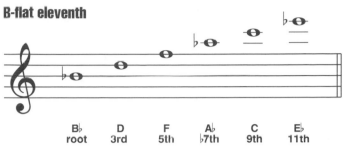

B♭	D	F♭	A♭	C♯
root	3rd	♭5th	♭7th	♯9th

B♭11

B-flat eleventh

B♭	D	F	A♭	C	E♭
root	3rd	5th	♭7th	9th	11th

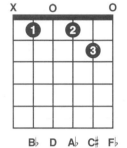

B♭ D A♭ C♯ F♭

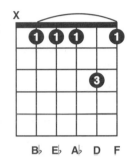

B♭ E♭ A♭ D F

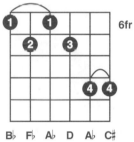

6fr

B♭ F♭ A♭ D A♭ C♯

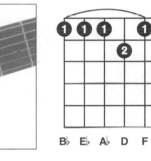

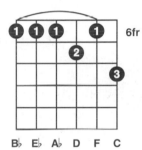

6fr

B♭ E♭ A♭ D F C

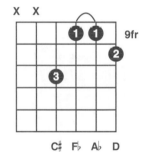

9fr

C♯ F♭ A♭ D

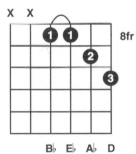

8fr

B♭ E♭ A♭ D

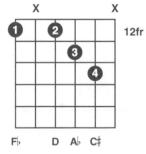

12fr

F♭ D A♭ C♯

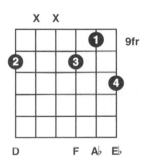

9fr

D F A♭ E♭

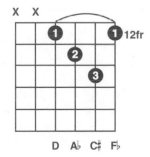

12fr

D A♭ C♯ F♭

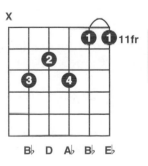

11fr

B♭ D A♭ B♭ E♭

B♭

B♭7#11 (B♭7+11, B♭dom7#11)
B-flat dominant seventh, sharp eleventh

B♭	D	F	A♭	E
root	3rd	5th	♭7th	#11th

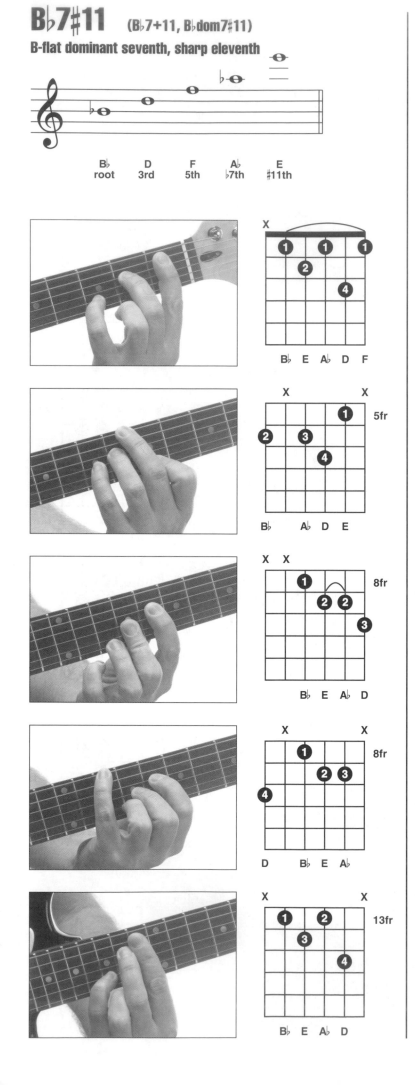

B♭13 (B♭dom13)
B-flat thirteenth

B♭	D	F	A♭	C	G
root	3rd	5th	♭7th	9th	13th

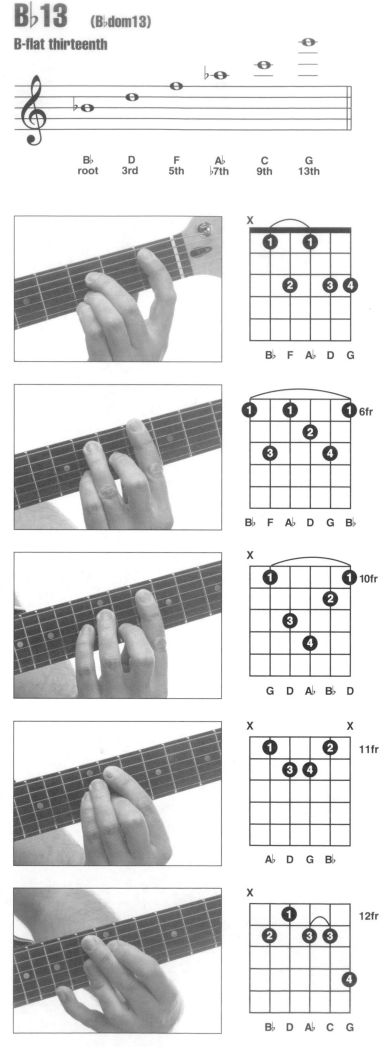

B♭13sus4 (B♭13sus)
B-flat thirteenth, suspended fourth

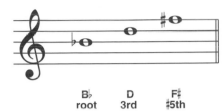

B♭	E♭	F	A♭	C	G
root	4th	5th	♭7th	9th	13th

B♭+ (B♭aug, B♭(♯5))
B-flat augmented

B♭	D	F♯
root	3rd	♯5th

X

B♭ E♭ A♭ C G

6fr

B♭ F A♭ E♭ G B♭

X

8fr

G B♭ E♭ A♭ C

X

11fr

A♭ E♭ G B♭ E♭

X

13fr

B♭ E♭ A♭ C G

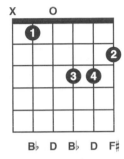

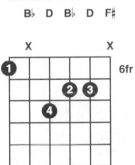

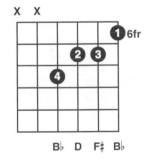

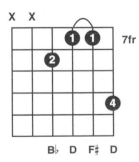

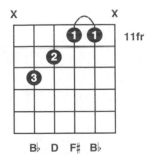

X O

B♭ D B♭ D F♯

X X
6fr

B♭ B♭ D F♯

X X
6fr

B♭ D F♯ B♭

X X
7fr

B♭ D F♯ D

X X
11fr

B♭ D F♯ B♭

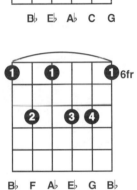
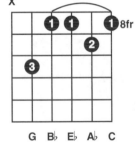
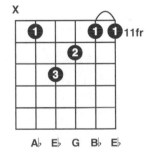
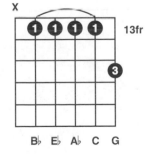

B♭

B♭+7 (B♭7♯5)
B-flat dominant seventh, sharp fifth

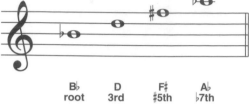

B♭	D	F♯	A♭
root	3rd	♯5th	♭7th

B♭ D A♭ D F♯

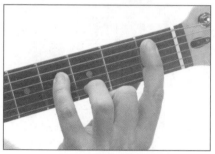

B♭ F♯ A♭ D

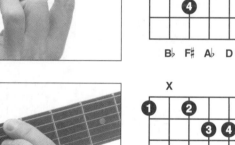

6fr

B♭ A♭ D F♯

8fr

B♭ F♯ A♭ D

11fr

A♭ D F♯ B♭

B♭+9 (B♭9♯5, B♭9+5)
B-flat ninth, sharp fifth

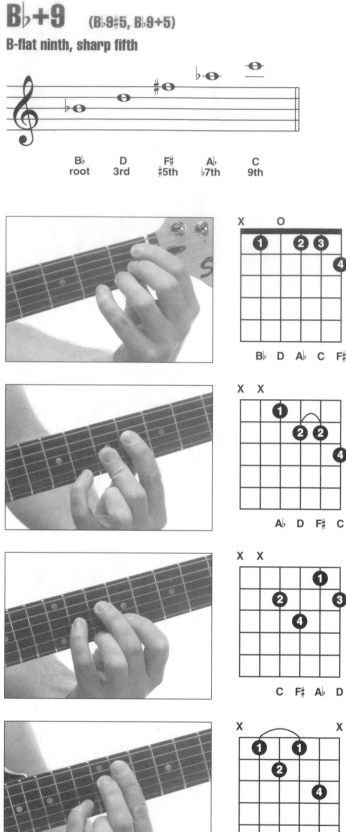

B♭	D	F♯	A♭	C
root	3rd	♯5th	♭7th	9th

B♭ D A♭ C F♯

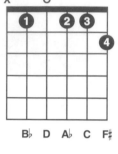

6fr

A♭ D F♯ C

9fr

C F♯ A♭ D

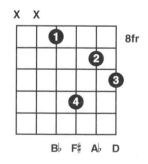

11fr

A♭ D F♯ C

12fr

B♭ D A♭ C F♯

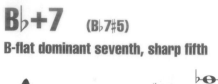
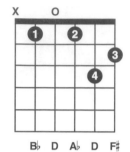
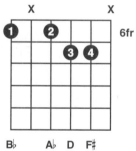
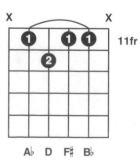
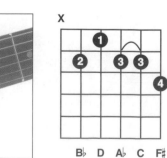

B♭+7♭9 (B♭7+5(♭9))
B-flat dominant seventh, sharp fifth, flat ninth

B♭	D	F♯	A♭	C♭
root	3rd	♯5th	♭7th	♭9th

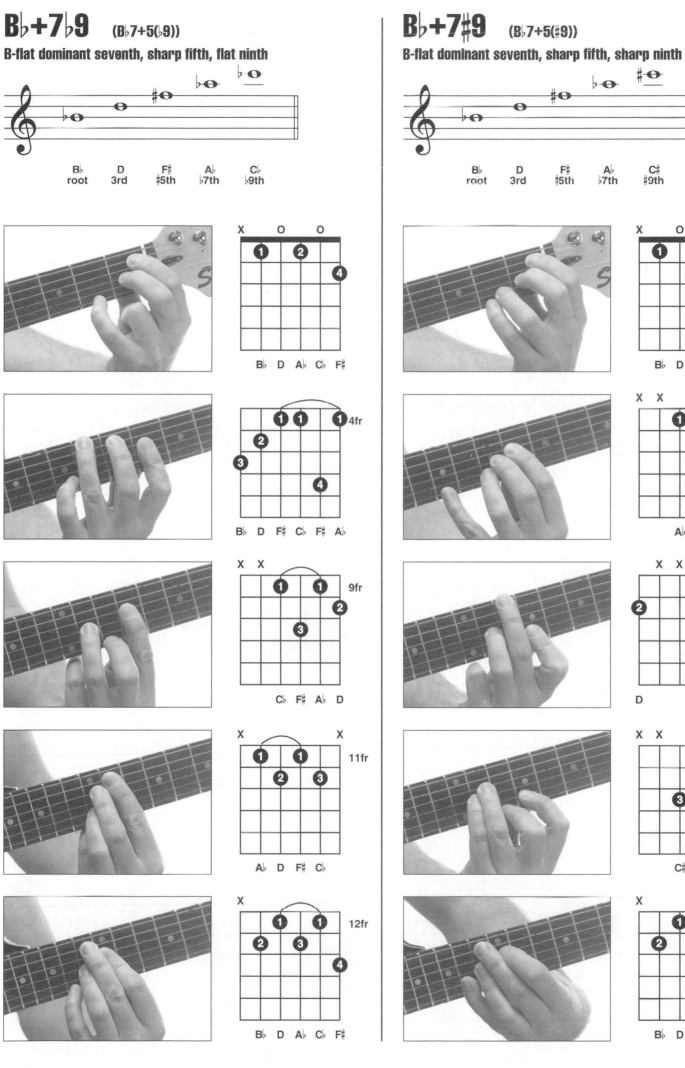

B♭ D A♭ C♭ F♯

B♭ D F♯ C♭ F♯ A♭ — 4fr

C♭ F♯ A♭ D — 9fr

A♭ D F♯ C♭ — 11fr

B♭ D A♭ C♭ F♯ — 12fr

B♭+7♯9 (B♭7+5(♯9))
B-flat dominant seventh, sharp fifth, sharp ninth

B♭	D	F♯	A♭	C♯
root	3rd	♯5th	♭7th	♯9th

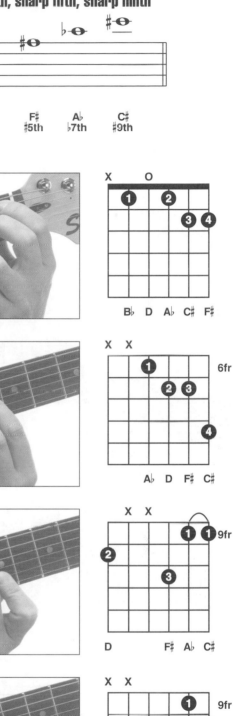

B♭ D A♭ C♯ F♯

A♭ D F♯ C♯ — 6fr

D F♯ A♭ C♯ — 9fr

C♯ F♯ A♭ D — 9fr

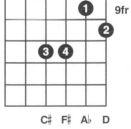

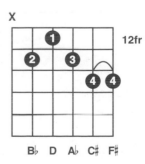

B♭ D A♭ C♯ F♯ — 12fr

B♭

B♭° (B♭dim)
B-flat diminished

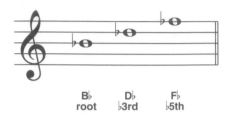

B♭   D♭   F♭
root   ♭3rd   ♭5th

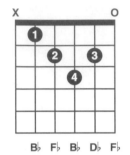

X   O

B♭ F♭ B♭ D♭ F♭

X   X

D♭ F♭ B♭ D♭

X   X

5fr

B♭   D♭ F♭ B♭

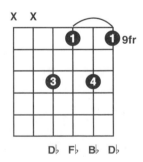

X   X

9fr

D♭ F♭ B♭ D♭

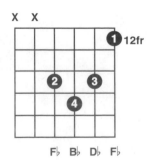

X   X

12fr

F♭ B♭ D♭ F♭

B♭°7 (B♭dim7)
B-flat diminished seventh

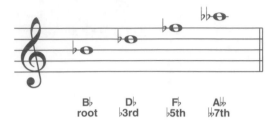

B♭   D♭   F♭   A♭♭
root   ♭3rd   ♭5th   ♭♭7th

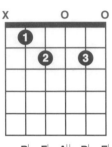

X   O   O

B♭ F♭ A♭♭ D♭ F♭

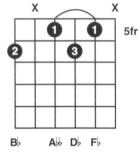

X   X

5fr

B♭   A♭♭ D♭ F♭

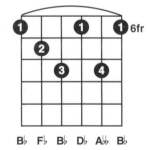

6fr

B♭ F♭ B♭ D♭ A♭♭ B♭

X   X

8fr

B♭ F♭ A♭♭ D♭

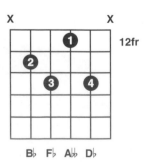

X   X

12fr

B♭ F♭ A♭♭ D♭

B (Bmaj)
B major

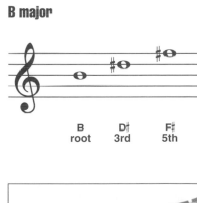

B   D#   F#
root   3rd   5th

B5 (B no 3rd)
B fifth (power chord)

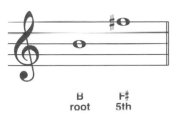

B   F#
root   5th

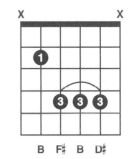

X   X

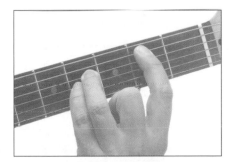

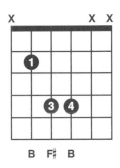

X   X   X

B   F#   B   D#

B   F#   B

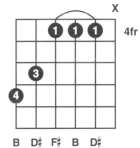

X

4fr

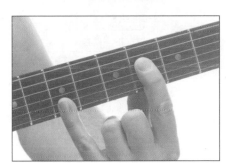

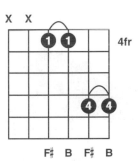

X   X

4fr

B   D#   F#   B   D#

F#   B   F#   B

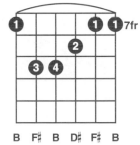

7fr

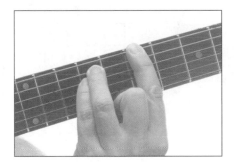

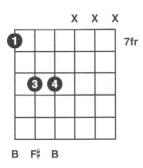

X   X   X

7fr

B   F#   B   D#   F#   B

B   F#   B

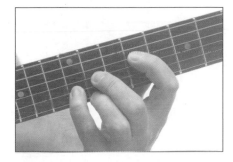

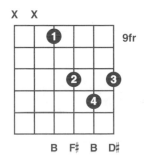

X   X

9fr

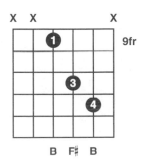

X   X   X

9fr

B   F#   B   D#

B   F#   B

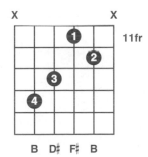

X   X

11fr

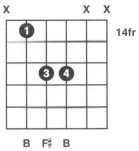

X   X   X

14fr

B   D#   F#   B

B   F#   B

Bsus4 (Bsus)
B suspended fourth

B E F#
root 4th 5th

Bsus2 (B5add2)
B suspended second

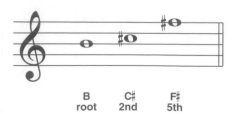

B C# F#
root 2nd 5th

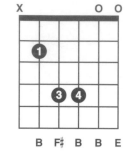

X O O

B F# B B E

X

B F# B C# F#

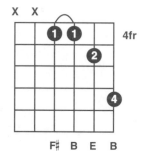

X X

4fr

F# B E B

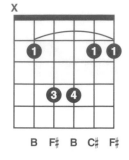

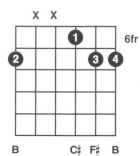

X X

6fr

B C# F# B

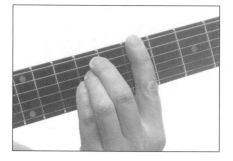

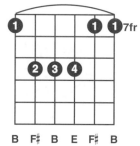

7fr

B F# B E F# B

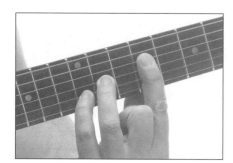

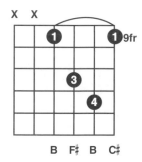

X X

9fr

B F# B C#

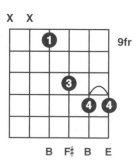

X X

9fr

B F# B E

X X

11fr

B C# F# B

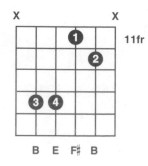

X X

11fr

B E F# B

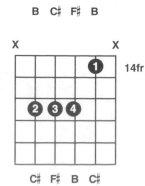

X X

14fr

C# F# B C#

Badd9

B added ninth

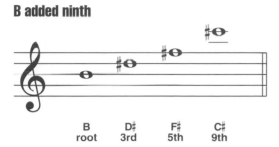

B	D#	F#	C#
root	3rd	5th	9th

X · · · · X

① ① ① ①

C# F# B D#

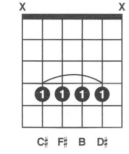

X

① · · ① 2fr

② ③

④

B F# C# D# F#

X X

① 7fr

②

③ ④

B D# F# C#

X X

① ① ① 11fr

②

C# F# B D#

X · · · · X

① 11fr

②

③ ④

B D# F# C#

B6

B sixth

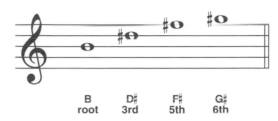

B	D#	F#	G#
root	3rd	5th	6th

X

①

③ ③ ③ ③

B F# B D# G#

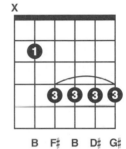

① ① ① ① 4fr

③

④

B D# F# B D# G#

X X

① 6fr

② ③

④

B G# D# F#

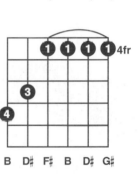

X X

① ① 9fr

③ ④

B F# G# D#

X X

① 13fr

② ③

④

B G# D# F#

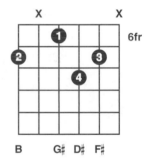

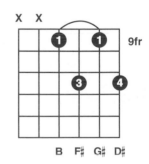

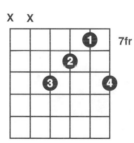

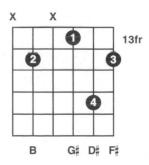

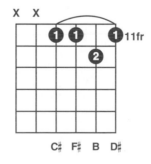

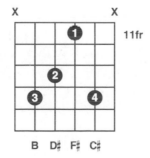

B

B6/9 (B6add9)
B sixth, added ninth

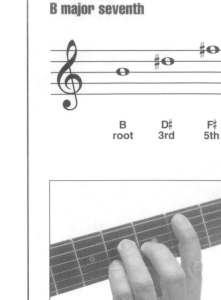

B root | D# 3rd | F# 5th | G# 6th | C# 9th

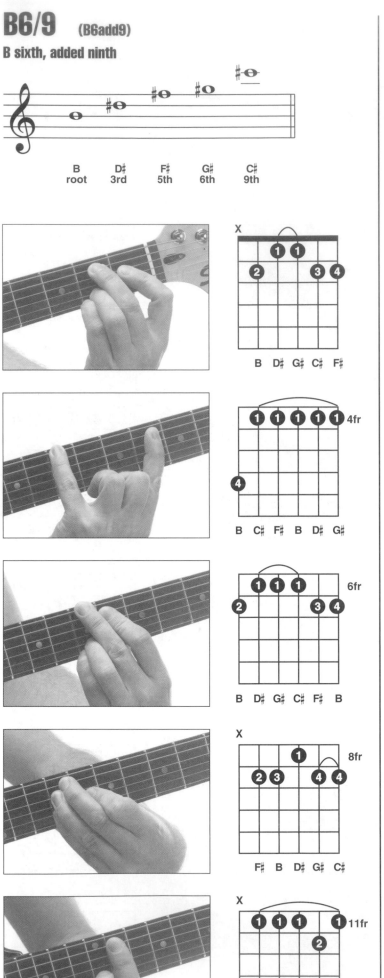

B D# G# C# F#

B C# F# B D# G# — 4fr

B D# G# C# F# B — 6fr

F# B D# G# C# — 8fr

G# C# F# B D# — 11fr

Bmaj7 (BM7)
B major seventh

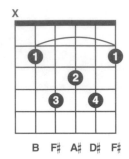

B root | D# 3rd | F# 5th | A# 7th

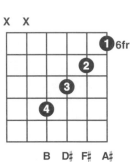

B F# A# D# F#

B D# F# A# — 6fr

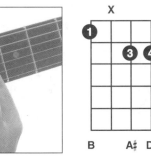

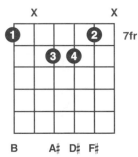

B A# D# F# — 7fr

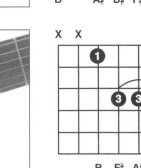
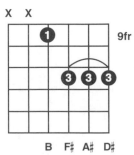

B F# A# D# — 9fr

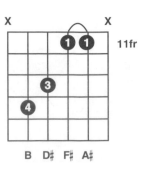

B D# F# A# — 11fr

Bmaj9 (BM9)
B major ninth

B	D♯	F♯	A♯	C♯
root	3rd	5th	7th	9th

B D♯ A♯ C♯

C♯ F♯ B D♯ A♯ 4fr

B D♯ A♯ C♯ F♯ A♯ 6fr

B D♯ A♯ C♯ 8fr

B C♯ F♯ A♯ D♯ 11fr

Bmaj7♯11 (BM7♯11)
B major seventh, sharp eleventh

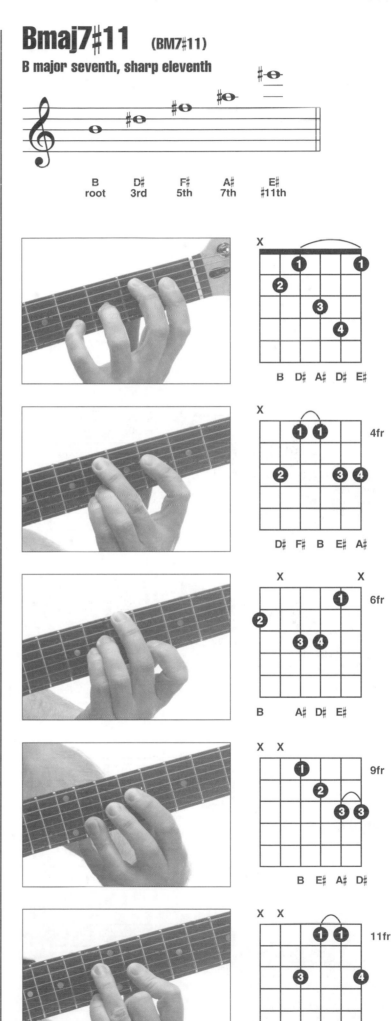

B	D♯	F♯	A♯	E♯
root	3rd	5th	7th	♯11th

B D♯ A♯ D♯ E♯

D♯ F♯ B E♯ A♯ 4fr

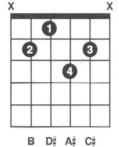

B A♯ D♯ E♯ 6fr

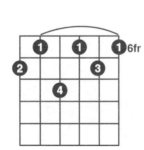

B E♯ A♯ D♯ 9fr

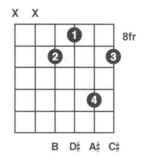
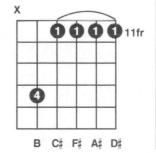

D♯ F♯ A♯ E♯ 11fr

B

Bmaj13 (BM13)
B major thirteenth

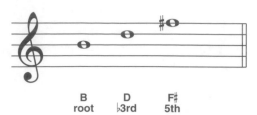

B	D#	F#	A#	C#	G#
root	3rd	5th	7th	9th	13th

Bm (Bmin, B-)
B minor

B	D	F#
root	♭3rd	5th

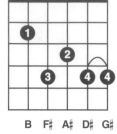

B F# A# D# G#

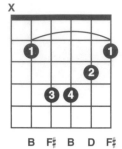

B F# B D F#

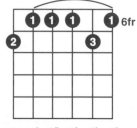

6fr

B D# G# C# F# A#

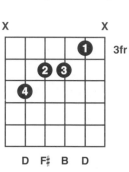

3fr

D F# B D

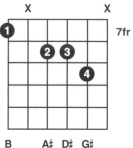

7fr

B A# D# G#

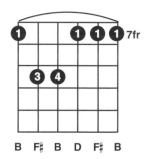

7fr

B F# B D F# B

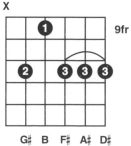

9fr

G# B F# A# D#

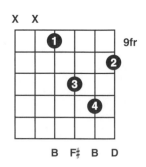

9fr

B F# B D

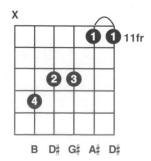

11fr

B D# G# A# D#

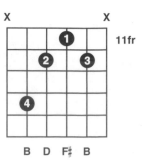

11fr

B D F# B

Bm(add9)
B minor, added ninth

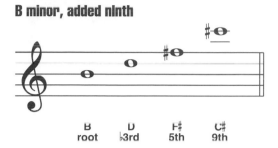

B	D	F#	C#
root	♭3rd	5th	9th

Bm6 (Bmin6, B-6)
B minor sixth

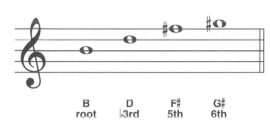

B	D	F#	G#
root	♭3rd	5th	6th

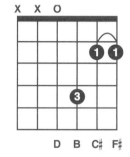
X X O

D B C# F#

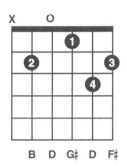
X O

B D G# D F#

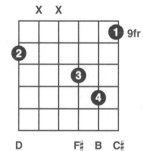
7fr

B F# B D F# C#

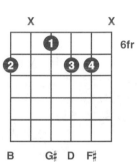
X X
6fr

B G# D F#

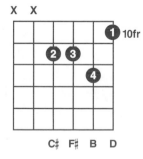
X X
9fr

D F# B C#

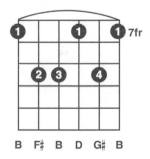
7fr

B F# B D G# B

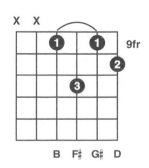
X X
10fr

C# F# B D

X X
9fr

B F# G# D

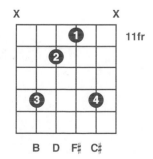
X X
11fr

B D F# C#

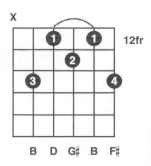
X
12fr

B D G# B F#

B

Bm♭6 (B-(♭6), Bmin♭6)
B minor, flat sixth

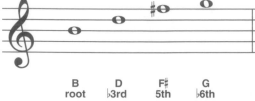

B	D	F#	G
root	♭3rd	5th	♭6th

Bm6/9
B minor sixth, added ninth

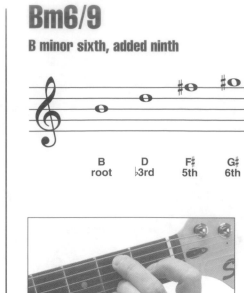

B	D	F#	G#	C#
root	♭3rd	5th	6th	9th

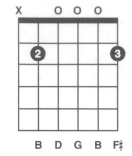
B D G B F#

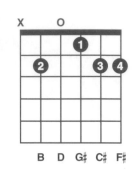
B D G# C# F#

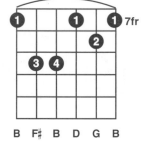
B F# B D G

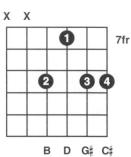
7fr
B D G# C#

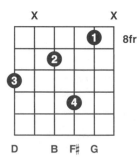
7fr
B F# B D G B

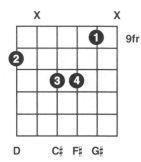
9fr
D C# F# G#

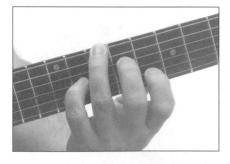
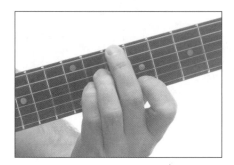
8fr
D B F# G

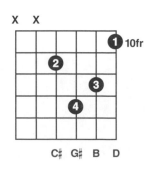
10fr
C# G# B D

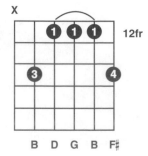
12fr
B D G B F#

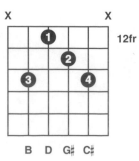
12fr
B D G# C#

Bm7 (B-7, Bmin7)
B minor seventh

B	D	F#	A
root	b3rd	5th	b7th

B D A B F#

B F# A D F#

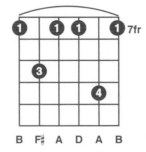
B A D F# 7fr

B F# A D A B 7fr

B F# A D 9fr

Bm7b5 (B-7b5, Bmin7b5)
B minor seventh, flat fifth

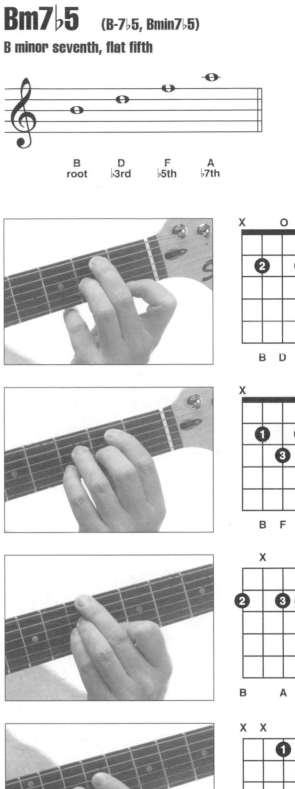

B	D	F	A
root	b3rd	b5th	b7th

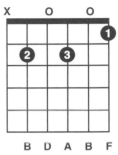
B D A B F

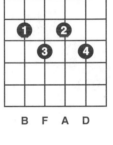
B F A D

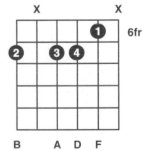
B A D F 6fr

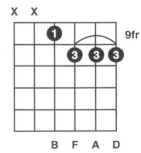
B F A D 9fr

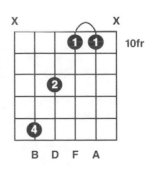
B D F A 10fr

B

Bm(maj7) (B-(+7))
B minor, major seventh

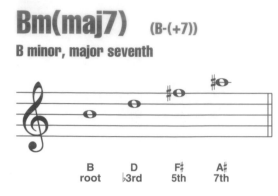

B	D	F#	A#
root	♭3rd	5th	7th

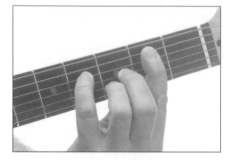 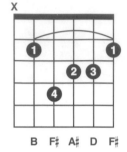

B F# A# D F#

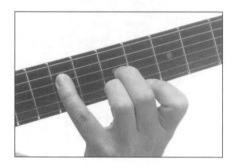 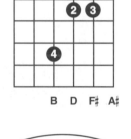

B D F# A#   6fr

 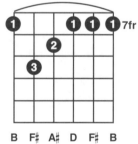

B F# A# D F# B   7fr

 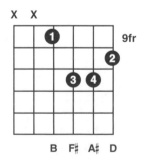

B F# A# D   9fr

 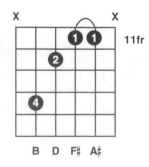

B D F# A#   11fr

Bm9 (B-9, Bmin9)
B minor ninth

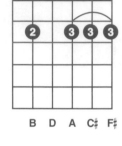

B	D	F#	A	C#
root	♭3rd	5th	♭7th	9th

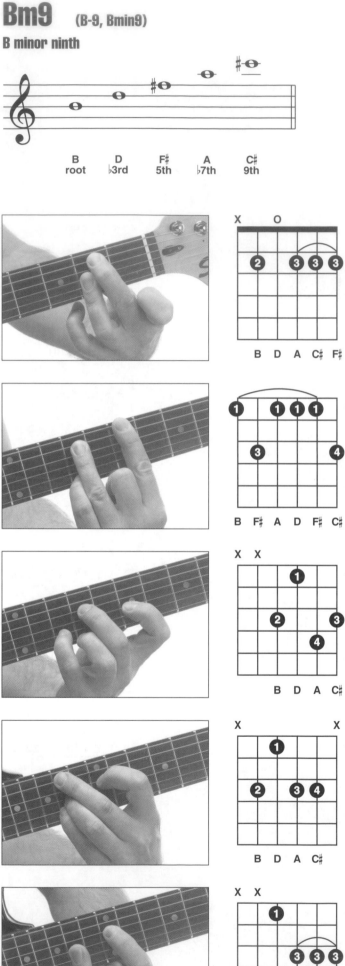

B D A C# F#

B F# A D F# C#   7fr

B D A C#   7fr

B D A C#   12fr

D A C# F#   12fr

Bm9♭5 (Bm9-5, Bmin9♭5)
B minor ninth, flat fifth

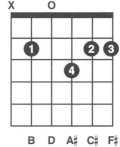

B	D	F	A	C#
root	♭3rd	♭5th	♭7th	9th

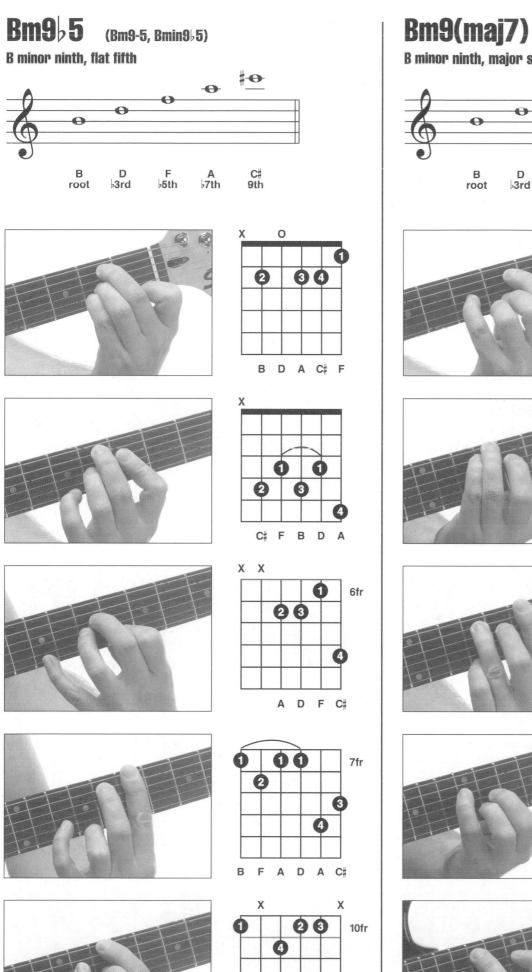

Bm9(maj7) (Bm9+7, B-9+7)
B minor ninth, major seventh

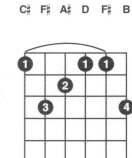
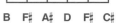

B	D	F#	A#	C#
root	♭3rd	5th	7th	9th

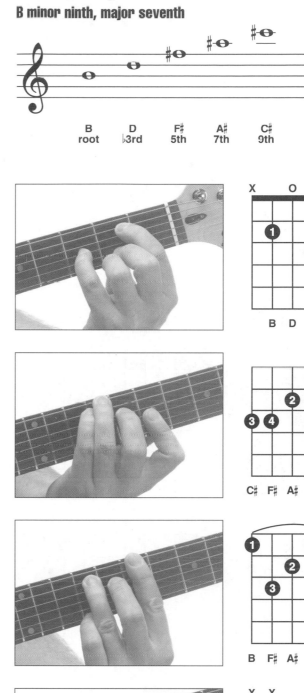

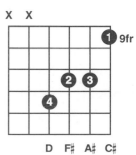

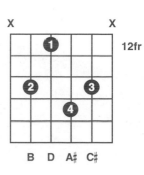

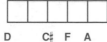

B

Bm11 (B-11, Bmin11)
B minor eleventh

B	D	F#	A	C#	E
root	♭3rd	5th	♭7th	9th	11th

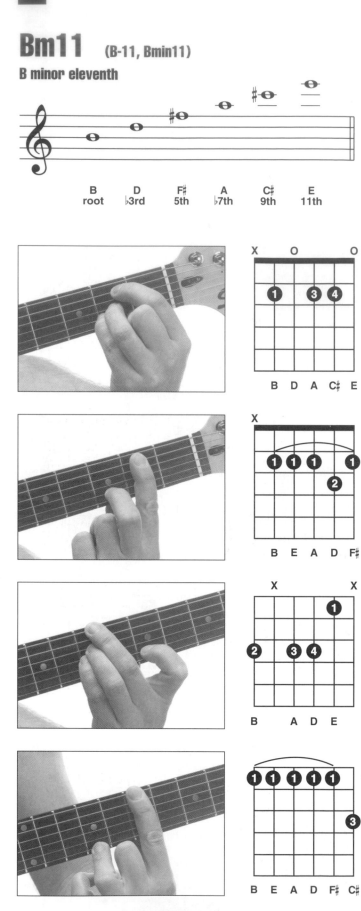

X O O

B D A C# E

X

B E A D F#

X X

5fr

B A D E

7fr

B E A D F# C#

X X

9fr

B E A D

Bm13 (B-13, Bmin13)
B minor thirteenth

B	D	F#	A	C#	G#
root	♭3rd	5th	♭7th	9th	13th

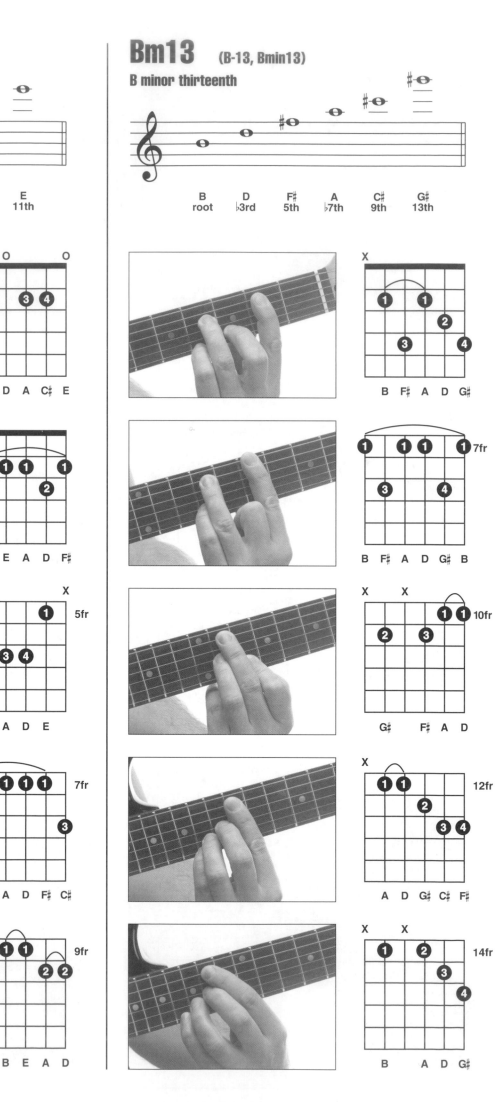

X

B F# A D G#

7fr

B F# A D G# B

X X

10fr

G# F# A D

X

12fr

A D G# C# F#

X X

14fr

B A D G#

B7 (Bdom7)
B dominant seventh

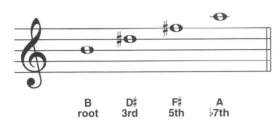

B	D#	F#	A
root	3rd	5th	♭7th

B7sus4 (B7sus)
B dominant seventh, suspended fourth

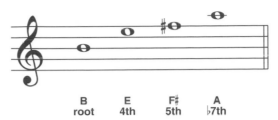

B	E	F#	A
root	4th	5th	♭7th

 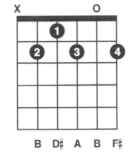

B D# A B F#

 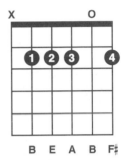

B E A B F#

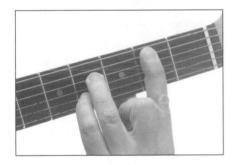 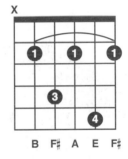

B F# A D# F#

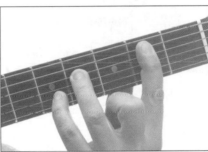

B F# A E F#

 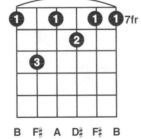

B F# A D# F# B

7fr

 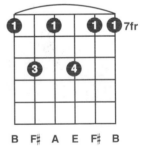

B F# A E F# B

7fr

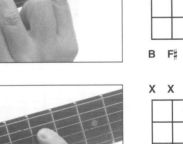 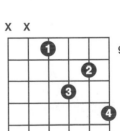 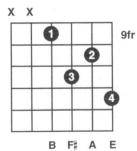

B F# A D#

9fr

B F# A E

9fr

 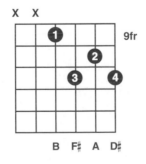

A F# B D#

11fr

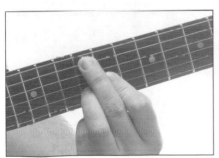 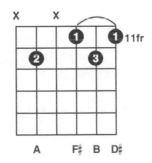

E A B F#

12fr

 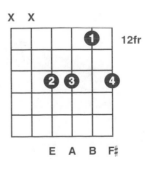

B

256

B7♭5 (B7-5, Bdom7♭5)
B dominant seventh, flat fifth

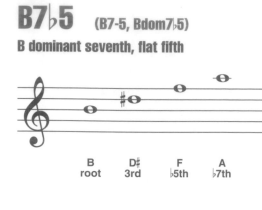

B	D♯	F	A
root	3rd	♭5th	♭7th

B9
B ninth

B	D♯	F♯	A	C♯
root	3rd	5th	♭7th	9th

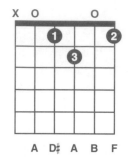
X O O

A D♯ A B F

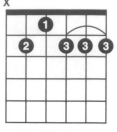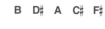
X

B D♯ A C♯ F♯

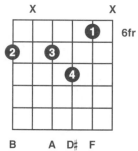
X X

B F A D♯

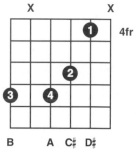
X X 4fr

B A C♯ D♯

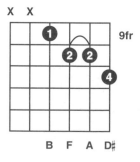
X X 6fr

B A D♯ F

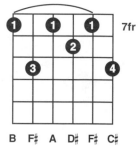
7fr

B F♯ A D♯ F♯ C♯

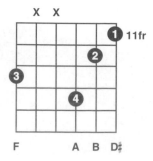
X X 9fr

B F A D♯

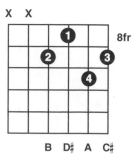
X X 8fr

B D♯ A C♯

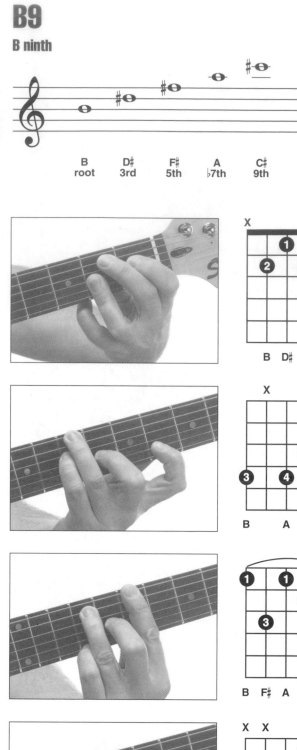
X X 11fr

F A B D♯

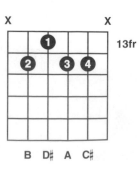
X X 13fr

B D♯ A C♯

B9sus4 (B9sus)
B ninth, suspended fourth

B	E	F#	A	C#
root	4th	5th	♭7th	9th

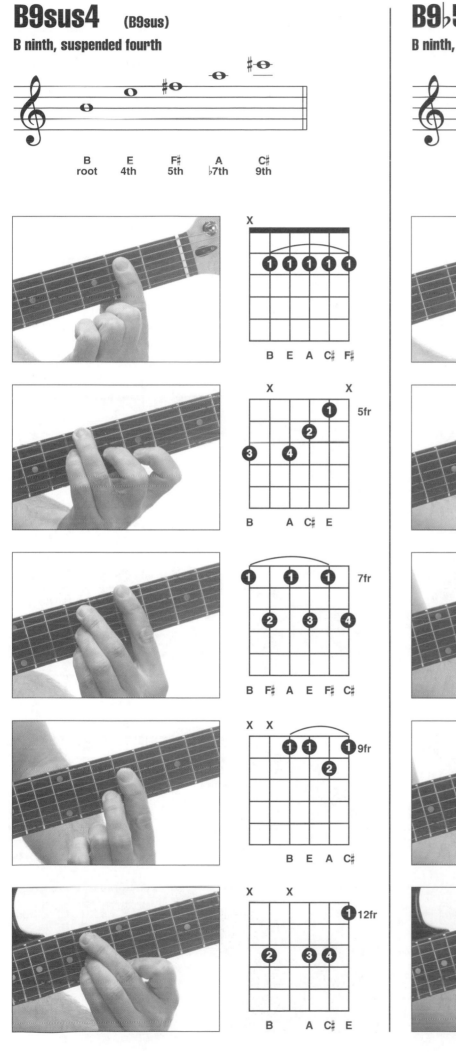

B9♭5 (B9-5, Bdom9♭5)
B ninth, flat fifth

B	D#	F	A	C#
root	3rd	♭5th	♭7th	9th

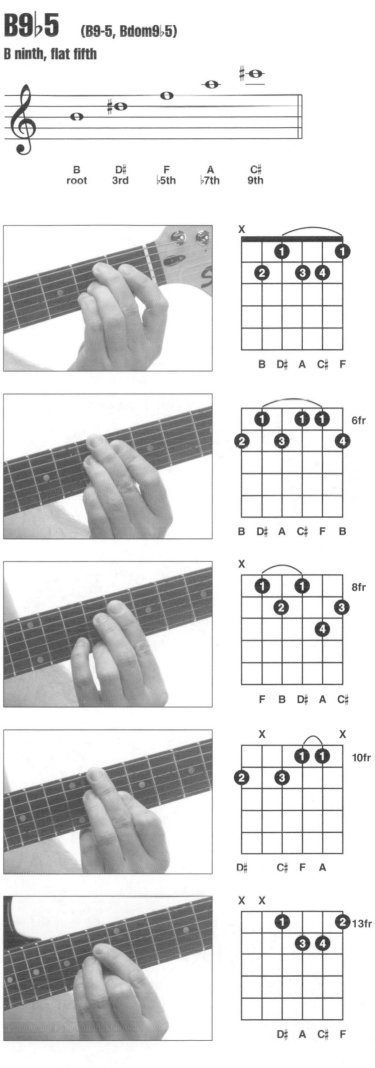

B

B7♭9 (B7-9, Bdom7♭9)
B dominant seventh, flat ninth

B	D♯	F♯	A	C
root	3rd	5th	♭7th	♭9th

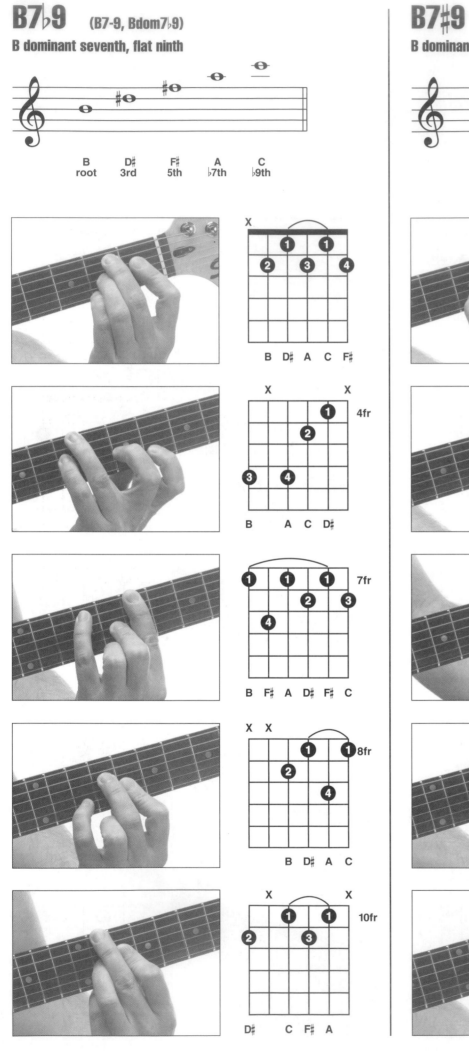

B D♯ A C F♯

B A C D♯   4fr

B F♯ A D♯ F♯ C   7fr

B D♯ A C   8fr

D♯ C F♯ A   10fr

B7♯9 (B7+9, Bdom7♯9)
B dominant seventh, sharp ninth

B	D♯	F♯	A	C𝄪
root	3rd	5th	♭7th	♯9th

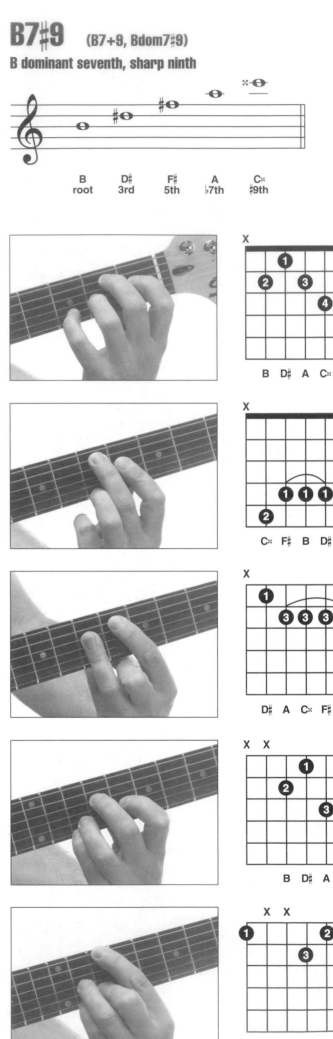
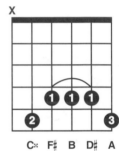
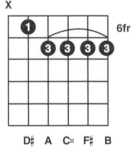
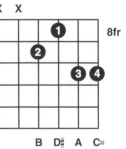
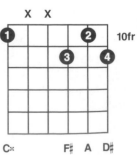

B D♯ A C𝄪

C𝄪 F♯ B D♯ A

D♯ A C𝄪 F♯ B   6fr

B D♯ A C𝄪   8fr

C𝄪 F♯ A D♯   10fr

B7♭5(♯9) (B7-5(+9), Bdom7♭5(♯9))

B dominant seventh, flat fifth, sharp ninth

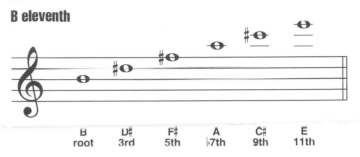

B	D♯	F	A	C𝄪
root	3rd	♭5th	♭7th	♯9th

B11

B eleventh

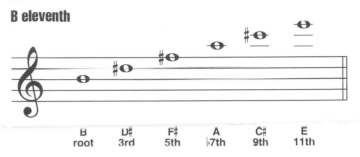

B	D♯	F♯	A	C♯	E
root	3rd	5th	♭7th	9th	11th

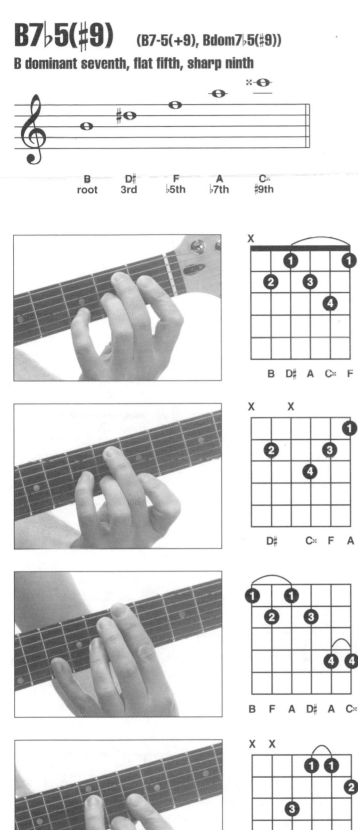

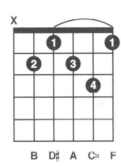
B D♯ A C𝄪 F

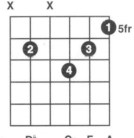
D♯ C𝄪 F A · 5fr

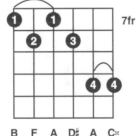
B F A D♯ A C𝄪 · 7fr

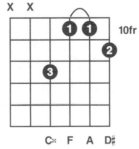
C𝄪 F A D♯ · 10fr

F D♯ A C𝄪 · 13fr

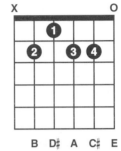
B D♯ A C♯ E

B E A D♯ F♯

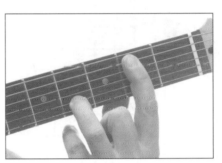
B E A D♯ F♯ C♯ · 7fr

B E A D♯ · 9fr

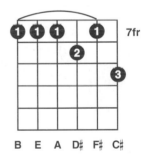

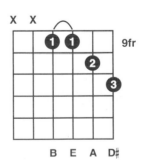

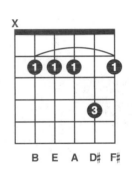

B D♯ A B E · 12fr

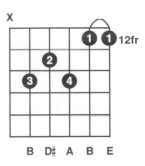

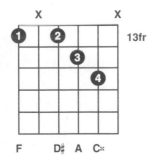

B

B7#11 (B7+11, Bdom7#11)
B dominant seventh, sharp eleventh

B	D#	F#	A	E#
root	3rd	5th	♭7th	#11th

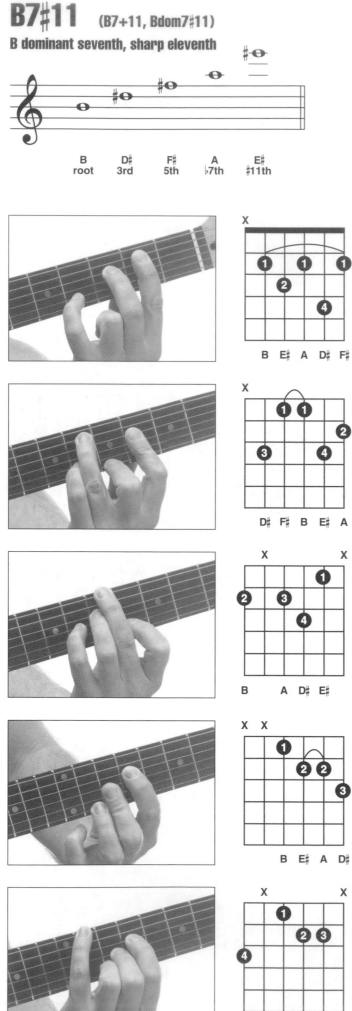

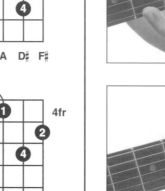

X
```
1 . 1 . 1
. 2 . .
. . 4
```
B E# A D# F#

X
```
1 1 .      4fr
. . 2
3 . 4
```
D# F# B E# A

X . . X
```
. . 1      6fr
2 . 3
. 4
```
B . A D# E#

X X
```
1 . .      9fr
. 2 2
. . 3
```
B E# A D#

X . . X
```
. 1 .      9fr
. . 2 3
4
```
D# . B E# A

B13
B thirteenth

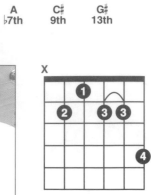

B	D#	F#	A	C#	G#
root	3rd	5th	♭7th	9th	13th

X
```
. 1 . .
2 . 3 3
. . 4
```
B D# A C# G#

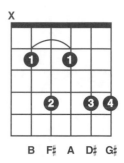

X
```
. 1 . 1
. 2 .
. . 3 4
```
B F# A D# G#

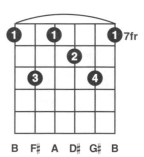

```
1 . 1 . 1   7fr
. . 2
3 . 4
```
B F# A D# G# B

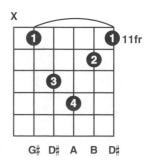

X
```
1 . . 1    11fr
. . 2
3 .
. 4
```
G# D# A B D#

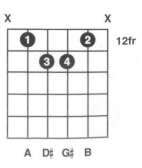

X . . X
```
1 . . 2    12fr
. 3 4
```
A D# G# B

B13sus4 (B13sus)
B thirteenth, suspended fourth

R	E	F#	A	C#	G#
root	4th	5th	♭7th	9th	13th

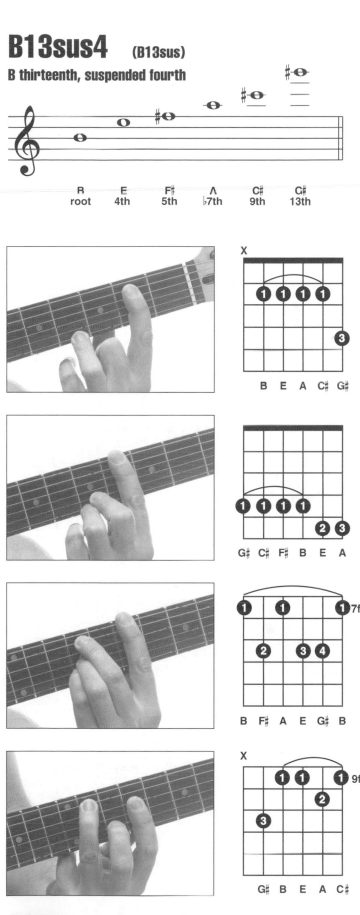

X

B E A C# G#

G# C# F# B E A

B F# A E G# B 7fr

G# B E A C# 9fr

A E G# B E 12fr

B+ (Baug, B(#5))
B augmented

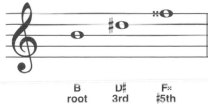

B	D#	F×
root	3rd	#5th

X   O O

B D# F× B F×

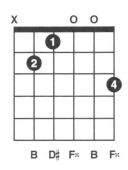

X   X 7fr

B   B D# F×

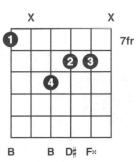

X X 7fr

B D# F× B

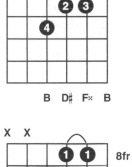

X X 8fr

B D# F× D#

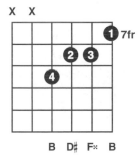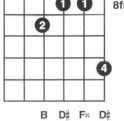

X X 12fr

B D# F× B

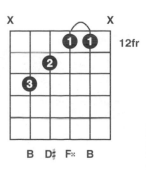

B

B+7 (B7♯5)
B dominant seventh, sharp fifth

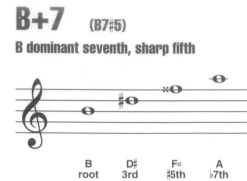

B	D♯	F✕	A
root	3rd	♯5th	♭7th

 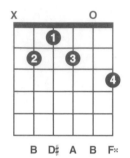

B D♯ A B F✕

 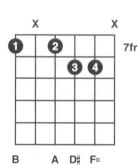

B F✕ A D♯

7fr B A D♯ F✕

 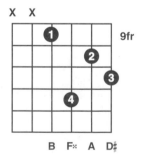

9fr B F✕ A D♯

 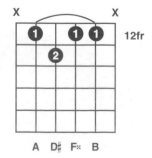

12fr A D♯ F✕ B

B+9 (B9♯5, B9+5)
B ninth, sharp fifth

B	D♯	F✕	A	C♯
root	3rd	♯5th	♭7th	9th

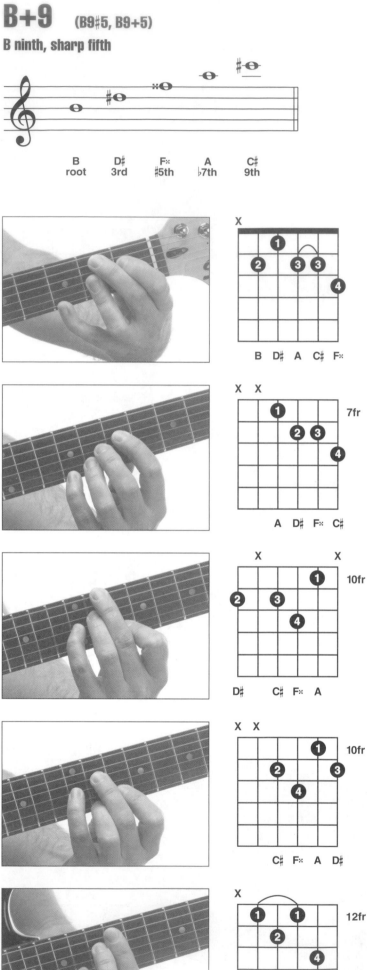

B D♯ A C♯ F✕

7fr A D♯ F✕ C♯

10fr D♯ C♯ F✕ A

10fr C♯ F✕ A D♯

12fr A D♯ F✕ C♯

B+7♭9 (B7+5(♭9))

B dominant seventh, sharp fifth, flat ninth

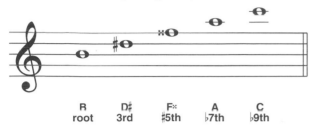

R	D♯	F𝄪	A	C
root	3rd	♯5th	♭7th	♭9th

B D♯ A C F𝄪

B D♯ F𝄪 C F𝄪 A

A D♯ F𝄪 C

D♯ C F𝄪 A

A D♯ F𝄪 C

B+7♯9 (B7+5(♯9))

B dominant seventh, sharp fifth, sharp ninth

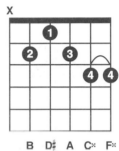

B	D♯	F𝄪	A	C𝄪
root	3rd	♯5th	♭7th	♯9th

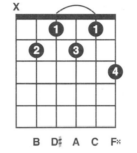

B D♯ A C𝄪 F𝄪

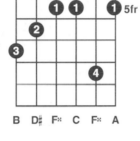

D♯ F𝄪 C𝄪 F𝄪 A

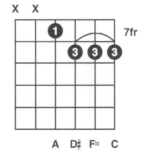

A D♯ F𝄪 C𝄪

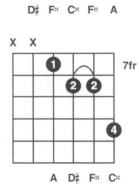

D♯ F𝄪 A C𝄪

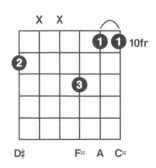

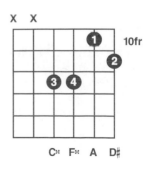

C𝄪 F𝄪 A D♯

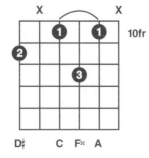

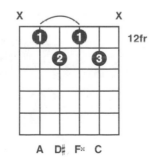

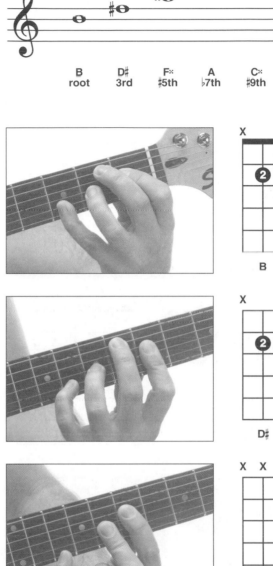

B

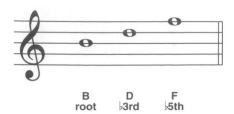

B° (Bdim)
B diminished

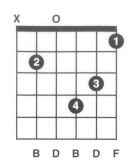

B	D	F
root	♭3rd	♭5th

B°7 (Bdim7)
B diminished seventh

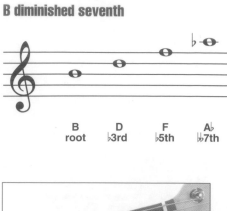

B	D	F	A♭
root	♭3rd	♭5th	♭♭7th

X   O

B D B D F

X

B F A♭ D F

X   X

B F B D

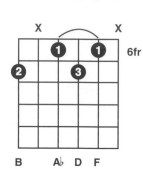

X   X 6fr

B A♭ D F

X X 6fr

B D F B

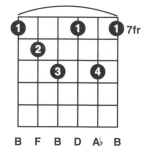

7fr

B F B D A♭ B

X X 10fr

D F B D

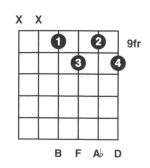

X X 9fr

B F A♭ D

X X 13fr

F B D F

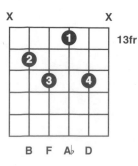

X   X 13fr

B F A♭ D

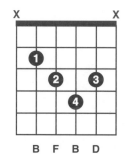
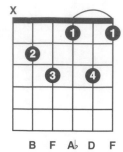

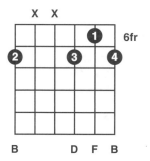

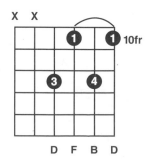
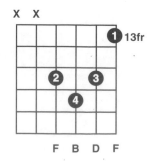

264